My Life

A COACH TRIP ADVENTURE

My Life

A COACH TRIP ADVENTURE

Brendan Sheerin

MICHAEL O'MARA BOOKS LIMITED

First published in Great Britain in 2011 by
Michael O'Mara Books Limited
9 Lion Yard
Tremadoc Road
London SW4 7NQ

ISBN: 978-1-84317-699-2 in hardback print format
ISBN: 978-1-84317-767-8 in EPub format
ISBN: 978-1-84317-768-5 in Mobipocket format

2 3 4 5 6 7 8 9 10

Designed and typeset by e-type

Plate section designed by www.envydesign.co.uk

Front cover photo of Brendan courtesy of 12 Yard Productions
Other front cover photography: www.shutterstock.com

Printed and bound by CPI Group (UK) Ltd, Croydon, CR0 4YY

www.mombooks.com

Contents

I dedicate this book to the lives and memory of

Les Beardsall, my life partner

Thomas Joseph Sheerin, my father

and

Dawn Shires, my dearest cousin.

Acknowledgements

I would like to thank the following people, who have helped me realize this book:

Lindsay Davies, my editor, for her guidance, assistance and help in editing this manuscript for me.

Kate Moore, Commissioning Editor of Michael O'Mara Books, for her tremendous patience and understanding while I was filming *Coach Trip*, but more importantly for guiding me through the writing of the pages of this book; and all the team at MOM Books.

Paula McKie, my agent, for always being there for me and for our fat rascal times.

All my colleagues at 12 Yard Productions and Channel 4, who gave permission for the scribing of this book and who generously supplied photographs to be used, especially on the front cover.

My dearest family and friends, who have always been there for me, listening to my fears and doubts and yet encouraging me to go forward.

And, finally, to all my talented and esteemed colleagues with whom I have worked on each and every *Coach Trip* programme I have made so far. For their support, guidance and friendship, which make the filming of each and every *Coach Trip* a unique, exciting and fun experience. A big thank you, guys… *fabulous*.

Brendan x

Malaga
August 2011

CHAPTER 1

The Land of the Leprechauns

MY DEAR FRIEND John Hoy calls me an Irish Yorkshireman or a Yorkshire Irishman, depending on which way you look at it. I have been travelling regularly to the west of Ireland from Leeds City railway station since the summer of 1959, having been born in Hunslet, Leeds, in February of that year. I was Tom and Maureen Sheerin's second child and a brother for Patrick, their firstborn. A sister and two more brothers were to follow me.

My maternal grandfather, Patrick Carden, lived next door to us in Leeds and used to regale me with tales of leprechauns with pots of gold and fairies at the bottom of the garden. Whenever he knew we were going to the 'wessshhht' of Ireland, as he pronounced it (with the emphasis on the 'shhh'), he would say, 'Ah, Brendan, the land of the leprechauns... the land of the leprechauns... Look out for them, lad, but if you see one, be sure never to take your eyes off him. For if you do, he will vanish... and the pot of gold will vanish too, as quick as clicking your fingers.'

I believed him. The west of Ireland, in particular County Mayo, possesses some of the most magical scenery in the country and has a remoteness about it that made it seem like it was somehow our secret. Even these days, mass tourism has not yet arrived, so in places it is just as unspoilt as it was when I was a child.

My father's family, the Sheerins, owned a farm in a beautiful area called Carrandine, just outside Kiltimagh, County Mayo, and it was to this farm we would make our pilgrimage every summer to see my grandmother Catherine and her son, my father's older brother, Paddy. Uncle Paddy was one of three bachelors who lived in Carrandine. Never having married, his sole responsibility was to keep the farm working and in profit. I am sure Uncle Paddy must have dreaded our visits when we were children, as our arrival always spelled mischief – and for a whole six weeks.

The journey from Leeds to Ireland took three days back then, and we used to make the trip with a huge number of our friends and relations from the Leeds area, all of whom were also visiting family back home in Ireland. The matriarchs of these families – the Sheerins, the O'Briens, the Hughes, the Fords, the Murphys and the Nolans – would each be armed with three or four children mostly under seven years of age, and would start their epic journey loaded down with suitcases, prams of all shapes and sizes, nappies and sandwiches of potted meat and cheese. The mothers and the children would travel out together and stay in Ireland for the entire six weeks of the summer holidays, and the fathers would join their families later for a fortnight or so if their work allowed.

The journey would start at Leeds City station, which in those days still ran steam trains. I remember on one occasion our friend Hazel Watson had purchased a beautiful pair of silver buckled shoes for the voyage – and then promptly dropped one of them between the platform and the carriage of the train.

'Ohhhh bejaaaysus, I've lost me new ficken shoe!' she shrieked at the top of her voice. Immediately, all the mothers started screaming at the guard in unison while making a human chain from platform to train, not allowing it to leave until Hazel had secured her shoe safely. The guard came along and retrieved the shoe with a large pole, watched by an admiring circle of women. He then whistled us off while Hazel cleaned the shoe with a handkerchief and paraded the new shoes up and down the carriage passageway, beaming with pride. Hazel was my favourite babysitter when my parents went out to the Irish dances at St Francis's school, and as a treat for me she used to put all our dining room chairs together and we would play trains for hours.

From Leeds, the steam train took us to either Holyhead or Liverpool, where we boarded an overnight B&I Line ferry to Dublin. A lot of the ferries also doubled as cattle boats, crossing the Irish Sea daily. They were not very comfortable and rolled horrendously; I swear they are where I got my seasickness from and I have suffered from it ever since.

On arrival in Dublin in the early morning of the next day, the various families would all go their separate ways to stay with their own Irish relatives. We would always start by visiting two of my father's younger sisters, my aunts Dymphna and Bernadette, who worked in the city. This would give us a day to rest and relax a little before heading to the 'wessshhht' the following morning.

Irish Railways operated a service from Dublin's Heuston to Claremorris, and immediately on leaving the city you would find yourself transported to a different world. Mullingar was the first station outside Dublin that we used to look out for; then Athlone, a large city on the banks of the mighty Shannon river – which seemed so wide as we crossed over it (the Shannon always gave me an idea of what the Amazon must look like); then Roscommon; Castlerea; Ballyhaunis…

Outside our train windows, beautiful green fields of cows or sheep would fly by, or vast stretches of bogland, where turf was piled in low stacks to enable the wind to blow through them and dry them out ready for the turf fire. Even today, as I travel through Mayo down to my mum's, I can distinguish the sweet smell of a bog fire from some house I am passing and the memories of my childhood come flooding back.

When we arrived at Claremorris, we changed onto the blue bus, which then transported us from Claremorris through the rolling emerald countryside down to Balla and then on to the Carrandine Post Office. Uncle Paddy would be there, waiting to help with the prams and the suitcases. Together we would walk up the tarmac road, onto the stone road and then past the woods over two stiles, until we were welcomed into the wide arms of my grandmother, who would then hold us away from her to see how we had grown and changed in the course of a year.

Dinner would be bacon and cabbage and lots of lovely floury Irish potatoes with butter (from our own churn), washed down with fresh milk from the cows. All followed by apple tart and ice cream for dessert.

Later, we children would be tucked up in bed, usually three to a mattress, top and tailed, as we often ended up sharing with some of our many cousins who would come to stay. We would find it hard to sleep, as we would be so busy planning our adventures for the next six weeks. But eventually, exhausted by our travels, we would doze off with the moonlight dancing on the window outside.

Living on a farm for six weeks gave us the freedom of playing in wide-open spaces with no traffic to worry about, and we could literally run wild. It was an enchanting place for kids. We even had a real fort on our land: a circular mound of earth built high around the surrounding fields on which we used to play war games. We would spend the day besieging each other and setting traps for the foxes that roamed the area. They were our enemy, as they were also responsible for attacking my grandmother's menagerie of fowl, including her hens and her lovely white turkeys.

But despite the freedom, there were still some rules we had to obey: we could not run after Uncle Paddy's cows, for example, as he had told us that the milk in their udders would turn to butter! We were also told we could not play with the other children who lived in Carrandine until our various chores had been completed.

Certainly there were plenty of jobs to do on the farm to keep us busy. There was no running water, for example, only a massive tank of rainwater at the side of the house, which was used to wash everything from our dishes and our clothes to ourselves. (My Aunt Bernadette swore her hair was better conditioned from washing in rainwater – she told me most French women did this and that's why they looked so chic.) So to get drinking water, we had to make a trek every day to one of two wells at neighbouring farms, either the Holsters' or the Toowheys'. My brother Patrick and I were given the task of filling the buckets morning and evening so that the kettle, which was heated on an open turf fire, could be kept at boiling point all day in case someone should call and want a cup of tea. I hated carrying the laden buckets because the water would splosh into my wellies and I would squelch all the way home. Our wellies were our pride and joy: we would wear them pretty much constantly for the whole six weeks so that we could stand in freshly laid cowpats and mud, as young boys like to do.

But of course the biggest task that had to be completed before we went home concerned the hay: the *blessed hay*, as it was generally known – or as my dear Uncle John would say, the *flipping hay*. Uncle John was my dad's younger brother who lived near us in Leeds, but he would also come out to the farm for two weeks over the summer with his own family to help bring in the hay. He always used 'flipping' instead of any other swear word so it was always 'flipping this' and 'flipping that'. I can still hear him now: 'Oh bejaaaysus, the flipping hay, the flipping hay, the flipping hay…' Of course, the full weight of responsibility rested on my poor Uncle Paddy, who would be a nervous wreck for weeks until we got all the hay into the massive hay barn across from the house.

When my own father came out to join us for his fortnight's 'holiday', he would have to start work virtually straight away. He would have the luxury of a single day off before setting out to

Ballinamore, where we had a large field away from the house. He would have half the grass cut before help would arrive in the form of Paddy, who had the cows to milk first and would take his own sweet time coming over. And who can blame him? It was hard work: the whole field of grass would have to be cut into long strips with a scythe, by hand. Occasionally, we hired a neighbour's tractor to make the job easier. Either way, the grass would then be left to dry in the golden summer sun.

The hay then had to go through certain processes before it was ready. We children would have the job of raking it over using wooden rakes, so it would dry evenly on both sides. Unfortunately, if you were heavy handed, you could break the teeth on the rakes and cause Uncle Paddy to have a fit or even two – which wasn't hard. When dry, the hay was then forked into dome-shaped haycocks, to dry it further and season it. Finally, it would be loaded onto a cart and drawn up to the house and the barn by our ever-faithful donkey, Lizzie.

The donkey and cart, as well as two bicycles, were the only form of transport we possessed in Carrandine. Safe in the complete seclusion of the countryside, we would leave the bicycles overnight under a tree on the stone road far away from the main house. We never used to worry about them being stolen.

As for Lizzie, she was an adorable old donkey. She knew her way to Ballinamore field and back, as every summer she would have to bring home the hay along that route. One year, when I was eleven, my younger sister Margaret and I were given the task of bringing Lizzie and the cart down to the field on our own. We were to bring the hay workers a picnic of sandwiches, apple tart and lashings of buttermilk, all homemade. So we harnessed Lizzie up and set off, passing through three sets of gates on the way. I was the driver and in charge, so I made Margaret get on and off the cart, open the gates then close them, three times in quick succession. The poor girl's face was as red as a beetroot by the time we were out onto the stone road.

But we were having fun: we were free and alone and full of mischief, making Lizzie trot and pretending she was Black Beauty, and we were doing well with our task. In fact, we felt we were doing so well that we had time to make a detour.

Ballinamore was a right turn at the end of the stone road, past the holy shrine dedicated to Jesus, Mary and Joseph where you would bless yourself as you passed or say a prayer or two if you had time. We would then pass the Ruanes' house and make a left turn into Ballinamore field. Well, this day we had sixpence to spend on sweets from our Aunt Frances and Uncle Patsy who had visited recently from Castlebar. (Aunt Frances made – and still makes – the best apple tart in Mayo.) The nearest shop was at the Post Office, a left turn and about three miles' walk away, so my plan was to arrive in style with the donkey and cart, greeting our friends the Begleys, the Kings and the Nicholsons on the way. But could I get Lizzie to turn left? Not on your nelly. That old donkey had had a lifetime of making the journey between our farm and the hayfield and she was not to be swayed off her usual route. She stood her ground and in the end we had to give way and continue, with no sweets, to Ballinamore.

Unfortunately, our troubles didn't end there. In the distance, I saw a flash of white and a donkey and cart advancing at some speed towards us on the opposite side of the road. As they approached, I recognized our neighbour, one of the Carrandine bachelors. It was Brian Moorhan, who was trying without much success to control a large white donkey. The creature was racing along and taking no instructions from Brian. In fact, as he sped nearer, I could see it was not a donkey at all – it was a large white ass. Poor Brian had been duped into buying the deranged animal from some tinkers, and unsurprisingly he could not control the creature. As soon as the ass saw Lizzie, he started to snarl, show his teeth (smiling in ass language), and bray and bray and bray a greeting. Even in donkey terms, I could see that Lizzie had begun to look extremely nervous.

She began pulling away from the ass, who in turn was clearly besotted with our pretty Lizzie.

'Oh bejaysus, this ficken thing is driving me wild! I will have to shoot the ficken creature!' cried Brian, whereupon the ass reared up, still attached to its cart, and tried to mount Lizzie (who was of course still attached to our cart), getting the reins, harness and all sorts of straps tangled up. Brian started thumping the ass wildly, shrieking curses at it. As he tried to pull it away, the braying and snorts increased and it looked like we would never untangle the two unfortunate beasts. Finally, the ass succumbed to Brian's cries and thumps, and eventually calmed down. Brian was forced to carry on up the road immediately, otherwise goodness knows what would have happened.

Of course, the whole incident was rather bewildering to my younger sister, who didn't understand what was going on. I explained that the ass wanted a date with Lizzie and she said no, which seemed to satisfy Margaret's curiosity.

Three days later, I was throwing the tea leaves onto the grass in front of the house to make a fresh pot when I saw Lizzie galloping down the field towards me in some distress. 'Oh sugar,' I thought, and sure enough, in close pursuit was Brian's white ass. The ass had escaped through the hedgerows that divided the neighbouring farms and was obviously intending to woo Lizzie in earnest this time. With no cart attached, he really fancied his chances – and his large state of readiness was apparent for all to see.

I ran into the house and cried, 'Brian's ass has escaped!' My dad and Uncle Paddy came racing out as Lizzie headed for the safety of the orchard. In the distance I could see Brian running down the field with his bandy legs, his trousers held up with string, far, far, behind his white ass. In his arms he was waving a lasso, and you could hear him roaring, 'Shhhtop the ficker... Shhhhtop the ficker!' He looked like an Irish version of John Wayne.

The ass did manage to corner Lizzie, but each time he tried to mount her she literally kicked him in the teeth, which clattered and clattered, much to our amusement. We all caught up with them – everyone was shouting; my father was trying to help a breathless Brian get a bridle around the ass's head; Paddy was trying to get hold of Lizzie, but he was also busy rowing with my father about getting us children inside. The ass was quite a big boy, as most asses are, and Paddy was worried that his nephews would start asking him embarrassing questions.

Oddly enough, no one spoke about sex during these summers, even though on a farm it happens all the time – heifers on heat, bulls going wild... Yet despite this, it's fair to say my Uncle Paddy did not take a very relaxed view of such matters. One time, when he was due to leave my Uncle John in charge of the farm to go off for a few days' holiday in Dublin, he became so paranoid that the heifers would be mixed up and mated while he was away that my Uncle John woke to find that Paddy had painted all the heifers' tails bright blue overnight, so that Uncle John would not get them confused.

Looking back, my childhood was an innocent time, particularly during those long, hot summers in Ireland. We had not a care in the world as we sampled the rural delights of County Mayo day after day, and growing up was the last thing on our minds.

CHAPTER 2

A True-Hearted Son

LIFE FOR THE most part was peaceful at my grandmother's farm. As children we always looked forward to Tuesday evenings and the arrival of Mr McDonald's blue van. He travelled the local farms selling such things as flour, salt, baking powder, and pots and pans. My grandmother was a good customer. She baked her own soda bread three times daily using only the coals of a turf fire. She also churned her own butter and looked after her turkeys and hens, as well as doing all the daily cooking, so she often needed to buy some extra kitchen supplies from Mr McDonald. At the back of the van was a small sweet section and we were given the opportunity to pick some toffee or a bar of chocolate as a treat. Naturally, we longed for Tuesday evenings.

There was a great deal of freedom for us children. Once our chores were done for the day and we had finished our tea, we were free to visit and play with the neighbours' children, being mindful that they had cows to milk first.

In fact, we often used to go and visit the neighbouring cows in their sheds. I remember one year when the Kellys' cow had given birth to two calves that were ginger in colour. They were called suck calves because they were constantly at their mother's udders, but if you held out your hand they would suck your fingers just like a child would suck a dummy or soother.

The Ruanes' house had its own attractions too: this was the place for football in the long summer evenings. Patrick, my older brother, was a very good footballer. The Begelys, the Kings, the Kellys, the Wards and the Holsters were our closest neighbours, and the lads from these farms would all play football until it got so dark you couldn't find the ball when it went under a hedge. There would be much talk about Leeds United, our home-town football team: Billy Bremner, Gary Sprake (Patrick was an altar boy at his wedding), Eddie Gray, Peter Lorimer and Norman Hunter, to name a few players. We would also chat about England and its big cities, and how some of the farm children might eventually follow in my father's footsteps and find work there. But there was no great desire among the children to move away. Although Ireland was a very poor country, most families survived by dint of hard work and enjoyed the simple pleasures in life, such as music and conversation.

The Holsters were our nearest neighbours and were made up of Jim Malee, his son-in-law Sonny Holster, who worked the farm, and Michael, Sonny's only son. Michael's mum had died suddenly, leaving Michael to be brought up by his grandfather and his father, so at five years old when we first met him, Michael was confidently talking about the weather, the price of bullocks and the state of the hay as he stood at his gate to welcome us all home for the summer holidays. We became good friends with the Holsters and of an evening over the summers that followed, I would often visit their house.

My relationship with Jim Malee was also close. He was a lovely old man who had been a policeman in Liverpool and returned home to Ireland to retire. He was a very good accordion player, so I would merrily dance jigs, reels and hornpipes while he played. Sonny and Michael would also play the tin whistle and the accordion, and I would often stay for supper before going home.

Jim would steal the evening with his rendition of the funny poem 'The Lion and Albert' by Marriott Edgar, made famous by Stanley

Holloway. It made us all laugh, but Jim used to be concerned about his broad Irish accent when he was reciting it. As we know, Mr and Mrs Ramsbottom in the poem were English northerners from either Yorkshire or Lancashire, so in time it was suggested that I should learn 'The Lion and Albert' myself, as it would sound so much better with a true northern Leeds accent. I can still remember it now, I used to recite it so much.

Michael's cousins, Paul and Janet Barrass, who lived in the Newcastle area, were often over for the summer and would come to our farm to play with Margaret and me. They would run through Paddy Ward's fields, which surrounded our land, to get to our farm, passing the abandoned Protestants' houses that were now used by Paddy's cows for shelter from the wind and rain. They were scared stiff that one of Paddy's bulls might chase them. Together we would take turns riding Lizzie, when she wasn't bringing in the hay or carrying the turf up from our bog.

This turf was essential for my grandmother as she used it as fuel. She would cook on an open fire with a massive pot, like a witch's cauldron, full of our staple diet of potatoes, accompanied by a bacon joint or a couple of chickens. Everything we ate was reared on the farm; the vegetables would come from the land, the eggs from the chickens (or turkeys if you were lucky; they were four times the size of normal eggs) and the milk straight from the cow, just sieved through muslin and served. As you can imagine, coming from the city to a farm, it was absolutely phenomenal; in fact the food was so rich it used to bring us out in spots when we first came over, until our bodies adjusted to it.

There was a huge barn where all the hay was brought up from Ballinamore and stored for the winter months to feed the animals. We discovered we could make one long slide out of the haystack by combining three or four chair-shaped slides, and we would spend all morning sliding, fighting and wrestling in the hay. Sometimes

Janet Barrass would give me a kiss there – I found out later she had a bit of a crush on me, though I didn't know it at the time.

One day, we found a great big nest of around a dozen fresh brown eggs in the barn. I ran into the house where my mum was with my grandmother working hard as usual, churning the butter, making the bread and doing the washing. I announced my find and quickly grabbed one of Uncle Paddy's hats to use as a container to bring the eggs to the house. There were so many they wouldn't all fit, so I put six eggs into the pockets of my shorts, three on each side.

Unfortunately, I then promptly forgot all about them and decided to have just one last slide down the haystack before I took the hat of eggs back. As I reached the bottom, I heard an almighty crack and immediately shoved my hands into my pockets in panic. I'll never forget the sensation of six egg yolks seeping down my legs. I got a smack when I got home, as wasting food was a big sin in those days.

This kind of mishap aside, our Irish holidays were very special, and I will always treasure the memories of day trips to the seaside with the Barrass family or visits to Kilsallagh in the north of Mayo to stay with our cousins the Walshes. However, every summer, eventually the awful day would arrive when we would have to go home to Leeds. The cases would come out and my mum would go around all the rooms packing up our belongings and getting things ready for the next day's departure. It was terrible – we all would have stayed in Ireland for ever if we could. But my father's work was calling him back and my mother had a cleaning job in England too. We had to say goodbye to all our friends and we would always promise to write letters and tell them what was going on with Leeds United until next summer, when we would undertake this massive pilgrimage all over again.

When the dreadful morning dawned, my grandmother would come out of her room all dressed up, clutching a bottle of holy water, and she would sprinkle us all with it and bless herself and bless us, and we would all have to bless ourselves, and then she would sprinkle the cases, sprinkle the prams… She would sprinkle everything in sight, would my grandmother, but it was just her way of bidding us a safe journey back home. She had only been to England once and that was when my father and my mother got married in 1955. I can remember seeing a photograph of her in a beautiful blue suit, which, later, she always used to wear to Mass.

Once we'd done with the sprinkling, my grandmother would kiss us all and then we would make our way down to Carrandine Post Office, the same route we took to go to church. Poor Michael Holster would be waiting for us at the end of his lane, very upset to say goodbye to us because he would have no one to play with once we'd gone. We would get to the T-junction and as soon as the first person saw the blue bus arriving from Kiltimagh, they would start to cry. And because they would cry, I would start to cry, and then my grandmother would cry, and then my Uncle Paddy would start getting upset, and then my mother would get upset too. It was like a Mexican wave of emotion running through the whole family. God knows what the poor driver must have thought, with this wailing family boarding his bus en masse.

It was on those occasions that I wondered how my father must have felt in 1947 when he'd had to emigrate to England. My father had to leave all his sisters and his mother behind and come down to that corner before boarding a bus and getting the train to Dublin, then the boat all the way to Liverpool or Holyhead, and then a train from there to Leeds – just like we did every year. It was hard enough for us, but this was his farm, his home, his family that he was leaving behind. I can only imagine how traumatic it must have been.

* * *

Ireland has always held a special place in my heart. Even today, whenever the Aer Lingus pilot asks us to prepare for landing on our approach to the runway south-east of Dublin airport, I look out of the window at the beautiful and intricate patchwork of green fields which make up this wonderful island, and my heart still skips a beat.

This is the land of my father and grandfathers and many lifelong friends: the Sheerins, the Cardens, the Walshes, the Gallaghers, the O'Briens, the Nolans, the O'Sheas and the Horkans, to name a few of the many families who have been a major influence on my younger formative years.

My father was born in Carrandine, County Mayo, and as a youth he worked on the farm with his brothers, John and Paddy. He also had seven sisters: Frances, Theresa, Mary, Pauline, Bernadette, Kathleen and Dymphna, the youngest.

My mother's father was a Carden from Steelaun near South Lackan, which is near Kilcummin in County Mayo too. He settled in Hunslet, Leeds, and later moved to Beeston, marrying Alice, a Catholic Yorkshire lass. Together they had four children: my mum Maureen, Kevin, Michael and Martin.

Both my families are recorded in the 1911 census of Ireland and all are registered as Roman Catholic. All my family members were at that time able to read and write, which was quite a feat considering education had to be paid for and many children would leave school to work in the fields at thirteen or fourteen years of age.

After the Second World War, my father left County Mayo to come to Leeds in West Yorkshire, England. At first he laboured on the land outside Leeds, along with many other Irishmen and women. My father then moved on to Monkbridge Forge, working in the treating plant and manufacturing turbine blades for gas turbines and Rolls-Royce engines. His younger brother John had come out to Leeds the year before and he helped my father to get a job there.

It is perhaps not surprising that so many young Irish upped sticks and left the country at that time. Ireland was a very poor country so many people had to travel to England to look for work. Many Irishmen ended up labouring on the building sites that proliferated in England in the post-war building boom. They stuck together, settling in cities like London, Birmingham, Liverpool, Manchester and Leeds, and creating new communities with their fellow expats. These were often built around the Catholic Church – literally in some cases. Certainly in Leeds, the local churches of St Joseph's, St Francis of Assisi and St Anthony's owe their existence to the generosity and faith of many of the Irish parishioners who raised money to build and maintain these churches.

As the song goes: 'Far away from the land of the shamrock and heather / In search of a living, as exiles we roam / But oh, how we like to assemble together / Like true-hearted sons from the County Mayo.'

And assemble they did, at large Irish dances with show bands led by such well-known names as Johnny McEvoy, Jack Ruane and Brendan Shine. They used to come over from Ireland to perform in the many dance halls of Leeds. Whether it was the Green Rooms opposite the Leeds Building Society, or later St Francis's Holbeck or the Trades Hall off The Headrow, the local Irish community would assemble together to chat with old friends, have a good dance and, of course, to drink.

I don't know how many couples met at these dances but there must have been hundreds, my parents included, who went on to court each other and then finally marry at the local Catholic churches, inviting most of the people they knew from the dances. My mother met my father at the Green Rooms. He was on the organizing committee, and would often be on the door taking the money, so she got in for free for most of the dances when they started courting. The resident band there was led by a man called Charlie

Burns, who would often fall asleep at his drums before the end of the dance.

It was a close-knit community with all the families knowing each other extremely well and living in each other's pockets. Work was often shared out among the menfolk when it came in. Many Irishmen worked as 'navvies' in gangs, building and repairing the roads, and whenever I cross the Pennines today I think of my relations who built the M62. These tough men worked in all sorts of conditions, but although times were hard, most people were happy and felt part of a supportive network of friends and family. Certainly from the moment I came into the world, I had not only my immediate family, but also a whole community looking out for me – including a very special woman whom I called Auntie Dolly.

CHAPTER 3

Auntie Dolly

I HAVE HEARD the story of my birth so many times that I feel like I can actually remember it myself. And of course, in every version of the story, my Auntie Dolly played a huge part, just as she was to play a central role throughout the whole of my childhood.

Margaret Hunter, or Dolly as she was called, had known my mother, Maureen, since Maureen was three. Dolly was about my grandmother's age and the families had always been great friends, as well as neighbours – Dolly lived just nearby on Pepper Road, near my parents' little back-to-back house at 21 Rumelia Street.

So it was only natural that Dolly was sent for as soon as my mother went into labour. Buttoning herself up against the cold wintry air on 23 February 1959, she raced over the road, fearful as to what she would find. In fact, the first person she saw was Alice, my maternal grandmother, who was nervously pacing around the small kitchen smoking a Woodbine and saying the rosary at the same time.

'Her waters have broken and the midwife is with her, Dolly,' she said, crossing herself. 'Oh Jesus, Mary and Joseph, you had better go up. You're much better than me at these things.' Alice then lit up another cigarette, having clearly forgotten whether she was on the Sorrowful or the Joyful Mysteries. It was evident she could not think properly – all she knew was that her only daughter was going through labour and she was frightened for her.

My mother Maureen was a fine young girlie, strong and hardworking, and she would endure her labour just like she had when she gave birth to my brother Patrick two years earlier, the first grandchild for both families. But that birth had taken place in a private nursing home run by the Sisters of Charity, which my father had insisted they would have for their firstborn. Now it was different: this was a home birth and there were no armies of holy nuns to help here. Hence Alice had decided the rosary was the best bet for a safe outcome, so she started another decade just for insurance.

As the story goes, Dolly climbed the steep stairs of the small back-to-back house, passing the red illuminated picture of the Sacred Heart of Jesus, and hoping the new baby would be a little girl. If it was a girl, she could go out and buy frilly lacy knickers for her and all sorts of lovely dresses. Why not? Dolly had the resources and she liked being part of the Carden and Sheerin families. As she arrived at the top of the stairs, the dark-haired figure of my worried-looking father was just leaving the room with a jug of water. 'I shall be downstairs if you need me, Dolly,' he said. Without saying a word, she took his hand and squeezed it and then entered the dimly lit room. There she heard Maureen, who was already beginning to push hard with the midwife's encouragement.

Dolly was the first person to hold me after the midwife. She even scolded the midwife about rubbing too hard to erase a birthmark, insisting it was 'not muck, but a tea leaf on his tummy, that's all'. Maureen and Tom called their second son Brendan and, in Dolly's eyes, he was going to become a very special little boy.

For Auntie Dolly was to be like a surrogate mother to me. Although she was not a relative, she was very close to my family and she was the perfect example of the genuine neighbourly bond that existed in those days. It was a bond that would last between the two of us until the day she died. She already had a fully grown son, Roy, who was a plumber with his own business, and her husband John was fully employed as a lathe engineer, so her whole life was already devoted to these two men and she looked after their every need. However, Dolly was on the lookout for a third man in her life and, fortunately for me, it turned out to be Brendan Sheerin.

Auntie Dolly was, to me, the perfect housewife. She would bake cakes, making coconut and fruit loaves on Thursdays; she would do all the shopping on Fridays, her purse bursting at the seams with cash (no credit for the Hunters, everything was paid in cash); and on Sundays she would make the best roast dinners with the crispiest and highest Yorkshire puddings I have ever seen in my life. They were even baked at the base to hold a reservoir of onion gravy. Once I took my best friend Liam O'Brien to Dolly's house for egg and chips after school, and to this day he still talks about how crispy and golden brown her chips were.

Dolly included me in everything, stating, 'If you ever end up living on your own, you will need to be able to shop and cook for yourself.' I wonder if Auntie Dolly knew something about me then that I did not know myself. I used to help her fill the copper boiler on a Monday to wash the bright white sheets from the beds, then rinse them in Dolly Blue, which made them even whiter.

Every Friday, we used to get the bus to the Grandways supermarket on Dewsbury Road. There we would purchase tins of John West salmon, laughing as we quoted to each other, 'It's the salmon that John West reject that makes John West Salmon the best!' I would steer the trolley, adding a few extra tins of Ambrosia creamed rice, made from cows in Devon. Dolly used to let me have a whole tin to myself, which was quite a luxury in those days. In our family, everything was shared out equally, and as my mum went on to have three more children – Margaret, Martin and Terence – in addition to Patrick and myself, a tin of Ambrosia went a long way in our household.

I was also allowed to pick out a little metal car or a bus from the toy section as another treat, but they were never brought home for fear of being hijacked by my younger siblings. I had learned this the hard way, when my train set was taken out while I was at school and then damaged beyond repair. I cherished my toys so became adept at guarding them fiercely.

One Christmas, my dad brought me a new bike from Watson Cairns in Lower Briggate, and thereafter on weekends I would ride over to Dolly's house on my own. When I arrived, on the other side of Pepper Road to her house, I would shout at the top of my lungs, 'AUNTIE DOLLY!' She would come out to guide me across the road and into her home, where I would spend the whole afternoon with her.

One day, Dolly was busy in the house and did not hear me cry out to her, so I decided – being quite a wilful child – to negotiate the road myself. Unfortunately, I was promptly knocked down by a milk float.

Auntie Dolly heard the commotion and came out to see me lying in the middle of the road, looking for all the world as if I were dead. She picked me up and brought me into her house, and sent an urgent message to my parents to let them know what had happened. They dropped everything to race over to me, fearful as to what they would find. When they arrived, they found me lying on Auntie Dolly's ample sofa, playing with a train that had been purchased from Longbottom's toy shop on Low Road. I was fine.

However, poor Auntie Dolly was blamed for not hearing me, especially by her husband, Uncle John, who gently but firmly said she should set a time to be there every day as my visits were becoming that regular. I suppose when I think back Auntie Dolly spoiled me, but for me her house was an oasis of peace and calm, and an escape from the noise of my own house and my four siblings.

Our families became inextricably entwined. My sister, born two years after me, was named Margaret after Auntie Dolly's real name. In gratitude, Dolly bought Margaret's entire christening outfit and was guest of honour at the ceremony. She was a very generous benefactor to our whole family and I loved her dearly.

But Hunslet was changing. The old steel works had closed down years ago and the area was redeveloping, with new industries being created. The copper works and other engineering firms were moving in, and there was prosperity in the air. As their circumstances improved, Auntie Dolly, Uncle John and Roy set their sights on a lovely semi-detached house in Grovehall Avenue, Beeston, Leeds 11. Oh, how I wailed when I saw my Auntie Dolly with their furniture van parked up outside the house. It felt like the end of my world, as if she were moving to Australia. In truth, it was only a 30-minute drive away, but to a young boy that was an insurmountable distance. My poor brother Patrick was given strict instructions to find out how to get to Auntie Dolly's new house by bus, and a plan was formed to get me there at least once a week to pacify me.

It was about this time that my father also decided to move us all, to St Luke's Crescent, Beeston. We were still some distance from Auntie Dolly, who lived further up the hill, but it was a fantastic move nonetheless. Our new home was a 'through house', meaning you could have a yard at one side of the house and a garden at the other, and you could walk through from one side to the next. It had four bedrooms, a living room and sitting room, a bathroom and two massive cellars. Patrick and I could even ride our bicycles around those cellars, they were that big. We would store our bikes there too, while Mam used the rooms for the laundry, spending all day boilwashing endless cotton nappies in Acdo detergent; the babies kept coming, and my younger brothers, Martin and Terence, were born in 1965 and 1967 respectively.

We would play all sorts of games with the lovely Hughes family, who lived close by on the same street. When the house next door to us became available, my dad bought that property, too, simply because my grandmother Alice and granddad Pat had been left behind in Hunslet and missed us. So they joined us next door, repaying my father over the years for the cost of the house. He must have been a man of means, my dad. After all, he paid for both houses in cash in the mid-sixties.

My weekly trips out with Auntie Dolly continued. Sometimes she would take me on the number one bus to Leeds city centre for a day of shopping. The bus would arrive at City Square and we would then walk down Boar Lane and turn right into Briggate, until we reached her favourite corset shop in the County Arcade, where they called her 'madam' and me 'young sir'. The ladies' lingerie was in lovely teak or walnut cases with matching drawers and everything was taken out discreetly and shown to madam before her purchase was put in the finest tissue, then wrapped in coloured paper before being placed into madam's bag. I used to love the way Auntie Dolly's money was put into a round cylinder and sucked up a pipe to the cash office and then returned with the change. As a result of these shopping trips, I discovered that Auntie Dolly wore suspenders with her silk stockings. I already knew about the corsets as I could feel them through her frock whenever I hugged her.

Auntie Dolly's strong Yorkshire accent used to take on the flavour of a well-to-do lady from Harrogate when she was in these upper-class shops. When she first got her new telephone installed at Grovehall Avenue, her voice changed to that of a Yorkshire Celia Johnson in *Brief Encounter*.

Across the road from the big department store, Schofield's, was a little street called King Charles Street, which was the site of my favourite shop of all time. This was called Beattie's and it was a model railway shop. If Auntie was feeling generous, I could choose a Hornby carriage or a goods wagon to add to my collection, but locomotives and steam train engines were reserved for birthdays and Christmas.

Lunch was always taken in the soup bar in the basement of John Lewis's store with a ride in the brass lift as a treat (rather than taking the quicker new escalators, which had just been installed). The lift was operated by a one-armed man who had fought in the Second World War against the Germans. Auntie Dolly told me he was very brave losing his arm like that for King and Country. She herself was very proud of her own war record, having contributed to the war effort by working day and night in the munitions factory in Hunslet, 'making bombs for Hitler and all his relatives and dear friends', as she put it.

The soup was served piping hot and packed with vegetables (including pearl barley, which Auntie Dolly told me was good for your bowels) and real ox's tail in the oxtail soup. But Auntie Dolly maintained we had to be careful with the chicken soup, as it was too creamy and would repeat on her.

After lunch, I could choose where to go as a treat, so we would visit two of my favourite arcades just off New Briggate and not far from the Grand Theatre. The first was the Grand Arcade, which had a moving clock that I was obsessed with. On the hour, the cockerel above the clock would flap its wings and crow, then a mobile Grenadier Guard would come out, followed by an Irishman, then a Scotsman, a Canadian and an Indian gentleman. They would acknowledge you with a bow or a raising of the hand and we would naturally return the compliment, to be polite. At the base was an inscription: 'Time and Tide Wait for No Man'. Auntie Dolly used to say this meant you should always live your life to the full and not let fear hold you back.

We would then make time to visit Leeds Market to go to Wildeblood's, who were purveyors of fine cooked meats, sausages, black pudding and chicklets, then deeper into the market to the nut shop. Here a lady called Jean, who had a huge beehive hairdo and bright red painted nails, would serve us with a mixed selection of nuts. Auntie Dolly would invariably triple the order over the

Christmas period with particular attention to walnuts, and also buy three packets of stoneless dates from North Africa. The date packets always featured a drawing of a handsome, tanned Arab gentleman, dressed in a beautiful white djellabah and turban, no doubt to protect him from the soaring temperatures of the desert. I would dream of leaving the comfort of his oasis and leading a caravan of Berbers over the immense sands of the Sahara with our packets of dates on the camels' backs, ready to be sent to Leeds Market for Christmas. He looked very exotic and I remember wondering why I found him so handsome and attractive.

We would then walk up the butchers' row of Leeds Market and out into Vicar Lane. From there we would cut through Queen Victoria Street back up to Thornton's Arcade, my other favourite destination, where we would wait for the hour to strike so we could see Robin Hood and Richard the Lionheart strike the bells on the Ivanhoe clock. At the side of Thornton's Arcade was our favourite coffee bar, which was owned by a lovely Italian family. This was our exotic treat as you could hear them all babbling away in Italian as if we were in Roma or Milano. We always had a milky coffee – 'not too much froth, love' – and a vanilla slice each.

Making our way to City Square, where a statue of the Black Prince sat majestically on his steed, we would catch the number one bus back up to Beeston and I would kiss Auntie Dolly goodbye and alight from the bus at the Malvern pub, which was my stop.

Auntie Dolly's kindness didn't just extend to me but also to the other children in her street. A little girl called Margaret McClellan lived next door to Auntie Dolly on Grovehall Avenue. She was one year older than me, and we often used to play together. One of Auntie Dolly's passions was the pictures, so she often used to take Margaret and me to see the Saturday morning children's foundation films like *Calamity the Cow* or *The Boy Who Turned Yellow* or *The Cat Gang Show* at the Malvern Picture House on Beeston Hill for sixpence.

Auntie Dolly and I also used to steal away together on our own sometimes, to watch a matinee in town. We loved the great romantic films: *Doctor Zhivago* with Omar Sharif at the Tatler cinema or *Brief Encounter* with Trevor Howard and Celia Johnson at the Plaza.

Other times, it seemed Auntie Dolly would take the whole street of children to the cinema. We would get dressed up and catch the bus into Leeds to the Odeon cinema on Vicar Lane or the top of New Briggate to go and see *Mary Poppins*, *Bedknobs and Broomsticks*, *Doctor Dolittle*, and *Oliver!* At the interval, we would have a tub of ice cream or a strawberry mivvy (a strawberry ice lolly with vanilla ice cream inside), the latter being our favourite.

Then one day, the biggest film of all time arrived at the Majestic in City Square: *The Sound of Music*! Wow, what a movie for a young Catholic boy! Auntie Dolly and I went to see it about fifteen times; we absolutely loved the storyline, the costumes and, most of all, the singing. Margaret McClellan and I would act out the scenes in Auntie Dolly's garden and sing all the songs upon our return to Beeston. Even today, I know all those children's names and I can recall the script at a moment's notice – which I often do when on location in Salzburg filming *Coach Trip*.

Catholicism, romance, comedy, a bitchy baroness and a woman struggling between love of her church and the love of a man. How perfect. Years later, when I was to see it again with my very first gay love, John, I realized how pertinent the film's message – to follow your dreams and be truthful to yourself – was for my life. As the clock's inscription in the Grand Arcade said, 'Time and Tide Wait for No Man.' I did overcome my fears and stay true to myself eventually, but my religion had a strong hold on me and was to shape the course of most of my childhood. Auntie Dolly's words of wisdom about living my life to the full would have to wait – for the moment.

CHAPTER 4

Altar Boy

To be an Irish Catholic boy growing up in the early sixties meant that your life revolved around the local church – in our case, St Francis of Assisi. The church played a big part in most people's lives, with its never-ending cycle of baptisms, confessions, Holy Communions, confirmations, weddings and funerals, all bringing together the lifeblood of the community. Priests, such as Father Stephen Corbally, had an enormous influence on my life. Although he was a stoic Yorkshireman from Selby, Father Corbally was passionate about serving his Irish brethren and helping them through life's difficulties, including poverty, tragedy and abandonment. He was an intelligent man and loved to regale us about St Paul – his favourite saint – during his Sunday sermons.

It was Father Corbally who suggested I follow in my brother Patrick's footsteps and become an altar boy. His curate at the time was a good-looking priest called Father Gath, who made most of the female congregation go weak at the knees when he first appeared at St Francis's.

Father Gath, being the younger priest, also breathed life into our church for us youngsters. He set up and ran a youth club and several football teams, and on a Sunday he would turn up in a van with Sister Hilda, calling in on the Sheerins, the O'Briens, the Thompsons, the Hughes, the Fords and the Jones, and gather as many kids as possible. Off we would go to Ilkley or Otley for the day, for an ice cream and a game of football. For many of us kids, it was the only way of getting out of the streets of Beeston and seeing something different.

I enjoyed playing football, but I was soon to discover that my natural talents lay elsewhere. In most large Irish families, there was a member who could sing, dance or play an instrument. Ours was no exception: my Uncle Francis was a tin whistle player, my Uncle Malachi could play the accordion, and my grandfather Pat Carden was a great step dancer. It seemed I had inherited my grandfather's genes, so one Friday night when I was around six or seven years old, my mother took me and my sister Margaret off to St Philip's in Middleton, where there was an Irish dancing school run by two ladies from Dublin.

The teachers were very kind, with fine Irish names: Philomena O'Brien and Mary O'Hara (the latter not to be mistaken with the famous harp player and singer). After introducing me to a few steps and playing me some music, Mary then proceeded to drag me around the floor at quite a speed – rather to my surprise – while I counted in my head and instinctively performed with my feet: *one* two three, and a *one* two three, and a *one* two three… Both teachers immediately noted that I was extremely light on my feet, which is a prerequisite for a good Irish dancer, although I did not know it at the time.

My dearest, darling sister Margaret was next to be whirled around the floor. She was not very happy about this and could not dance the steps (in fact, to my great amusement she was described as being 'heavy-footed'). She lasted the lesson but didn't really show any interest at all so did not go back. I, on the other hand, could not get enough of dancing. I loved the music and the steps and even today I can turn a head or two when on the floor. The last time was at the YMCA Theatre in Scarborough. It was a fund-raiser for a local

Scarborough Irish dancing school and I did quite well, if I say so myself.

While I was at the dancing school at St Philip's, I was introduced to Margaret Ford and Marie Cosgrove, who were already family friends, although I didn't realize they were also such good dancers. The only other boy was a guy called Bernard Smith, from Middleton. There were enough girls to partner so we got on well, and I immediately felt at home in the company of my fellow dancing students.

Quickly I advanced through the ranks at the dancing school and was soon able to dance slip jigs with Margaret and Marie, and also two-hand reels, hornpipes and jigs. When we were asked to dance at the St Patrick's Day celebrations at the Mecca ballroom in the Merrion Centre, Leeds in 1967 – well, this was the big time. We took the place by storm. I have never drunk so much pop in one night in all my life, and the cheese with pineapple was so exotic I thought I was at the Ritz.

Becoming a proficient dancer would bring other benefits, too. It dawned on me that I would be the only Irish dancer in the Sheerin family, available to perform at a moment's notice at weddings, birthday parties and those times when my Uncle Francis would visit my grandfather on a Sunday after Mass and start playing his tin whistle, after first flicking off any fluff from the inside of his Harris Tweed jacket. I was immediately excited at the prospect of becoming an important part of these family celebrations – although occasionally my legs would dance me into trouble.

One summer, several years after I had first learned to dance, when I was about thirteen or so, I was over in Ireland for my holidays as usual. Our friend Paul Barrass, who was three or four years older than me, had learned to drive in England during the year and had passed his test at the age of seventeen, so he had brought his Ford Escort over to Carrandine. He was so proud of it and was always working on it. He would chauffeur us younger kids around the small country lanes, driving fast and showing off. Sometimes we would be a bit scared, as the roads weren't too brilliant in those days.

One night, however, he took me into Kiltimagh, which was the nearest town to us, about six miles from our family farm. We ended up in a big public house called the Raferty Rooms. Inside, you could hear all these American and Australian tourists who had come home to their roots: 'Hi, I'm Patrick and I'm from Chicago.' There was a little ceilidh band in the corner, who were playing all those morbid Irish ballads like 'Galway Bay' and 'Danny Boy'. Paul was on the hunt for some local girls, so we went in and ordered two half lagers because we couldn't afford anything else. All of a sudden, the band started up again and they began to play reels and jigs. Everybody's feet started to tap along, but nobody was dancing, so Paul thought it would be a good idea if I got up and started everyone off. I said, 'Oh no, I couldn't,' as I was quite shy and obviously there were a lot of people in this pub. But Paul was older than me and could be very persuasive, so eventually I got up, pointed my toe and waited for the music, and once the rhythm and the beat were correct, I shot off around the empty dance floor, executing a perfect reel.

Well, people started to stop their conversations and look up, the cameras started clicking and soon they started to clap to the beat of my steps and the music. The whole pub was up on its feet as the reel came to a finale and I ended with a little bow. I returned to a beaming Paul who was cheering like everybody else and immediately the owner of the establishment, Paddy Raferty, was at my side offering me a contract to dance every night for the summer months. Of course, the Americans and Australians absolutely loved it. They thought it was fantastic that this young boy could dance an Irish jig – not that I was old enough to be in the pub in the first place.

Paddy Raferty then asked if I would dance a jig and started whipping up the crowd: 'We want to see this little boy dance a jig, don't we, ladies and gentlemen? The people that have come all the way from Australia and America, they all want to see this little boy dance a jig, don't they?' Of course, the whole place erupted. So I started to perform a slip jig and immediately our table started to fill up with free drinks. Well, Paul's face was beaming; he thought it was the absolute best thing since sliced bread. I had never really drunk alcohol before, but as the free drinks kept coming, I started to sample a few and before long began feeling a bit strange.

Luckily Paul, being older, realized what was happening and somehow managed to get me home in one piece just before midnight – only to find my Uncle Paddy sat waiting up for me, saying his rosary. My mother had long gone to bed. He asked where I had been and I said we had been to Kiltimagh though I didn't tell him exactly what we had been doing because I knew he wouldn't have approved.

I went to bed dreaming of spending the rest of the summer entertaining the visitors of the Raferty Rooms with my dancing, and earning heaps of money in the process. But it was not to be.

The next day, Sunday, we all went to Mass – and as luck would have it, one of the first people we saw was a neighbour who had been in the Raftery Rooms the previous evening. Of course he told my Uncle Paddy that his nephew Brendan had been dancing in the pub all night. Uncle Paddy was disgraced, absolutely disgusted. My father had gone back to England by this point so my uncle talked to my mother, saying that no Sheerin should ever dance for money in an establishment like that in Kiltimagh. So that was the end of my first foray into the world of entertainment.

Nonetheless, I took great pride in my new skill. Good Irish dancers move in time to the rhythm of the music and are tremendously light on their feet. Their steps are executed with extreme accuracy and grace, and their arms must be straight down and not moving around at all. That is how I was brought up to dance, with none of this Michael Flatley arms-in-the-air nonsense. I wouldn't have been seen dead in those loud, flamboyant blouses either. I always wore a crisp white shirt bought from the back of Leeds Market, and I looked a right bobby-dazzler, as they say.

The only downside to Irish dancing was the ensuing fallout with my older brother, Patrick. He was a very good footballer and used to play all the time with his mates Michael Ford (with whom I served Mass; he was very kind and nice), Paul O'Brien and Kevin Jones. They were all the stars of the older team.

One day, Father Gath organized a five-a-side football game for my age group of under-tens, and made up a team that consisted of Liam O'Brien (my best friend), Michael Parkinson, Steven Child, Paul Newton and me. As always, I was to be put out of the way, somewhere safe and out of trouble, so I was given the goalkeeper's position. As usual, the game proceeded at the other end of the field as my teammates kept the opposition very busy.

So what do you do when you're bored and in an empty goal? With my thoughts drifting, I remembered a *fesch* (Gaelic for a traditional Irish dancing competition) that I was to be entered into next weekend. A jig tune formed in my mind and I started humming, then I decided to act out the steps with my feet while keeping my eye up the field. There was still no sign of any life at this end of the pitch, so I continued and then thought it was safe to practise a full circle. After all, they were all safely down the other end. I got so carried away – *der* der der, *der* der der, *der* der der – I did practically a full circle of an Irish jig as the football shot past my head and straight into the unoccupied goal. Well, all hell broke loose. You would have thought it was the World Cup.

My brother Patrick was not amused when he heard the news and hung his head in shame. I had disgraced us all, and my teammates, while Father Gath had no option but to send me off. That was the end of my football playing, but looking on the bright side, I won a gold medal for a jig at the St Bridget's *fesch* in Leeds that following Sunday – at the tender age of just eight years old.

* * *

Luckily, Father Gath forgave me. In fact, he quickly realized that although I was not much use on the football pitch, I was capable of being a very useful member of our church community. As an altar boy, I was expected to know by heart the wording of the Mass, the cornerstone of the Catholic faith – which, in those days, would all be spoken or sung in Latin.

It was the duty of Father Gath to teach me, and quickly I became word-perfect in the calls and responses that make up the Mass. I found I took great pleasure in the way the Latin phrases would flow so beautifully together. Father Gath would say: '*Dominus vobiscum*' (the Lord be with you). I would reply: '*Et cum spiritu tuo*' (and also with you). We would then confess our sins: '*Confiteor Deo omnipotenti, istis Sanctis et omnibus Sanctis et tibi frater, quia peccavi in cogitatione...*'

I loved the drama of striking your breast with your clenched right fist, admitting your sins while saying, '*Mea culpa, mea culpa, mea maxima culpa*' (my own fault, my own fault, my own most grievous fault).

The Kyrie, then the Gloria that followed, were quite difficult to learn, but nothing previously mastered prepared me for the time when I first heard Father Gath intoning and singing the Credo. This long statement of faith can be sung or spoken, and is an important part of the Mass for every Catholic.

'*Credo in unum Deum, Patrem omnipotentem, factorem coeli et terrae, visibilium omnium et invisibilium...*' (I believe in one God, Father Almighty, Maker of Heaven and Earth, seen and not seen...) The Credo was a massively long text for a boy of eight to learn in Latin, but learn it you did, through endless hours of repetition.

Sometimes with Father Corbally I would say it under my breath, raising my voice at the sections I could remember so he could hear, and then lowering it again at the ones I couldn't, until eventually I had mastered it completely.

In those days, the priest faced the stunning high altar, with his back to the people, so his words were sometimes hard to hear. As an altar boy, you had to speak exactly in time with the priest, down on the sanctuary, so that the faithful congregation could follow you and everyone would be in sync. There was a lot of business moving lecterns from one side of the priest to the other, and nothing could occur on the altar without a genuflection every time you passed the tabernacle (the box in which the consecrated Eucharist is kept). Your right knee had to bend and touch the floor. With your back ramrod straight and a heavy lectern in both hands, it was quite a tricky feat for a boy of eight – and of course it had to be performed with due seriousness and no laughing or falling over.

The 'Credo in unum Deum' was always intoned in a lovely tenor voice to the glory of God, and was and still is a solemn and beautiful piece of music – if sung correctly. But God help you if your resident fathers were having an off-day vocally or you had a visiting priest who could not sound a note (or, worse, thought he could sing like Matt Monro). The Credo would start too low, which would immediately put the priest's nerves on edge, the 'in' would then be too high, followed by a wobbly 'unum', and then the 'Deum' would be down the aisle and out of the door. Even as a child, you knew how it should sound properly, so any deviation or wobbles would start fits of laughter among us altar boys for all the congregation to see. If they were in on the wobble, there would be a moment of humour in what was, in those days, a very solemn hour of prayer and incantation.

A quartet of brass bells on one single handle and a big brass gong were our favourite toys to play with on the altar, and we used to have tremendous fun ringing and banging the gong. We would even have a competition to see who could hit the gong the loudest during the most important part of the service, the Consecration.

On one memorable occasion, at 7 a.m. Mass, I hit the gong so hard that the sound ricocheted around the church, bouncing off the Gothic arches and hitting the side altars of Jesus and Mary before coming back to the main altar. Poor Mrs Manning nearly had a heart attack, as by this stage she was in a deep spiritual trance and full of the Lord's Spirit. During my subsequent Spanish Inquisition-style trial, Father Gath stated for the prosecution that you could probably hear the gong in Canterbury Cathedral, which was miles and miles away and near London (my friend Phillip Gleeson told me). I was found guilty and my bottom was slippered, and I was told once and for all to hit the blessed gong with reverence and grace from that moment onwards.

By the time I was ten years old, Michael Ford, Kevin Jones and our Patrick had retired from the altar. These vacancies enabled us younger boys to be elevated to the position of readers, which meant we were responsible for reading the Epistle and the Responsorial Psalm (the readings and supplication before the Gospel).

Both Phillip and I became the favourite readers for Father Corbally, and as a result we became very good at reading aloud at an early age. We would read most of the letters of St Paul to the Colossians or the Corinthians or the Thessalonians or the Hebrews or the Romans, and we decided he really got around all over the place, did that St Paul – whereas boring old St Peter just went to Rome and became Pope.

But it was at Easter that we really shone, during the Passion of St John's Gospel. I was always given the job of Narrator; Christ was played by Father Corbally, being his representative on earth; and Phillip always played Pontius Pilate, the Pharisees or the crowd. The service used to last at least an hour and a half, but we enjoyed reading and re-enacting Christ's final walk to Calvary.

As a result of my sterling performances, I was eventually promoted and given the position of thurible bearer during the services. The thurible was a beautifully decorated silver incense burner, which was carried at the front of any procession around and onto the church altar. It was apparently required to perfume the church in the Middle Ages to disguise the smell of unwashed pilgrims, but later it was simply used to purify the altar. The smoke was meant to remind us of God's divine mercy and our prayers going up to heaven.

The charcoal was never left to go out, as that would mean there would be no smoke, so I became extremely good at leaving the altar and topping up the charcoal and adding the odd bit of incense myself. One Easter, it got out of hand when a few of us put too much incense in, and we all started coughing and spluttering as it got in our eyes. Luckily, Father Corbally let that incident ride.

Later, when I was eighteen and living in Spain, some dear friends from back home started taking the mickey about my continuing service as an altar boy whenever I was back in England for Christmas. Father Corbally would always call me the moment I got home to ask would I serve for him at Midnight Mass, and I could never say no as I had so much respect for him. My non-Catholic friends would refer to my thurible as 'Brendan's smoking handbag' and come to the church to gawp at me in action. To get my own back, I would unleash a blast or two of incense down their pew as I passed in pious procession, making them cough and splutter. It may not have been very reverential of me, but at least I had the last laugh.

CHAPTER 5

St Patrick's Day

A S WELL AS the weekly Mass, we altar boys would also serve at weddings, christenings and funerals. We all knew the members of the mainly Irish congregation, so it could be hard to hide your feelings sometimes, especially at funerals.

Once the Requiem Mass was complete, the body of the deceased was re-blessed with holy water, incensed, carried out of the church and put into the hearse. The family would then get into the cars behind and off they would go to the cemetery. How many cars the family could afford would give us a good indication of what kind of tip Liam, Phillip and I would get afterwards. One car was low, two decent and three or more cars was bonus time, tip-wise.

We then had a frantic rush back through the church – with Father Corbally still dressed in his black-and-gold embroidered vestments and us in our red cassocks and white surplices – into the presbytery, out the other side and straight into Father's light-blue Vauxhall Viva.

I always made sure I had the thurible and the incense boat while either Phillip or Liam got the brass bowl of holy water and the sprinkler. These were used to re-bless the coffin and the grave when we got to the cemetery.

Father would set off at top speed with me in the front and Phillip and Liam in the back, along with Father's dog Trixie, who would be wagging her tail in excitement at another sojourn to the cemetery.

Father's driving was quite erratic at times and we had to frequently remind him which way to go and tell him if anything was coming from my direction, so that he could pull out into the busy Leeds traffic without causing an accident. It was quite difficult driving in his full set of vestments but somehow he managed it.

Father was never very good at judging traffic lights. In fact, come to think of it, his braking could be a bit heavy too. But you have to remember that the hearse and mourners had got a head start on us and we had to catch up, otherwise the body and the mourners would be left waiting for us at Cottingley Cemetery.

The cemetery was at the top of Elland Road, just past the Leeds United football ground. There was a set of traffic lights by the football ground and on one occasion Father was so busy talking to Liam in his rear-view mirror about last Saturday's match – in which Billy Bremner had scored a brilliant goal – that he didn't notice that the lights had changed to red. He then decided, a bit late in my view, to apply the brakes – and stopped with such force that the holy water shot out of the brass bowl which was nestled carefully in Phillip's lap, soaking him through, blessing Trixie (who thought she was being given a drink of water) and blessing myself in the front in the process.

Father called Phillip a cabbage and we started to laugh, but we then realized we had only a few drops of holy water left. This was a problem as Father liked to be generous with the holy water, especially as the *poor craiture* was to be laid finally to rest (the 'poor craiture' being an Irish term for the body). Not only would he bless the coffin, but also anyone within fifty yards would be blessed with an abundance of holy water. In addition, Father would need to have enough left over so that the family could bless the coffin as the final act at the end of the committal.

While Father continued to drive, we came up with a plan. As soon as we arrived, Phillip, in his sodden state, had to walk slowly past the mourners and the coffin to a tap in the corner of the cemetery. He then had to fill the brass bowl and return forthwith, while the coffin was being very, very slowly incensed. Father would quickly bless the tap water, therefore making it holy. The situation would be saved.

Luckily, the plan worked perfectly and we all got £5 each, which was a good funeral really; weddings usually paid £10 if we were lucky, depending on whether the groom or best man was tight or not. The tips were important; they were our main source of income at the time.

Father Stephen Corbally was really like a spiritual father to us boys. He used to call us 'dobbins' if we were silly, told us to use our 'savvy brains' to pass our exams and get on in life, and he loved us all dearly. He also loved his church, and the new St Francis's Church in Leeds, and the Catholic school of the same name, bear witness to his dedication as a priest to provide for his flock.

He was a kind man, and very observant. One morning, he noticed my hungry expression after Liam and I had served the 7 a.m. Mass. He asked if we had eaten anything and, on hearing that we hadn't, promptly sent me to his housekeeper – a lovely round Yorkshire lady called Mrs Needham – to tell her that there would be three for breakfast. Rolling her eyes to heaven she set to, providing us all with a beautifully cooked fry-up of bacon, sausage, mushrooms and eggs, washed down with lashings of tea. This became a regular treat for us boys and we would always demolish Mrs Needham's breakfasts with gusto.

Over breakfast, Father would do some intelligence gathering about his flock: who was working, who was not, who needed a job, who was in any kind of trouble, who would appreciate a visit. He knew his congregation and they knew him; he was honest with them and helped them through life in any way he could. Liam and I used to chuckle after breakfast on our way to school about how Father would first put his hot tea into his china saucer to blow on it, then slurp it down with such a noise that we dared not look at each other for fear of bursting out laughing. I was also intrigued by the way Mrs Needham cooked her fried eggs in a separate pan, so that the whites of the eggs were as white as snow. Most families only possessed one frying pan and everything was cooked together so your eggs were tarnished with bits of bacon, so this was something I had not seen before. Liam and I would hear the school bell sound as our lovely breakfast hit the table, and think, well, we don't mind missing Maths or Physics for this.

In truth, we also used to relish our ensuing interrogation by Sister Concepta, who was a Sister of Mercy. She was a very tall Irish lady who was also our headmistress, and whose office looked out over the playground so that she could keep a beady eye on latecomers.

Nuns were nuns in my day – all wimples and black habits. You could spot them a mile off, and the only part of their body you could see was their face. Sister Concepta was just like Reverend Mother in *The Sound of Music*. She was a strict disciplinarian and ruled the school with a rod of iron. Her one redeeming feature was that she could sing like an angel and could be heard over and above everyone else.

Once you'd entered the school, you had to climb a flight of stairs to get to your classroom. Sister Concepta's office was at the top of the stairs, and she would wait for us there with a long cane hidden in the folds of her habit, along with her massive pair of black rosary beads. She would wait till we had nearly passed her, then she would suddenly materialize to ask why we were late for school. We took great pleasure in telling her that we had been serving Mass for Father Corbally and that he had insisted we stay for breakfast: a truly watertight defence for us both. However, she still always questioned me at length as to my identity, going through my genealogy there and then in her mind as she had also taught my mother when she was young. I had to tread very carefully indeed – in those days, if you were punished by a nun or a priest, they might also inform your parents, so that you would get punished by them, too. It was a double whammy. One way or another, you learned quickly to keep your mouth well and truly shut.

Sister Bridget was my favourite. She was a young, bubbly, Irish nun, who was in charge of Home Economics, a subject I loved. She was extremely pretty and had a beautiful freckly complexion with piercing green eyes. You could just about make out that she had a lovely figure through her nun's habit. She used to love having the radio on when we were baking cakes and would sing along to the hits of the day. She was very progressive in a way and all us children adored her.

Then, one day, she simply disappeared from our lives. It was a great mystery. No one mentioned her and the religious ranks of our school closed – it was as if she'd never existed. Eventually, we plucked up the courage to ask directly what had happened to her, and we were told that she was ill. We all missed her greatly so we quickly formed a plan. If she was ill, we needed to find out which hospital she was in so we could all go and visit. But when I informed Sister Concepta of our idea, it went down like a lead balloon and we never dared mention it again.

Luckily, we had other events to distract us from Sister Bridget's disappearance. St Patrick's Day was soon approaching to break up the monotony of the forty-day period of Lent, and an air of excitement rippled through the school. There was to be a St Patrick's Day dance at St Francis's (there was a big assembly hall at the school that was used for community dances) and one of the leading show bands was coming over from Ireland.

Now, Father Corbally didn't have many problems in his flock, but one of them always arrived two weeks before St Patrick's Day in the shape of Lizzie O'Hara. She was a lovely Irish lady who owned a massive boarding house on Cemetery Road, and she looked after the many Irish construction workers who came to Leeds to find work. She would cook a meal for them every day, do their washing and generally look out for them until they found a wife and settled down like most lads did. She would also help them out midweek if they were short of the price of a pint or two, but she always made sure the repayments were made and was a shrewd businesswoman at heart. Apparently, she had money stashed away all over the place, and when she had had enough of looking after 'her boys', as she called them, it was said she would return to Galway to her family cottage, and wouldn't want for anything for the rest of her life.

One of the most noticeable things about Lizzie was that she had a strange habit of biting her tongue while it lay at the left-hand corner of her mouth – constantly, not just now and again. Most folk who did not know her thought she would chew her tongue off, but then it would go back into her mouth to be lubricated and then pop out again.

She cycled everywhere on her Dublin-made bicycle, calling motor-car drivers 'fickers' if they crossed her. Thus it was, two weeks before St Patrick's Day, she would come flying down on her bike over Nineveh Bridge to St Francis's to haunt poor Father Corbally.

She would come to Mass and then, as soon as it was finished, she would make her way into the sacristy, where Father would be de-robing and I would be washing the cruets. The conversation would go like this:

'Top of the morning, Father, and how are ye today?' (She always replaced 'you' with 'ye'.) Looking very concerned, she would then ask: 'Have ye ordered the shamrock, Father, for St Patrick's Day?' At this, her tongue would switch sides momentarily and start doing overtime with excitement.

'No, I haven't,' would be Father's measured reply.

'Oh, but I think ye should. Mary O'Rourke has told me St Anthony's have already ordered theirs, Bernadette O'Riley says Corpus Christi Parish have theirs paid for, and Marie O'Shaughnessy says Father Murphy has ordered his fresh and already blessed from the base of Croagh Patrick [St Patrick's mountain in Westport, County Mayo] at great expense.'

'Well, Father Murphy should know better. It's two weeks away yet,' Father Corbally would retort. 'I cannot order it too early, Elizabeth' – he always called her by her rightful name – 'It would go off and wither if I ordered it too early.'

'Couldn't ye keep it in the fridge, Father? Like lettuce?' Her tongue would be going back in and out by this time in expectation.

'I haven't got a fridge big enough, and besides, the shamrock pickers of Ireland are not starting till next week!'

'Oh well, I shall call in tomorrow, Father, just to check ye have ordered it.'

Every day, Lizzie would remind Father about the relevance of shamrock and its importance to the Irish of Leeds… and every day he would say it was far too early to order it.

Lizzie would then start her shamrock-ordering campaign with anyone who would listen to her, the length and breadth of Beeston.

'Well, you would think he would have ordered it by now. St Anthony's [etc., etc., etc.] and Bernadette O'Riley…'

Then finally, just before 11 a.m. St Patrick's Day Mass, with the church overflowing with faithful Irish families, proudly wearing green in recognition of the homeland they had had to leave behind, I was dispatched to find Elizabeth O'Hara, with explicit instructions to return with her at all costs.

As Lizzie and I entered the sacristy, we could see Father Corbally, with his back to us, arranging something on a large silver platter. When he turned around, behind him there was the biggest bunch of shamrock I have ever seen. Lizzie's eyes lit up with delight and pride.

A large piece of shamrock, representing the patron saint of her home country, was blessed in front of her alone and laid in her hand, still wet with holy water.

Lizzie's eyes glazed over and a large tear descended down her left cheek and onto her tongue (which she still chewed). 'Oh, TANK you, Father. TANK you!'

'God bless you, and happy St Patrick's Day,' replied Father Corbally.

She took out a large emerald Claddagh pin so that Father could attach the shamrock to her chest and she proudly turned to go and show it off to the waiting congregation, who would receive their shamrock after Mass had ended. Just as she got to the sacristy door, she spun around and placed a fifty-pound note into Father's hand, and with a smile in her Irish eyes and her tongue not far from Father's face she said, 'And a happy St Patrick's Day to YOU TOO, Father!'

After the Mass, the big excitement was the St Patrick's Day dance, which was held in the evening for adults only. My father asked Phillip and me to man the ladies' cloakroom. Chris Gleeson, Phillip's dad, was to be on the door with my dad as they were old mates.

Phillip and I were to charge the ladies 50p per coat, and of course any takings would be split between ourselves 50:50. It was a very lucrative proposition for us both and we were very busy.

We knew a lot of the ladies from our parish who came regularly to the dances, but we also knew a lot of Irish families who lived in and around Leeds too, so we felt very at home at these events. All the women would be wearing their finest clothes for this special night and looked immaculate – to my eyes at least. It amazed me how every lady still touched up her make-up or checked herself in the mirror before descending down the stairs to the dance floor. Many were met at the bottom of the staircase by their husbands or long-term boyfriends, all of whom also wore their Sunday best.

Phillip and I watched everyone from the balcony. They danced the waltzes and foxtrots, which gave way to rock'n'roll and jiving and twisting. Everyone was having a great time. My dad supplied us with orange squash and crisps to keep us going.

After a while, a lady arrived at the counter and I went to take her coat. She had striking red hair, a beautiful freckly complexion and piercing green eyes. She wore a very smart, expensive-looking green two-piece suit with a frilly white blouse and a string of pearls around her neck. She was very beautiful indeed and I thought I knew her, but could not think how. She gave me her coat and said, 'Thank you, Brendan,' which puzzled me still further. I took her coat and gave her a ticket, staring and taking in her face. How did she know my name? I could not for the life of me work out who she was, despite racking my brains.

The lady smiled, obviously reading my mind. Laughing, she said, 'Won any medals lately, Brendan?' Well, as soon as she said that, I recognized her. I was totally floored and confused: it was Sister Bridget, the nun who had disappeared overnight, the nun who had taken an interest in my Irish dancing, and also the nun who had taught me Home Economics! And oh my goodness, she did not look like Sister Bridget any more! In fact, it took a few seconds to dawn on me that she was not actually a nun any more.

She introduced herself as Claire. 'Oh, Sister, it's so nice to see you,' I said, stupidly, and continued to address her as Sister even though, with all good humour, she kept telling me she was no longer a nun. But once you have addressed someone in that manner for all your life, it's hard to change it in a matter of minutes. She asked how I was, how all my family were keeping, and if I was going on to Corpus Christi High School, which I was. Eagerly, I asked her about her health and whether she had made a full recovery from her illness, telling her that we had all been so worried about her and that we had wanted to visit her in hospital. I explained that no one would tell us which hospital she was in, and that we'd been informed that she was not receiving visitors anyway, even if we had gone.

A thoughtful smile came over her face and she paused before replying. Eventually, she said she was very well indeed, thank you, and that she had made a full recovery. She told me she had decided a nun's life was not for her any more, but that it was lovely seeing me again. She wished me happy St Patrick's Day and turned to go.

As she made her way to the top of the stairs, I called after her impulsively, using her proper name for the first time. 'Claire, are you happy?'

She turned back and smiled. 'Extremely.'

I could not contain my excitement. I told Phillip all about it, but more importantly I rushed over to the balcony. Looking over, I saw Claire waltzed away in the arms of a tall, dark-haired, suited and handsome Irishman. Looking at her radiant expression, I knew she was in love, and far happier in her new life than she could ever have been in her old one.

CHAPTER 6

Playing Netball with Nuns

I WAS A late starter at school academically. Having not passed my 11-plus, I was given the opportunity through Leeds' 13-plus educational scheme to move from St Joseph's Secondary School to Corpus Christi High School, a mixed-sex Catholic school on the other side of town. The move would enable me to achieve an O- and A-level standard of education, rather than being limited to the CSEs that St Joseph's offered.

It was quite a feat for a thirteen-year-old to travel from Malvern Hill in Beeston to City Square on the number one bus, then to change onto the number six in front of the statue of the Black Prince. This took you down Boar Lane to the Corn Exchange then via the Old Leeds Market out to York Road, continuing up to the Shaftesbury picture house, where you always had a look to see if they had changed the programme.

Passing through the Halton Moor estate, everything would change and became rougher. The houses were more run-down, and some children didn't have the uniforms and shining shoes that we possessed. You could see the kids who had literally just been pulled out of bed to get the bus on time. These council-house kids were poorer than us, but all the same we Catholics stuck together. Rich or poor, black or white, it did not matter to us. We were all God's children, even if some would have to shoplift a Mars bar or a KitKat for their breakfast. Who was I to judge?

By now, I was also attending a monthly school for budding young priests, organized by the Diocese of Leeds, at a house owned by the Poor Clare Sisters in Headingley. I had confessed to Father Gath that I thought I had a vocation to the priesthood, which at the time was very real to me. I was serious in my faith and believed my future would lie down this path.

On these monthly visits, we would travel to other parishes within the Leeds Diocese, to meet the local priests and learn all about the different parishes. We would also meet other boys of our own age to talk to and confide in. It was here I met another candidate for the priesthood, Terry Docherty. He was cock of the third form at Corpus Christi, and immediately put me at my ease by assuring me I would have no problems at the school, as he would be my bouncer and personal bodyguard. He was as good as his word and I never had any problems at Corpus. Kitted out in my beautiful new purple blazer, I loved every minute of it and made many new friends.

Our spiritual studies increased, with more time spent in prayer and meditation, but we also had free periods during which we would play records, hold snooker tournaments or play netball with the nuns. The nuns would hit us while playing and cheat constantly so they always ended up winning the game, as we would never dare strike a nun back. They used to get away with murder.

As it was a mixed-sex school, naturally relationships began to form between the girls and the boys. Eileen Roach became my first girlfriend but she soon chucked me – perhaps I had been two-timing her. Being chucked was a common practice amongst the third form at that time so I wasn't very bothered. Also, I was starting to understand that my tastes were changing. I was beginning to notice men more than girls, which was quite a worrying development for a future priest. I reassured myself that this was a phase that every boy goes through and in the meantime I tried to educate myself a little more about the subject. You could look up anything you wanted at Leeds Reference Library, including all about the Romans and the Greeks.

My friends Matthew Kent, John Enright and I started smoking, and whoever had some money would buy three Park Drive cigarettes to share between us. Sometimes, during cross-country running, Matthew and I used to hide behind the bushes and smoke while our fellow classmates did ten laps around the football field. On the last lap, we would join the stragglers and move up through the ranks to avoid being spotted, continuing on the final run back to the changing rooms.

We had several rows regarding our tobacco supplies: I would often save two ciggies for John and me to smoke on our long bus journey home, leaving poor Matthew to cadge another ciggie from someone who owed us. Poor Matthew always claimed I put John first in the ciggie stakes of friendship.

Matthew used to love going to Leeds City station to look at the trains; access was quite easy in those days. By purchasing a penny platform ticket you could spend all day there, dreaming of going to London on the 11.50 to see Buckingham Palace, Trafalgar Square and Carnaby Street, where all the hippies smoked drugs and got high, or so they said. Matthew spent so much time looking at trains he ended up driving them for a living.

I was very good at French and should have gone on to study it at O level, but it was not in the same options group as Geography and Geology, which I was also good at. So I had to drop French and study those two subjects, along with RE, History, Home Economics, and of course English Language and Classics (more Greeks). Mr Lucas was our Geology teacher and he was superb and very dedicated, as they all were. He always used to say with a sparkle in his eyes, 'Remember, boys, stalagmites go up... but stalacTITES come down!' He ended up taking me for an A level in the subject and through the whole book of *Holmes' Geology*.

When it came to studying the creation of the Earth, he would explain the Big Bang theory necessary for the syllabus, but at the end of his lecture, he would say there was no real answer as to the how and why of it all, as all the theories were simply hypotheses. 'As you are all of the Catholic faith,' he would add, 'it is where my science finishes and your faith in the Creation begins.'

When I was about fourteen years old, my father accompanied me to an interview with both Bishops of Leeds. Bishop Wheeler I knew, as he had visited our church, St Francis's, on many occasions to confirm candidates. I had served on the altar with him several times. I had also rescued him on his last visit from several fervent Catholic ladies who had targeted him for plenary indulgences. In Catholicism, the more you genuflect in front of a bishop and kiss the ring on his finger, the more of your sins will be forgiven. Well, Maureen O'Rourke and Bernadette O'Riley must have had a mountain of sins, as they never left the poor man in peace. As he wandered through the crowds of happy parishioners, at each corner he would stumble upon them lying in wait for him on their knees, genuflecting and kissing his ring, with the poor Bishop trying to catch Sister Hilda's eye to get a refill of his china cup of tea. He was a lovely humble man and very gentle in his demeanour.

Bishop Moverley, on the other hand, the Auxiliary Bishop of Leeds, was a bit too posh and stuck-up for my liking. He was more of a theologian than a man of the people. Luckily for me, as I entered the room for my interview, Bishop Moverley went out with my father to go through the reports about my family and school life.

Bishop Wheeler, six other monsignors and a parish priest then proceeded to question me about my vocation, my favourite subjects and my sporting life. The latter was one area in which I failed miserably, and I was forced to admit I liked to dance more than play football. I was always more artistic than sporty.

Although he never said anything to me, my father was quite

worried about this turn my life was taking. His sister Mary had briefly become a nun at a Poor Clare convent, but had left after she became ill, so he knew what a hard and austere life it could be. He also felt I was too young to be making such a big decision at my age. But my mind was set on becoming a priest and that was that.

The following Monday morning after assembly, I was approached by the secretary of the school and asked to attend a meeting with Mr Rossiter, my headmaster. I entered the office with some trepidation as it was normally only the naughty boys who went to see Mr Rossiter or the deputy head, Mr Odridge, who was the one who dealt out the slipper as punishment. But in this interview, I was to find out about my ordination as a priest. It turned out that I had passed: the school had submitted reports about me to Holy Mother Church from all my teachers regarding my ability and conduct in the classroom, and I was told that I should continue my studies and a review would take place between my O and A levels.

I thanked Mr Rossiter and said I would consider the opportunity, but that I still had a long way to go. Nevertheless, rumours soon started flying around school that I would be ordained in the private school chapel. I knew it would be an honour for the whole school and I began to feel a certain pressure to continue down this path. But at the same time my sexuality was continuing to confuse me, even though I had a new girlfriend in the form of Nina Krupianka, an Italian-Polish girl who was becoming one of my closest friends.

Nina was also studying Home Economics, and we were taught by two lovely teachers called Mrs Fry and Mrs Owen. They were in the 10 per cent minority of teaching staff who were not Catholic, and therefore represented a different, refreshing view of the world. They were aghast at the thought of me becoming a priest and told me so during one of their many lunchtime tastings, held for their favoured students and friends. Speaking as frankly as they could, they explained that what they described as my 'natural personality' would go against the Church's teachings. They told me that I would be like a piece of paper pulled from both directions until it split down the middle. This was quite an insight into my character at that age and I will always remember their honesty, thoughtfulness and kindness.

In fact, it was at school, during Religious Education, that I first heard about the subject of Papal Encyclicals, letters from the Pope that addressed various issues of concern to the Church. Our teacher, Mr McGivern, a tall, dark Northern Irishman, was very progressive and he told us to ask questions of our faith. It was rumoured that he had married a Jewess and had had to leave Northern Ireland as they were both persecuted for falling in love with each other.

It may sound odd now, but at the time I really knew nothing about the Church's stand on abortion, birth control and homosexuality. Sex education was virtually non-existent so the subject didn't exactly come up – yet with my regular visits to Leeds Reference Library, I was beginning to become much more interested in the topic.

It was therefore a huge shock to me when Mr McGivern taught us about the 'Humanae Vitae' encyclical of 1968, reaffirming the Church's strict, uncompromising stance prohibiting all abortion and birth control, and condemning homosexuality as unnatural. Disturbed by what I had learned about my faith, I visited the Carmel bookshop opposite St Anne's Cathedral to purchase a copy of what I called 'the bastard encyclical'.

As I read through it, I began to feel both angry and revolted. The thought of all this regulation being enforced upon a God-fearing, honest and hard-working Catholic population was, to me, quite outrageous. If God was Love then this was not showing it. What about all those lovely Irish ladies I knew who had had six or seven children and were already struggling to feed and clothe them, often being forced to take two jobs to make ends meet? Was it right that they should be asked to bear more offspring? And if I was made in the image of God, as my Catholic Catechism stated, then surely I was welcomed in God's eyes and not suffering some mental stigmatism for my natural sexual inclinations? Describing homosexuals as being mentally unstable was the final straw for me. This issue would definitely not go away and I was not going to let it until I had all the answers I needed to quieten my conscience.

A Catholic uprising was within me and the smell of revolution was in the air. My comrade-in-arms came in the form of a lovely boy called John, who became my first gay friend and companion. He was slightly older than me but kind, loving and very intelligent. He was studying ballet and wanted to be dancing at the Royal Ballet by the age of twenty-two. This was a boy with goals and ambition and I warmed to him instantly. We used to laugh a lot and he used to dance a lot. I have never seen anyone jump so high in all my life. He could clear twenty steps in front of Leeds Town Hall in one dramatic leap and he did not care how many people on The Headrow saw him do it. In fact, Yorkshire ladies passing on their way home from work used to applaud this feat and say, 'Isn't he grand?'

And grand he was, for me. He told me I could do anything I wished, as the world was my oyster. We used to argue playfully over our respective passions for dancing – he always told me he could not be an 'Oirish' dancer as 'the arms are too restrictive, darling! Whereas in ballet, my dear, one can do *this* and *that*...' And he would display the movement of his long, strong arms like a graceful swan on the Leeds and Liverpool Canal, in response to me showing off with my jigs and reels. We revelled in our time together and at last I had a friend who knew my secret. I could now act out as a 'puff' and not just feel like one in secret.

So why were we so close? Well, he was another Catholic schoolboy, from St Michael's, and he just *understood*. I had met him at Leeds Reference Library looking at the books on ancient Rome and Greece, just like I was – but he was studying Roman orgies and I was not that advanced. I didn't even know what an orgy was, never mind what it entailed, much to his amusement. He took great delight in corrupting my innocence and regaling me with illicit information while I threatened him with six to eight Hail Marys as penance – or a whole decade of the rosary if he was really naughty.

John also told me a very interesting fact, which was that you had to be twenty-one to be a puff or, as he put it, 'to have sexual relations with another man – or *homme* in French; they do it all the time'. So apparently I had to wait six years and he had to wait four years. However, we reasoned, we could still be puffs in secret. Thus the Leeds Reference Library Puffs Society was formed, with us being the two founding members. We were a clandestine organization, just like the French Resistance in the Second World War.

Two days after we met, we were in the library as usual, with John teasing me and asking me if I'd ever snogged anybody. Well, of course I hadn't – I'd never had the chance. So that very same afternoon, John led me into the stacks of books of Leeds Reference Library, winding his way through the rows and rows of shelves until we got lost amongst the dry volumes and found ourselves in a quiet reference section that no one ever visited. There was absolute silence all around. I looked deeply into John's eyes. He had the darkest eyes I'd ever seen; they were like two massive lumps of black coal. And with those big black eyes boring into my soul, he confidently leaned forward and kissed me firmly on the lips. And then he whispered, 'Shall we do it again?'

The second kiss was a proper kiss. I closed my eyes and felt the world fall away and just lost myself in that kiss. It felt like the most natural thing in the world. Afterwards, John led me back out through the rabbit warren of bookshelves, and as we emerged into the main, populated part of the library, I caught the librarian's eye. She was your stereotypical reference librarian, with schoolmarmish spectacles and a straight-laced pencil skirt. Her eyes were peering at me over her lenses, and in my paranoid state I thought, 'She *knows*.' I blushed beetroot red all the way to my toes and got out of there as soon as I could. But as I passed the people on the steps of the library, and boarded the number one bus to Beeston to find more people on the top deck all staring at me, and then looked out of the bus's window and saw passers-by gazing curiously at me as the bus whizzed past, the feeling that *everyone knows* intensified until I simply had to stare at my hands and avoid the looks that were flying all around me, while inside my world was ablaze with my new discovery.

Of course, no one knew anything. As I grew more confident with our secret, my friendship with John slowly blossomed into something more. It was never a romantic relationship, but our passion for each other was intense. We had a physical connection that blew me away. I was fifteen years old and my hormones were the same as any other boy's of that age: running absolutely wild.

We used to swim together every week at the Olympic swimming pool in Leeds city centre. Even now, every time I see Michelangelo's *David*, I will always remember John; he had the body of a ballet dancer, strong, tall, firm and muscular. He trained religiously every day and he was the most beautiful athlete I had ever seen in my whole, young life.

We both took our responsibility as founding members of the Leeds Reference Library Puffs Society seriously. The first operation of this clandestine organization was to seek out other puffs. John said we had to find a gay pub, but with him being seventeen and me only fifteen, this was going to be some mission. How do you find a gay pub at that age? Who could we possibly ask?

In the end, we were forced to put that operation on hold, as I was doing my O levels and John had to attend an audition to further his ballet studies. We nearly had our first argument as, despite his objections, I forced him to go into St Anne's Cathedral with me to light a candle to Our Lady, so that he would get into ballet school with her assistance. In fact, he was very successful at the audition and after that day he always carried a small statue of her around with him for luck. He called it 'My Lady' and used to kiss it before every performance.

It was at Corpus Christi that my love of all things musical and theatrical began, and it was Mr Richard Bloodworth who started it all off. He was a lovely man: blond, fit and very handsome. He was also funny, kind and very artistic; naturally, I had a crush on him. It was during his music lesson that I first heard Sibelius's *Finlandia*. I loved it and immediately bought a copy with my pocket money from a very posh record shop in the Arcade on Briggate in Leeds city centre. It cost me an arm and a leg and I still have it today.

Mr Bloodworth decided to fill the school with music, starting with an old-time music-hall show. His wife, Megan, came up from London. She was a proper London actress but what I really loved was her rendition of the songs from *My Fair Lady*, especially how she could change her accent from posh English to Cockney. I was very impressed.

I suppose I identified with her as I had this knack of taking off Maggie Smith's role in *The Prime of Miss Jean Brodie*, so my Scottish accent was rather good. I could be extremely posh too, not opening my mouth too much and speaking in an Etonian accent. I used to have my cousins Sean and Marie and my dear sister Margaret in stitches. But my party piece was my father's Irish accent, which I had off to a fine art. Consequently, Mr Bloodworth asked me if I would take on a part in the school show, singing 'Paddy McGinty's Goat' with six dancers, whom I would choreograph. We danced a reel dressed up as leprechauns with green tights, the lot. It went down a storm. We ran for a whole week and made a fortune for the school, which was of course the whole objective.

Sadly, my dear grandfather, Patrick Carden, passed away on the morning of the last day of the show. The news was kept from me till the last curtain. I was heartbroken.

The school continued to ride the theatrical wave of success, assisted by the tireless dedication of our teachers and, of course, the outstanding talents of the pupils. During a run of *Joseph and the Amazing Technicolor Dreamcoat*, Terry Docherty's Pharaoh – a part that required him to perform like Elvis – was an absolute knockout every night; a talent I think he took with him into the priesthood. *Jesus Christ Superstar* and *West Side Story* followed, again with tremendous success. Corpus Christi was to become the school of the diocese not just for academic ability but also for theatrical and musical excellence. I cannot remember a single day of unhappiness there.

The time came to take my O levels and I sat them with all the nervousness of any student facing up to his future. I got mostly Bs and Cs, which allowed me to progress to my chosen A levels – but, spectacularly for an altar boy and priest-in-training, I failed my Religious Education exam, being marked 'Unclassified' by the board. Well, Mr McGivern was spitting mad. He thought my mark was disgraceful. He immediately put me in for a resit and quizzed me on what I had put in my first paper that had made it all go so horribly wrong.

Having been somewhat inspired by my reaction to the 'bastard encyclical', I confessed that I had used my O-level paper to present a rather controversial argument on the topics of sex before marriage and homosexuality. I suppose I was just trying to rebel. But to get the grade I deserved in the subject, I would have to stick to what was preached and put the Catholic viewpoint in my answers. This approach worked: I figuratively bit my tongue and I jumped right up to a B grade in the resit.

It was around this time that an important decision – whether or not I wanted to continue with my training for the priesthood – was taken out of my hands. Not because of the disastrous Religious

Education exam, but rather because the school for priests was wound down by the Diocese of Leeds. I think there were funding and venue issues, but whatever the reason behind it, it released me from a path that had clearly been the wrong one for me to be on. None of the Fathers tried to persuade me to continue training under their guidance. I think they could see that I was growing up, and that my life was not destined to be one of religious vocation. I kept up with my altar-boy duties on Sundays, however. I enjoyed them and, besides, I could never say no to Father Corbally.

CHAPTER 7

On the Scene

S o I SETTLED down to my A levels, particularly enjoying Mr Lucas's Geology lessons. I found him a really inspiring teacher, and with my vocation to the priesthood now a dead end, I started to think that maybe I would become a teacher instead. I loved both Geology and Geography, so I thought one of those might suit for my specialist subject, while the personable interaction demanded by the teaching profession seemed to be a good match with my outgoing and friendly nature. To become a teacher now became my main ambition and I knuckled down to work.

There were new developments outside school too. John told me he had met a university student at the library who was called Dominic. He had another student friend called Isaac, so now our Leeds Reference Library Puffs Society had four members. Isaac was Jewish – well, with a name like Isaac he would be, wouldn't he? He was a cantor at Jewish ceremonies so couldn't come out with us on some of our trips to town as he would be stuck in a synagogue chanting all day. There was also a problem with the name of our society, as the new members insisted it had to be changed (rather to mine and John's annoyance). Apparently, 'puff' was not the right word to use any more, so we had to become the Gay Society: gay liberation was on the up and the subject was on everyone's lips at Leeds University. Indeed, John had found a gay bookshop on Clay

Pit Lane. It sold a paper called *Him* and could get the odd copy of a London paper called the *Gay News*. Of course, this was all totally illegal at the time so it could have been raided by the police at any minute. I was just about brave enough to go in with John, but we could not afford the books and papers. Besides, they were too risky for us: we could not hide them at home as our families might find them and there would be all hell to pay then.

John and I were growing closer still. Our attraction had deepened over time, and while we remained friends in terms of our emotions, we were still drawn to each other physically, and happily experimented with our newfound desire. One day during the school holidays, John's mum was due to be out of the house from morning till evening, and so he invited me round for breakfast.

Well, I needed no wake-up call that morning. I was up bright and early and keenly awaiting the 9 a.m. bus to John's house before the vehicle had even left the depot.

When I arrived, John was still in his dressing gown, a luxurious, silken robe that was exquisite. John always loved to wear dramatic clothes, and this outfit was no exception. We ate coffee and toast together at the kitchen table, and then John languorously stretched his arms and said, 'Shall we go back to bed?'

I wasn't nervous; I was just really excited. Everything felt so natural and it seemed somehow just right that it was my lovely friend John who was introducing me to this brave new world. Afterwards, I glowed with the secret knowledge that only that kind of experience can bring. John and I continued our dalliance with each other over the coming months, but we were both aware of our youth, and the adventure of life that stretched out long and beautiful before us, and so we kept our feet firmly on the ground and our emotions tethered, and went forwards just as friends.

Along with Dominic and Isaac, we found a coffee shop called Brills, at the top of New Briggate, which was frequented by gay men, but we could only afford one or two coffees so couldn't spend much time there. In any case, we were constrained by the restrictions of school and ballet training and – in my case – my Saturday job. I had no choice but to work so that I could supplement my meagre pocket money.

My first weekend job was collecting the milk money around Beeston for a local dairy. The owner, Gordon, had faith in me handling such large amounts of money as I had come highly recommended by Gerard, another altar boy who worked there.

Gordon would calculate the weekly bills then off I would go on Friday teatime, collecting his money for him. If I did not manage to collect it all on Friday evening, I would resume the following Saturday morning until it was all in. I would walk for miles. It was not long before I was shown how to drive a milk float around the yard by the resident milkmen and put in charge of one.

During the school holidays, I would be allotted to a milkman to help him on his round, which of course went quicker for him as he had an extra pair of hands. I had to be up at 4 a.m., but I would be finished by 10 a.m. at the latest, so it wasn't so bad. I eventually got my own round, which was great fun, and because I could collect quickly, I got to take on extra rounds, which meant more money in my own pocket.

The money allowed me to buy platform shoes, Oxford bags (fashionable baggy trousers) and flowered shirts with matching ties, which were all the rage in those days. It also meant that I could afford to go out in Leeds city centre. My friends from Corpus Christi, Matthew Kent and John Enright, both had Saturday jobs too, so the three of us would often go out to the pictures and then on to a Wimpy bar for a burger afterwards.

Eventually, Gordon sold the dairy and I moved my employment to Leeds Market, where I worked in Wildeblood's, selling cooked meats: boiled ham, corned beef, spam, chicklets and cow's stomach.

I loved working in the centre of town and being part of the city. Matthew worked around the corner in a haberdasher's opposite the Post Office, so during our lunch breaks we would meet up and go to the café in John Lewis on The Headrow. We used to have a big bowl of soup and a bread roll for our lunch, then run down the whole length of Briggate back to the market for the Saturday afternoon rush.

Gordon called at my house one night and said he would pay me double what the market was paying if I came to work at the grocer's store he had just bought in Beeston, opposite his old dairy. So soon I was busy selling potatoes and various seasonal vegetables and, in the summer, salads and strawberries.

He then bought a newsagent's in Dewsbury bus station, where he had me weighing out sweets and selling chocolate, newspapers and cigarettes. I always maintain it was good for me to work, partly so that I could become independent and have my own money, but also so that I could perfect my communication skills, which I would need for the future. My A levels were nearly upon me, and my career in whatever I chose to pursue would, with luck, soon blossom and bear fruit.

What I did not realize, when John called me one Saturday to say that he had at last found a gay pub we could go to in the centre of Leeds, was that in a few short weeks I was about to meet someone who would have a huge influence on my life, and who would ultimately ensure that my future career was not in Leeds, nor even in England.

* * *

John, Isaac and I decided to meet that very Saturday night outside the Queen's Hotel in City Square, Leeds, for our first attempt at going to a gay pub. Dominic could not or would not come until we had given him a full report on the proceedings. He was just not ready to venture into a gay venue at that time; he was the most fearful of us all and was terrified of being arrested and sent to prison like Oscar Wilde. John and I did not know who Oscar was but, true to form, we looked him up on our next visit to Leeds Reference Library. John, of course, was comfortable looking up everything – 'homosexuality', 'vagina', 'penis', 'testicles', 'sperm', you name it – whereas I tended to look up things like 'granite' and 'trilobites' and 'volcanoes' in Arthur Holmes's books. I was a bit behind John like that. Yet we both thought Dominic was being too careful – you had to take risks in life otherwise it was boring – not to mention being far too dramatic for his own good. Prison indeed! This was the 1970s.

City Square was central for all of us, though Isaac was coming from the Etz Chaim Synagogue on Harrogate Road, Moortown, so he had the furthest to travel. Nevertheless, he arrived early, wearing jeans with black boots with a zip at the side and a crisp white shirt with a denim jacket. He looked very 'cassh' indeed (hip-speak for casual).

Isaac had been cantoning all day and had told his mother he was going to a birthday party. In fact, we had all told our parents we were going to a (non-existent) birthday party, and had explained away the fact that we did not have a present or a card by saying that we were all sharing the expense to keep costs down, so one of our friends had bought it. Isaac told me his mother was suspicious and kept asking questions. He suspected that she knew he was deceiving her.

He asked me earlier if Catholic mothers were like the Gestapo. I replied that my mother was far too busy looking after my younger brothers to worry about me, plus Catholic trust ran high in the Sheerin household. I don't think this comforted him; it was clear he felt guilty and upset about what we were about to do. I told him to say four Hail Marys and the guilt might subside, as that always worked for me, but unfortunately this was no help to him as he did not know what a Hail Mary was. I told him not to worry. St Sebastian, the patron saint of gays, would look after us all; he was a Roman soldier who was pierced by a hundred arrows by his comrades, who persecuted him for being gay and a Christian. Although Isaac wasn't a Christian, St Sebastian should cover him for the gay bit. Anyway, we had to keep it all in perspective: we were not planning a robbery or going to kill anyone.

I had come all the way from the newsagents at Dewsbury bus station via Beeston to have the quickest and soapiest bath at my house, soapsuds flying everywhere. My dad had kindly made me a boiled ham sandwich and a cup of tea to drink with a Penguin chocolate bar, all of which I bolted down while I was getting changed, such was my urgency to exit the house in record time. I had been to Class, a fashionable shop in Lower Briggate, to buy some new cream-coloured Oxford bags and a flowered shirt with matching tie. This I wore with a pair of two-inch brown platform shoes, which I may add were all the rage when I was seventeen in January 1977, crowning my outfit with a bottle-green velvet jacket that my mum had bought me from Richmond's the tailors. After a massive splash of Brut aftershave from its distinctive green bottle, I ran for the number one bus to town and arrived just after Isaac.

While we stood waiting for John, we started watching all the posh people arriving at or exiting the Queen's Hotel, which was the premier hotel in Leeds. There were ladies getting out of Jaguar cars in their fox furs and long frocks and men dressed in dinner jackets – it was another world. Before long, we were fantasizing about the caviar and smoked salmon that rich people ate as a starter (almost like the prawn cocktail that I had had at my Uncle Martin's wedding to Marie Lemondine last summer) and dreaming about the glamorous lives we would lead if only we had some money. But it was cold and drizzly and here we were waiting in the rain as usual for flaming John.

John was, typically, twenty minutes late and came flying down Park Lane like Rudolf Nureyev, full of apologies. His ballet class had apparently overrun that day as they were rehearsing *Swan Lake* and some of the girls were crap (his words not mine). He was wearing some tight-fitting, light-grey flannel trousers that his mother had taken in for him to fit his lean figure. She was a whizz with her sewing machine and would spend hours on her black Singer altering things for people, from curtains to clothes. She could charge as much as £5 for a pair of altered curtains, which is why John always had a lot of money and didn't have a Saturday job like us. 'Mummy's money' he would say, kissing a fiver. He often paid for coffees for us, and when I objected he would laugh and say that I was 'a poor boy from Beeston' so he was merely helping me out.

Along with the grey trousers, John was wearing a black polo-necked sweater and a white scarf draped around his neck. He looked very theatrical, as usual, like Maurice Chevalier in *Gigi*. Over the top, he wore a black wool Crombie coat that was his dad's, though he never told us that. We only knew because Isaac had noticed that his dad's name was sewn into the lining. Isaac never missed a trick; you had to be careful with him as he saw everything. Perhaps that's why he became a forensic scientist with the police later in life. In any case, John looked very dashing with his jet-black long hair and his polo neck. There are people who can wear polo necks and those who can't, and John was one of those who looked completely fab in one.

In the shadow of the Black Prince, we all greeted each other, moaned about John being late for his own funeral, and then set off, past the Tatler cinema to the Majestic bingo hall and down Wellington Street to the army recruitment office. Here we all paused for a moment, overcome with fear, excitement and guilt – both Catholic and Jewish – before we started heading towards the pub next door, known as the West Riding. This was to be our first glimpse into the very new and very unfamiliar world of gay bars. Apparently the gay scene had moved here from the Wellesley Hotel, or the Great Northern Hotel as it was in those days, further up Wellington Street. So here we were now, about to make our debut as budding gay men.

Of course, we had to actually go in first. Unfortunately, on arrival at the entrance of the West Riding, we could not agree who would be the first to walk through the door, so to save embarrassment we simply carried on striding purposefully down Wellington Street, turning right into King Street past the Metropole Hotel and then behind the Post Office, which was heaving with red delivery vans, and around the block, back to the Majestic and the army recruitment office and the entrance of the West Riding again. We then enacted the same procedure at least four times, until eventually John suddenly plucked up his courage and darted in the door on the fourth round, on his own, leaving Isaac and me outside looking at each other like a couple of lemons.

After ten minutes standing idiotically in the cold, fearful of someone seeing us outside this den of iniquity, we followed John's example and proceeded very quickly through the straight bar that was at the front of the building. There were a few old folk in there, supping their drinks, but no one took a blind bit of notice of us as we walked through. Finally we opened a black door into the back room, where John was stood holding a pint of lager, beaming at us. We were in our first-ever gay pub! (Or back room of a pub anyway.)

We ordered ourselves a drink and surveyed our surroundings. One thing was immediately apparent: we were the source of everyone's attention. I suppose this was not surprising. After all, we were young, handsome, fashionably dressed and available, with the added bonus of being only in our late teens and not yet legal. This was quite an incentive for the older men in the back bar of the West Riding on a Saturday night.

We found a table near the jukebox and I put on Julie Covington's rendition of 'Don't Cry for Me Argentina', which was about to become number one in the charts. She had just appeared on *Top of the Pops* and we were all in love with the song, and the whole bar seemed to be in agreement with my choice as it was a very popular record amongst my peers. Barbra Streisand's 'Evergreen' followed and then 'Don't Go Breaking My Heart' by Elton John and Kiki Dee. I had all the records and played them constantly on my portable at home.

Slowly and quite tentatively, we began to be introduced to these men. A young handsome teacher named Ian was the first person to come over to talk to us, though it was clear he particularly had his eye on John. For the first time in my life, I felt that awful pang in my stomach known as jealousy, even though John and I had agreed to spread our wings: we were too young to tie ourselves down by being faithful when we were just starting out on this exciting adventure. And although John knew what a *ménage à trois* was, I was having nothing to do with it. He was reading too much at Leeds Reference Library that was not good for him, as far as I was concerned, and those French had a lot to answer for.

A vicar named Colin joined us, along with Peter, a blond bus driver who evidently fancied Isaac like mad and kept asking him if he wanted another pint. We were all underage drinkers so we had to be careful, and given that none of us was twenty-one, we could not officially go out with anyone anyway. But that didn't stop them trying. Some more men came over: a firefighter known as Fireman John, a theatre manager called Maurice, and a man named Paul who had come from Harrogate. One by one, they all introduced themselves and asked us what we did, how our studies were going and if our parents knew that we were gay.

Well, that was an easy one: God forbid that our parents ever found out. No, we now belonged to a secret, hidden world of nods and winks and word-of-mouth discos held in back rooms of pubs. That night, we learned that there was a big club in Huddersfield called the Gemini, which held over 500 men, all dancing and having a great time. I longed to go there one day, but for the moment this little room in the West Riding was enough: this was our first night out in the gay world and I intended to relish every minute of it.

The night was a tremendous success. For the first time, we realized there were normal gay men who lived in Otley, Adel, Bramley, Beeston, Swarcliffe and Middleton – not just in London or the bigger cities like Birmingham or Manchester. I also found out that a lot of guys went to Amsterdam. It was a gay Mecca, I was told: the Dutch were very liberal and you had gay bars, gay discos, gay clothes shops, gay saunas and gay everything there. Apparently, we were not alone in this world.

Moustaches were the fashion in those days, along with tight jeans and white T-shirts designed to show off toned bodies. There was no shortage of such men there that night. A builder named Phillip took a shine to me and we laughed and talked until the last orders bell put a stop to our laughter. As far as Isaac and I were concerned, it was essential that we caught the last buses to Beeston and Moortown. We knew we could not be late, nor could we risk arousing any suspicion in our parents; after all, we knew we would be wanting to go to another 'birthday party' the next Saturday. John was by now talking to a guy called Steve, who told him he had a white van from work and would drop him off in Headingley. Isaac and I, however, had no such luck and had to get the bus.

We ran into City Square feeling exhilarated, liberated and not alone any more. We had a following of about six men, who all said they would love to see us next Saturday, and we knew that from now on this is what we would live for... next Saturday. Oh, the feeling of freedom was intoxicating – and yet when I got off the bus and started to walk home, the shroud of secrecy enveloped me like a London fog.

As wonderful and special as it was, I could not share this sense of freedom with anyone. Not my parents, not my brothers and sister, not Auntie Dolly, not my friends, and definitely not my Church. It was a sobering thought. But nonetheless I had leaped over the first fence into my new life: I had found a place where I could meet other men and be a part of something, instead of feeling set apart from life. I kept thinking over and over, 'I am not alone, *we* are not alone.' The Leeds Reference Library Gay Society was to be dissolved with immediate effect; we had no need to be part of a secret society, as we had at last joined the wider world. We did not need to be secret any more – well, not on a Saturday night, at least.

The following Saturday, the West Riding was heaving with men. John and Steve seemed quite close that night. They had started meeting during the week at the Brills coffee shop at the top of Briggate. Dominic was with us for the first time and was nervously eyeing everyone and everything in case the police raided the place. He had already told us about the window in the gents' loo that we could get out of if there was a raid.

Isaac, meanwhile, had fully embraced his identity as a gay man and had come up with a new name for himself, Zac, by which he now wanted to be known. It was more modern and very gay, he said. Unsurprisingly, his mother had gone apeshit when he told her about his new moniker, so he was happy to be out of the house that night. He and his mother had a difficult relationship; she was very demanding and could read him like a book, and he was desperate to escape from her influence.

Luckily, there was plenty of entertainment on hand to divert him. That night, we met a character called Bernard, who was also known as Bernadette. He looked stunning, with rouge on his cheeks, a dab of lipstick to enhance his features and a big beauty spot on his left cheek. He was as camp as a row of tents and quite outrageous. Someone explained to me that he was a secret transvestite, but I didn't know what that meant. I didn't even understand why he had two names.

Gradually, I began to learn the ropes. Apparently there were effeminate men who would scream and act like women, then there were men who were just normal like us, and finally there were really butch men who wore leather jackets and acted very tough. It was an eye-opening business learning about this new way of life. Mostly, though, there was simply a lot of laughter and fun, as if everyone had stored up all their emotions and let them all fly on a Saturday night. Before long, we all felt very at home with all the camp innuendo, with its references to cottages, chickens, stuffing (not Paxo, I hasten to add), being camp and bona or butch and straight.

Later that evening, I was standing at the jukebox, looking for my beloved Julie and 'Don't Cry for Me Argentina', when a handsome, black-haired man came in through the black door of the bar and looked at me. 'Oh Jaysus, Mary and Joseph,' I thought. He was lovely, with piercing blue eyes. He wore a car coat and scarf and he went over to stand with Ian, the teacher who was also sometimes called Ida in camp language. He had a wonderful tan, given it was deep in wintertime, and I thought he was one of the most striking people I had ever seen. He kept looking over at me and smiling, and eventually he came over and bought me a Coke.

His name was Les. Little did I know when he approached me that night that he was going to be the man, the one, the person who would change the course of my entire life.

CHAPTER 8

All You Need Is Love

L ES WAS WORKING in Greece as a relief resort manager when I met him that night in the West Riding. He was home for just a few weeks, after having narrowly escaped an earthquake on the island of Crete. Normally based on the Costa Brava in Spain, he covered other resorts during the winter months. In truth, he had not really wanted to come out that night as he was due to go down to London on business then back off to Greece, but his friend Ida had persuaded him to call in at the West Riding for a pint. Lucky for us both that he did.

We chatted easily. Les told me all about his travels and I related my stories about my trips to Ireland. He also told me about the Greeks – the real Greeks, not the Reference Library sort – about the lamb they ate, the dolmades, the beaches and the resort of Mykonos, which was an openly gay resort that was just developing. I found him extremely interesting and we had an immediate connection, despite him being fifteen years my senior.

I agreed to meet him for lunch before he went back and he took me to the Flying Pizza on Roundhay Road. The Flying Pizza was a lovely pizza house in the smart district of Leeds, and it was very chic. Italian food was all new at that time, you have to remember; my idea of exotic fare was a Vesta ready meal of chicken curry and rice, so I was easily impressed. I would have been swept away by a simple spag bol, so the Flying Pizza was the absolute epitome of haute cuisine in my opinion. In this modish setting, I told Les that I was thinking of applying for a summer job through Ivey Travel in Leeds, as I was interested in going abroad at some stage. In my long-term life plan, though, I still wanted to be a Geography or Geology teacher, but I couldn't decide which. Not that I needed to just yet: I was only seventeen and I still had my A levels to complete that coming summer.

Les agreed with me that my education was important. However, he suggested that maybe after my A levels I could come out to Spain to work for the summer months on the Costa Brava, before I took up my teacher-training course in London. He said he might be able to offer me a position in Spain as an admin assistant.

I leaped at the idea. I couldn't speak Spanish but my French was very good and I was willing to learn. I also knew I was very good with people – after all, I had helped so many deaf old ladies in and out of our Church and served on the altar, so I was quite confident about dealing with people.

We agreed to exchange addresses and keep in touch, and I left, excited by the possibilities that were opening up ahead of me. It seemed like the whole world was out there, waiting to be grabbed as soon as I'd finished my studies.

Les went back to Greece and during the next few months we wrote to each other constantly. I shared a lot of my hopes and aspirations and told him about my Geography and Geology coursework. I also described our days out on field trips to Malham Tarn to look at the limestone pavement, and to Flamborough Head to study coastal erosion, boulder clay and chalk, and finally to the Lake District to focus on glaciation. On that particular trip, we went in Mr Lucas's Simca sports car and he treated me to lunch in Grasmere and bought me some Kendal mint cake.

In turn, Les told me all about life in Corfu, Crete, Athens and

Rhodes, as he travelled the Greek islands. I began to trust this man completely; we had a fondness for each other and a mutual respect and honesty that I found totally natural. Whenever he returned to Leeds, we met for lunch or dinner, usually going over to Bradford in his car, as I was concerned about being recognized in Leeds by nosy neighbours or friends.

Meanwhile, life went on in Leeds, and my comrades and I continued to explore the opportunities that awaited us in the city. One day, John announced we were all going to Charlie's, which was a rather insalubrious gay nightclub on Lower Briggate, around the corner from the infamous Penny pub. The Penny pub was the gayest pub in Leeds and everyone knew it was the gayest pub in Leeds; therefore you never went in. The main reason for avoiding such an openly gay establishment was that all the buses to Beeston, Middleton and Dewsbury Road left from the side of Leeds Market, then came down The Calls and passed right by the front door of the pub. You could easily be spotted by one of your neighbours or your mates going in or out and we just couldn't take the risk. No, the Penny was just too gay for us. It was also a bit rough, and I was told it was frequented by rent boys from the poorer areas of Leeds as well as an array of drag artists led by the infamous Vikki Graham and Patrick, her partner in drag crime. I didn't know what either a rent boy or a drag artist was, so it was back to the Leeds Reference Library on Monday for me.

In the meantime, here we were at Charlie's on an early summer evening in May 1977. The club was up a single staircase and the entrance had a door with a grille. It looked and felt highly illegal, and we were very lucky to get in given our age. However, the stairway was full and the entrance was just too busy for the owner to keep tabs on everyone, plus he was more bothered about the pound notes coming into his till than worried about any young chickens squawking about. And yes, that's what we were, apparently, according to the wisdom of John: a chicken is a boy of thirteen to eighteen years old in gay language. I was learning and learning fast.

The dance floor was upstairs from the main lounge and a small bar was located on both floors. The lounge was where people cruised by, looking at each other and chatting. We were more interested in dancing and we couldn't wait to get upstairs to the dance floor. All four of us had our first-ever dance together to ABBA's 'Dancing Queen', which became a very special record for us. Each of us had come on a different journey, from a different background and with a different future ahead of us, but at root we were all the same. It was a moment that will stay with me for ever, and whenever I hear the song now it brings back those happy and carefree days when I was seventeen and had my whole life ahead of me, feeling at home for the first time with a new group of people who understood me and accepted me for what I was.

Les was back in England that night and we danced together. We had become very close over the intervening months, both through our heartfelt letters and the time we spent together during Les's visits back home. Whenever we saw each other, our relationship deepened. I was struck by his goodness and his kindness, and I could really feel myself falling for him. It was a brilliant evening, interrupted only by a couple of lesbians fighting on the dance floor, which apparently happened every week. Once that was sorted out by the bouncers – who were also gay and from Seacroft – the night flew by. I left at 1 a.m., with Les dropping me off as I had to serve Mass at 10.30 a.m. the following morning. I practically skipped to church the next day, such was the depth of my happiness.

However, I was acutely conscious that I was living a double life – to the extent that I even still had my public 'girlfriend', Nina Krupianka. She was a dear friend and we spent hours at her house in Moortown, not far from Isaac's, and I am happy to say that we are still friends to this day.

Inside, my heart and mind were divided about my faith and my sexuality. I just could not tell anyone about my secret life outside of my circle of gay friends – and even if I did pluck up the courage, would I be understood or rejected? Sometimes, I would suffer crippling periods of guilt and remorse, my mind whirring round, wondering if what I was doing was 'wrong' or 'evil'. I had never told a priest of my sexual inclinations, despite my desire to unify my gay life with my faith, so I struggled privately with this issue, constantly questioning myself. Yet I kept coming back to the fact that the ultimate tenet of my faith was that 'God is Love', so surely it should be OK to love whoever you want, no matter what their gender may be? The greatest commandment of all was to love thy neighbour as thyself, after all.

Eventually, I decided to act out an experiment I had thought of while Father Corbally was preaching about love in his sermon one Sunday, quoting St Paul's letter to the Corinthians. I knew I could not talk to Father Corbally himself about my dilemma, as he was far too close to home. Also once, during my confession as I was about to leave the box, he asked me how many people were left in the queue, and when I told him four – with Mrs O'Hara bringing up the rear – he sighed heavily and said, 'Night, night, Brendan, see you tomorrow.' I was deeply shocked: I had always been under the impression that he could not recognize my voice through the purple curtain. Silly me – the man had known me all my life. Obviously he knew who I was!

So, no, I could not talk to Father Corbally. But what was to stop me trying further afield? Somewhere like, say, St Anne's Cathedral in the town centre? I enlisted the help of my friend Patrick, who was also gay. Patrick was a family friend who was a couple of years older than me; we had attended the same school, the same parish church and caught the same bus to Corpus Christi for years. We had both shyly admitted to each other that we were gay and now, together, we decided to collect some evidence regarding our Church's attitude towards our sexuality.

We chose St Anne's Cathedral as the venue of our experiment, as none of the priests knew us there and we could run out into the anonymity of Leeds city centre if they decided to chase us out of the cathedral. So, over a period of two weeks, we went in and spoke to various different priests about the dilemma of being gay and Catholic.

The results were mixed. One older priest told us it was a mortal sin and we would go to hell. Another suggested that we should shower in cold water while praying. A third advised us to get electric shock treatment from the doctors.

However, one more worldly and well-travelled priest, a young missionary called Father Andrew, gave us the advice we wanted to hear. He told me it was up to my own conscience and I was to stop crucifying myself and live the life I wanted to live with dignity and pride. Wow – and this from a priest of the Roman Catholic Church! Patrick and I were over the moon. We danced out of the cathedral, up to the Merrion Centre and down to Brills coffee shop and treated ourselves to two cappuccinos and a couple of vanilla slices.

Meanwhile, Saturday nights would now find our gang at the Peel in Boar Lane, at the C&A entrance. Sadly, the landlord had changed at the West Riding and it was no longer gay-friendly. The good news was that the Peel was nearer to walk to Charlie's afterwards, when we could afford it, for our dance to either Baccara's 'Yes Sir, I Can Boogie' or Elton John's 'Don't Go Breaking My Heart' or any of our other old favourites from ABBA, Barbra Streisand or David Bowie. New friends also came onto the scene: a football referee named Alan, an accountant called Phillip, and Jimmy from Glasgow who worked in Debenhams. As far as I was concerned, these guys were an example as to how to live your life no matter what your career path or where you came from.

Around this time, as the final countdown to my A-level exams began, I had an interview with Owners Services Limited or OSL, a leading international villa and apartment company, which had originally been set up to provide flights and transfers to the British owners of Spanish villas and apartments. It was the same company Les worked for. My interview took place at Ivey Travel, a local travel agents just off Commercial Street in Leeds. Happily, I was successful and it became official: I was to join Les on the Costa Brava that summer after I'd taken my last A-level paper, and work the summer season there.

To celebrate, Les took me with some friends to the Gemini club in Huddersfield, which I had been hearing about for so long. I was so, so, *so* excited. The thought of going to the biggest, most famous gay club in the north of England was amazing and when I walked in and climbed the stairs, I felt almost overwhelmed. I stood still and surveyed the crowd. The place was packed with men, some in T-shirts, some in checked shirts, all wearing casual jeans and dancing the night away. I had arrived and was going to stay and dance here all night. As Les went to the bar to get the drinks, there was a cry of excitement as the DJ put on ABBA's 'Waterloo'. The dance floor exploded and I went straight out there to join them. I defy anyone to dance to this anthem with a crowd of gay guys and for it not to be the best dance of your life. The sense of union with the other dancers, the music, the beat and the rhythm all came together and I felt I belonged at last. When Les joined me on the dance floor, my happiness was complete.

There was a yard at the back of the club where men would seek out partners and be intimate with one another. Les and I didn't need to do that; we already had each other. In any case, the yard was a dangerous place as the police used to raid the club by opening the yard doors and coming in the back way to arrest anyone who happened to be getting close to another person. Les and I had an emergency exit sorted if one were needed, as Lilly Law were always raiding the Gemini just to let you know they were watching you. It was a great problem if you were caught, as they would publish your name in the paper and then everyone who read the *Evening Post* in Leeds would know you were gay. There was talk of men committing suicide if a court case was looming in front of them, such was the fear of being found out and losing your job or worse. It's hard to believe now, but in those days the police used handsome blond police cadets as agent provocateurs to entrap you. It was a different world.

Summer approached in 1977. Our lives would soon be changing, quickly and dramatically. My friends and I had all reached eighteen years of age and our thoughts were turning to our future careers. It was John who first announced his plans: he had a place at the London School of Ballet and would be leaving Leeds the following month. I'm pleased to say that he eventually did become a ballet dancer, fulfilling his long-held ambition. However, while I was working in Tenerife some seven years later, I received a letter from his sister, Philippa, with some devastating news. John had died of a mysterious cancer-like illness while dancing in New York, at just twenty-six years of age. My eyes are filling up even now as I write this; at the time I heard the news, I think I cried for a week.

But in the summer of '77, such sadness was a world away, another lifetime. We were all full of dreams of the future. Isaac was going to university in Manchester to study Criminology, while Dominic was going into town planning; he had already had an offer of employment from a big company based in the Merrion Centre Tower, right in the very heart of Leeds. As for me, I still had my A levels to complete and then, with my parents' permission, I was to go to Spain and work there for the summer, before returning in October to start at teacher-training college.

Mr Lucas, my Geology teacher, gave me my final Geology A-level practical paper, handing me four types of rock that I had to identify and describe. I can still remember them today: limestone, granite, basalt and gneiss. I identified them, describing their creation, structure, location and what geological process they represented. I then looked at Mr Lucas, who smiled at me positively. It was hard to say goodbye to him. As I walked down the long drive of Corpus Christi School that July afternoon, I looked back to savour my time there. I had been extremely happy and my teachers had been remarkably talented people, to whom I am still grateful to this day. But tomorrow was to be the start of a new adventure – because tomorrow I was going to Spain.

CHAPTER 9

Viva España

M Y FATHER TOOK me to Leeds City railway station for the midnight train to London. He gave me an envelope with £200 in it, which was a lot of money in those days, and said it was to be used in an emergency to come home with if I was unhappy. He hugged me and put me on the train with a warning to watch out for the loose women in London who frequented King's Cross station. Little did my father know that I would never engage in talking to a lady of the night, so I was safe on that score at least. My mum had packed me so many sandwiches and chocolate bars you would have thought I was setting out on an expedition to climb Everest.

I found myself a carriage and slept most of the way to London. From King's Cross, I got a taxi to Victoria station to wait for the Gatwick Express. There I noticed a young boy on a bench, trying to sleep. He only had some trousers and a T-shirt on and although it was summer, it was chilly in that station, so before I got the first train at 6 a.m. I left most of my mum's sandwiches and chocolate bars for him. At least he would have some breakfast when he woke up.

I had to travel via London as all the flights from Manchester were full, but I was overjoyed: I was going to fly with British Caledonian and it was a DC-10 plane. I had studied the various aircraft used by different carriers for my interview and I was really excited to be flying in a McDonnell Douglas DC-10. It had three engines, one on either wing and one in the tail, and it carried 380 passengers, so it was a big plane as far as I was concerned. I checked in early and very politely asked for a window seat. I wanted to see everything we flew over, particularly Paris and the Pyrenees.

The stewardesses wore a lovely tartan uniform and they looked extremely smart. I have never forgotten how it was to fly in those days of Dan-Air and Britannia Airways. In the late seventies, not everyone could afford to travel by aeroplane and I was lucky to be able to enjoy the glory days of flying when it was still glamorous and special. It was a different world in those days. Firstly, when you checked in you were given a boarding card, and asked if you smoked or not (smokers sat at the back of the plane). Secondly, when you took off, a free – yes, *free* – bar service was offered to all passengers and, thirdly, you were given a hot – yes, *hot* – meal of beef, chicken or fish, with vegetables, a roll and butter and a dessert, followed by tea or coffee. The only extra things you had to pay for were the duty-free cigarettes and perfumes, which were usually cheaper on the plane. This deal was good news for everyone; the cabin crew were also happy as they got commission from the sales.

In those days, the stewards and stewardesses all spoke at least one European language, and they would wear a small, gold flag pin on their uniform to denote the country in whose language they were fluent. I do despair these days at the state of some of the cheaper airlines. Today, most of the announcements in a foreign language are all predictably taped for take-off and landings, but what happens if someone is ill and none of the cabin crew speak Spanish or French?

Once the plane was in the air, my tiredness caught up with me, and while I battled to keep my eyes open for my first-ever flight, I gave up the fight after we passed over Paris and allowed myself to slip into a rejuvenating nap. After two hours' flying time, I woke from my doze to hear the announcement that we were making preparations to land at Gerona, our destination. The DC-10 had to descend quite steeply after passing over the dramatic peaks of the Pyrenees into the new Gerona airport. Gerona had superseded Perpignan airport as the gateway to the Costa Brava; the latter had been the nearest, but using it entailed long transfers over the French border, including a change from Spanish to French coaches and back again, so the Spanish government had built Gerona to service the Costa Brava resorts from Blanes in the south to Portbou in the north.

After passport control, I retrieved my luggage and was met by Les and his coach driver, Tomas, who put my suitcases in the coach and told me to hop on board in broken English. It was lovely to see Les again, particularly on his 'home turf', but I was very aware that he was working so we were quite formal and reserved as we greeted each other, though as our eyes met unspoken excitement passed between us. The journey to L'Estartit was to be an hour and a half, via Flaçà and Torroella de Montgrí. After all the holidaymakers had been safely delivered to their villas and apartments, I was taken to my own, where finally Les and I could greet each other properly with a hug and a kiss. I would be sharing a three-bedroom apartment with Les and his senior representative/guide, Alfredo, who was from Madrid. Alfredo was an outgoing and yet rather formal man; he came from a noble family and had studied English in Harrogate.

The apartment looked out over the stunning harbour of L'Estartit and the island of Las Medes. I quickly settled in, playing my beloved 7-inches of 'Don't Cry for Me Argentina', 'Evergreen' and 'Dancing Queen', which I had brought with me for those times when I felt homesick.

It was, of course, the first time I had ever lived with a boyfriend. It was brilliant right from the off. I loved learning little things about Les, from the vegetables he hated (swede) to the records he had in his collection (a lot of Julio Iglesias). He was a very laid-back person, with a calm and easy-going attitude, and from the very beginning we conducted our cohabitation with give and take and compromise, so there were never any rows. Sleeping with another person at night was a different and very new experience for me. It was wonderful to curl up with Les, knowing that we were free to do it, that no one would intrude or come banging on the door. I found that Spain – newly free itself after the collapse of the Franco dictatorship – was a place that encouraged all freedoms, and so Les and I were able to develop our relationship without judgment or prejudice, without the watchful eyes of friends or family on us, in a country where liberty was honoured and embraced. We were never once questioned about our bond, even by the British expats who lived in the town, who seemed to be more open-minded than their fellow countrymen back home. Our love blossomed that summer and I fell head over heels – not only with Les, but also the country that made it all possible.

L'Estartit, our new home, was a small fishing village that was developing into a charming little resort. It boasted a long curvaceous beach with a mixture of small family-run hotels in the centre, the larger Panorama Hotel on the Avenida de Grecia, and lots of lovely villas dotted around. There were a few apartment blocks too, but overall it was small and I found I could bike round the whole village in thirty minutes flat using Alfredo's bike. The centre was dominated by Santa Anna Church, which was set within a large square.

Our employer, OSL, was based at number 67 Calle Santa Anna, and the Spanish agency we were working with, Viajes Florida, was at number 50 on the opposite side of the street. It was run by a man called Salvi, whose family also owned the Santa Anna Hotel. I soon found out that practically all the families were related to one another by some means and they all owned different parts of the town – an apartment here or garage there. They all spoke Catalan as their first language. Eventually, I started to meet other English people too, such as Betty Wilson, who owned the Lladro shop, assisted by a woman called Nora and her husband George, who also ran a second-hand bookshop around the corner from our office. Not forgetting

Jenis and Jackie who ran the Fisherman's Bar, and Theresa and Pat who ran Kim's Bar on the seafront.

The Guardia Civil (Spanish police force) in 1977 wanted all foreign visitors registered within twenty-four hours of their arrival in L'Estartit, so one of my regular jobs was to take the ledger to the *cuartel* (police station) and get it stamped, so that all new holiday-makers were legally resident in Spain for either one or two weeks.

My other duties included selling excursions and answering enquiries by phone and on the front desk. The properties were self-catering and I quickly learned the Spanish words for 'taps', 'toilet', 'grill', 'oven' and 'sink'. I then had to pass on the information about repairs to the agents who serviced the properties. Pedro Parri was our agent in L'Estartit and would speak to me in Castellano (Spanish), but to his wife and daughter in Catalan.

The Catalans were fiercely proud and held themselves apart from Madrid and the 'devils' they claimed worked and lived there. As I've mentioned, Spain was at that time going through the journey from dictatorship to democracy, after the death of Franco a couple of years previously in 1975. It was a time of discovery for most of the Catalans of the region, and being able to talk Catalan freely in the street, and not be shot at like they once had been, when the language had been banned under the Franco dictatorship, was a particular source of pleasure.

I really enjoyed my time in the office and loved the siesta period, when we would close for three hours. Les and I would go for lunch or spend some time on the beach, or just relax and have a nap during the heat of the day, and then we would go back and work from five o'clock till eight o'clock. It was a charming dilemma to decide which restaurant to eat in after work – usually we would stay in L'Estartit, but sometimes we would go further afield to Pals, Ullastret or Foixà. The latter had a restaurant in someone's house that used the front lounge as its main dining room. There we would try all sorts of Catalan dishes, from snails to stuffed squid to veal in wild mushrooms, not forgetting the desserts of *crema Catalana* or *recuit amb miel*, both of which I grew to love.

There is a saying that things happen to you if you are in the right place at the right time, and so it was with me one Monday morning about six weeks after my arrival. Les had been down the coast to nearby Calella de Palafrugell to see Sue, a colleague and overseas representative of ours who covered the resorts of Calella, Bagur, Llafranc and Tamariu. Unfortunately, that day she was very sick and needed to go back to the UK urgently.

I was asked to cover for Alfredo, who looked after most of the properties in L'Estartit, and in turn he would cover Sue's resorts until a solution could be found. It was a massive promotion for me and I was thrown in at the deep end: it was sink-or-swim time. Alfredo came round the properties with me for two days, then a secretary named Gill assisted me until I got a handle on the list of duties. Then, on the Saturday, Les gave me a transfer list and told me that I was to pick up some clients who were flying in on the Monarch Luton flight that morning at eleven o'clock, and also some others who were coming in on a Britannia Manchester flight that afternoon. He gave me a checklist of things I had to remember, but otherwise I was on my own. I was handed an OSL clipboard and sent on my way.

I got changed into some smart clothes and met Tomas at the church square and we started our departing transfer together. We picked everyone up, checked them in at Gerona, said our goodbyes, received loads of tips and then went around to the arrivals hall to greet our new clients. Thus began my career as an overseas represent-ative, or courier. The new clients were to be delivered to their respective villas or apartments and I would subsequently visit them during the week to make sure everything was satisfactory. I would sell them excursions and even take them out on the trips myself too. It was the start of a very happy career that was to last well beyond that first summer.

I looked after groups of passengers when we had horrendous air-traffic delays, sometimes of up to fourteen hours, taking them out of the airport and touring Gerona and Lake Banyoles with them, against the advice of the airport representatives, Damien and Patrick, who were always furious with us for breaking the rules. We used to call the passengers from the departure lounge and bring them back through passport control and out onto the coaches and away from the airport, while other operators did nothing to help their clients. The delays could be horrendous; we reps used to carry toothpaste and alarm clocks whenever we picked up clients, as sometimes at night the planes were so late that you could fit in a few hours' sleep before your arrivals landed from Manchester or Gatwick or Luton.

We also had a supply of airline tickets that could be written out for passengers who had lost theirs – we used to carry supplies of the different charter airlines' blank tickets in our briefcases. I still have some Dan-Air and Britannia ones as souvenirs.

The donkeys, bulls and sombreros we used to have to check in were amazing; sometimes Gerona airport on a Saturday morning looked more like a stable than an airport, as everyone grappled with their straw-filled donkeys. It would be unthinkable these days, of course; it would cost you more in excess baggage fees than the donkey was worth. In Tenerife, later in my career, everyone used to purchase and bring home the native birds of paradise to let their neighbours know they had been somewhere exotic.

Les and I spent a lot of weekends in Pineda, which was down the coast from us, just south of Lloret de Mar. Les's best friends Flora Carretero, her husband Luis and son little Luis (who was two years younger than myself, so not so little) lived there, and we spent hours at their house sampling Flora's fantastic cooking. Paella and roast lamb were her specialities. Flora's house was like a school of Catalan culture, and she gave me lessons in shopping, telling me what to buy and what to avoid in vegetable markets, always touching this and feeling that to see if it was ripe or not. I also started to learn Catalan and Castellano from the Carreteros. Being part Irish, I loved to talk – and the lack of communication with my hosts was killing me.

Not only that, but with my new role as a courier it was becoming increasingly important that I could communicate with my coach drivers, who were all Spanish. They would try their best to help me – but as this often involved teaching me swear words while telling me the phrase meant something innocuous, they weren't the most reliable of instructors. I lost count of the number of times I'd come out with a Spanish phrase and Les would chuckle and put me right, while in the background the drivers would bang their hands on their steering wheels with mirth.

So, I stepped up my efforts. Every evening at nine o'clock I would listen to the news and the weather forecast on our black-and-white television, and I would translate it all to Les, who corrected me and gave me advice on pronunciation. Les was fluent in both French and Spanish and I had a tremendous respect for his language skills. He, in turn, was generous with his time and expertise as he helped me to master this new language.

One day, I was sent with a list to buy some meat from the butchers, as an exercise to test my linguistic capability. We were having some friends round for a barbecue – Gil Brookes Parry, the new girl at our Spanish agency; Les's old friend Trevor Butterfield, who had come over from the UK; and Betty Wilson, from the Lladro shop in L'Estartit – so I was asked to fetch supplies. Trevor had only come over so that he could check me out and report back to Les's friends in the UK. The intimacy Les and I shared had not been lost on those close to us and there was a great deal of interest in our relationship and how it was developing.

To allow me to practise my Spanish fully, I was sent to the butcher's alone. On entering any shop, particularly a butcher's in 1977, a man stood out like a sore thumb. A man never went shopping:

it was not the done thing amongst the Spanish or Catalan, as the shops were seen as being entirely the domain of women. So there was already considerable interest in me as I entered the shop and took my place in the queue of ladies, and even more so when my neighbour Mercedes singled me out and greeted me with a '*bon dia*' (good day). She then enquired what I wanted to buy and I said, '*Carne* [meat] for the barbecue.' Mercedes hung around a while after she'd placed her order, talking to another lady who was just as intrigued, so what with them and the women in the queue behind me, I had quite a little audience when it came to my turn.

Confidently, I asked the young butcher Jordi for some *chuletas de cerdo* (pork chops) and some *botifarras* (Catalan sausages): so far so good. Next, I asked for meat for *pinchos* (kebabs) and *chuletas de cordero* (lamb chops), and then I asked for a *polla*: '*Dos y media en kilos y cortado en quats.*' Well, the whole queue of ladies immediately started to scream with laughter. Poor Jordi was practically on the floor too. I had no idea what I had said. After I'd stumbled back to the house, I told Les what had happened and we went through my order together. When I got to the *polla* bit, he stopped me. 'Oh no!' he exclaimed. 'You just ordered a penis weighing two and a half kilos and chopped into four pieces!' No wonder the whole place was in stitches.

This incident did not deter me from mastering this new language, although I still encountered the odd mishap. On another visit to our favourite restaurant, which did *macaronis* as a starter, I somehow managed to mispronounce the name of the dish in my haste to impress the handsome young waiter, and asked for a plate of *maricones* instead. With a raised eyebrow, he laughed and said, 'I shall go and check with the chef to see if we have a new dish on tonight.' I hadn't realized I'd accidentally ordered a plate of gay men.

CHAPTER 10

Today Spain...

THAT FIRST SUMMER in Spain was the stuff that dreams are made of. As it drew to a close, I started to face up to the reality that I would soon be leaving this idyllic place. Come September, I was due to return home, ready to take up my place at the teacher-training college in London, for the course started in October.

But it was not to be. As the season came to an end, and OSL started to review the feedback from clients, it turned out that my customers had given me fantastic comments. Consequently, I was offered a job to work the winter season in Portugal, where I would receive in-depth training to be a travel rep and consolidate the fantastic experience I had already gained in L'Estartit.

Although OSL had originally been set up to cater to the Spanish market, it had since developed into offering holidays in resorts beyond Spain too, in places such as Portugal, the Canaries and the Balearic Islands, so they started to need reps in those areas too. I was headed to the Algarve, which was just starting to grow as a tourist destination, to Albufeira, near to Faro. I was told by OSL that if I got my driving licence, I would be able to have my own resort areas too.

At this point, I still thought that I might yet train to be a teacher, but I was earning good money and I loved the lifestyle of living in another country, so I reasoned that if I took a year or two out, I would have plenty of funds to draw on in the future if I wanted to go to college then. I wrote to the principal of the teacher-training school in London and he replied with a nice letter to say that there would still be a place for me if I wanted to attend the following year. As it happened, though, I passed my driving test and thus my future of being a tour representative was mapped out for me. I ended up working in the Algarve, in Tenerife, in Agadir in Morocco... but always returning to the beautiful Costa Brava for the summer months. Most years I worked in Calpe, Calella de Palafrugell, Tamariu, Llafranc up to Begur, and other years I stayed in Rosas and Canyelles Petites, working all along the north-eastern coast of Spain at these resorts.

Perhaps the best thing about my new job was that Les would be joining me. He had already signed up for the winter season in Portugal and so the two of us had another exciting adventure ahead of us.

We had really grown on each other that first summer living in Spain. We had a freedom and a trust of each other that, it would transpire, would continue throughout our lives. He did not look like Robert Redford – but I was not looking for a Robert Redford to love, just someone normal. We were comfortable around each other and seemed to like the same things. I respected him too for being fifteen years my senior; he was a wise guy whom I could ask anything of and he seemed to know the answer, or several answers depending on your viewpoint. The age difference never seemed to matter to either of us, as we were of one mind, so to speak. He was a quiet, gentle man: kind, loyal, trustworthy and considerate. He loved anything to do with travel, which I did too. Perhaps most importantly, every time I saw him I got a heart-thumping sensation that would take my breath away.

And so it was that, in November 1977, during a visit home to Leeds, I found myself entering St Anne's Cathedral with my partner for life. We pulled out two wedding rings that we had bought for each other at H. Samuel, the jewellers on Commercial Street, and I dipped them both in holy water. I said prayers for us and then we slipped the rings onto each other's fingers: rose and white gold for me, and a herringbone-weave ring for Les. We chose our own rings as a sign of our respect for the other's individuality. Under the stone arches of the cathedral, we both made a commitment to each other then and there that would remain solid for as long as we both would live. We then lit some candles, and wished for our relationship and our hearts to burn as brightly all our lives.

While in Leeds, we took the chance to catch up with our families. My sister Margaret, my brothers and my mother had all been out to visit me while I was in Spain; my siblings came for a holiday, but I think my mother came to check out my new living conditions (my father couldn't visit as, as usual, he'd had to go to Ireland to help with the 'flipping hay'). I actually caught my mother running her finger along the surfaces, checking for dust – but luckily we had a maid who came weekly, so it was all absolutely pristine and got the Maureen Sheerin seal of approval.

My mother couldn't help but notice how close Les and I had grown, however. So on this visit home to Leeds, she chose her moment to ask me about it. We were in Leeds City station, on the platform, a few short minutes before I had to catch a train to Manchester on my way to Portugal. Margaret had come to wave me off too, but she discreetly made herself scarce as my mother spoke to me.

'You know this Les guy,' she said to me calmly, her voice steady, her eyes as alert as any mother's when they know their own sons' hearts, 'he's more to you than just a friend, isn't he?'

I nodded slowly.

'I'm going to ask you a question, and I want an honest answer,' she said. 'Are you gay?'

Well, what a blessed relief it was to say it: 'Yes.' And I explained that the word was 'gay', not 'puff' or any other term she might have heard.

'I'm going to ask another question, Brendan,' she said next. 'I want the truth. Are you happy?'

I smiled broadly and said that I was, the happiest I had ever been, and she hugged me with a mother's love, and said she was pleased for me, but that I was not to tell my sister or my father as they wouldn't be able to cope.

Well, Margaret already knew the truth, having seen Les and me living in Spain together, but I kept my word: I never explicitly told my father I was gay. But he knew; he wasn't a stupid man. And every time that Les came round to the house, my dad would jump up from his chair and shake his hand warmly and get a big glass of whiskey for him to drink, pressing it into his hand and making his welcome as warm as could be. All those years spent worrying about my sexuality, and how I would tell my family, and it turned out to be as easy as telling them I was me. Really, they already knew.

It was lovely having family over to visit us abroad. After the winter season in Portugal, Les and I returned to the Costa Brava for the summer of 1978, this time renting a four-bedroomed rustic villa called Villa Les Acacias, which had a lovely terrace for dining. With only the two of us living there, there was plenty of space for people to visit and my sister Margaret used to come over with our cousin Dawn for a holiday of sun, sea and sand. Dawn and Margaret were the same age – about seventeen – and they were like two gorgeous peas in a pod. Dawn worked for a playgroup while Margaret was a secretary for TSB bank, and they used to come over for their holidays and enjoy our wonderful villa, which was just around the corner from the beach.

One of the most welcome aspects of my job as a rep was to accompany the tourists on their excursions. My favourite coach trip was to the stunningly beautiful city of Barcelona. We left at 7 a.m. every Thursday and stopped for fifty *cafés con leche* and fifty croissants as soon as we reached the motorway services, as it was a three-hour journey. I loved visiting Gaudí's Sagrada Familia, which you could walk around and under for free in those days. It was still twenty-three years from completion; the Pope finally consecrated the church in 2010. We would then visit the old Gothic cathedral, followed by a walk through the old Gothic quarter of Barcelona to the Ramblas, while I chatted away to my group all the while, highlighting the points of interest and giving the history of the amazing sights we were seeing.

We would pass the famous Boqueria market and rejoin the coach to go to the Plaza de España and up to Montjuïc to see the views over to Tibidabo and the port of Barcelona. At the Plaza de Catalunya I would leave the ladies to go shopping in El Corte Inglés (this was in the days when you could get 145 pesetas to the pound). Most of the men would be put into taxis to the Camp Nou stadium to see the pride of Barcelona's football club.

We would all rejoin each other in the Plaza de Catalunya for our final walk down the Ramblas to the port. Passing the Liceu Theatre where Montserrat Caballé started her career, we would then stop by at the Plaza Real before arriving at the port, where the statue of Christopher Columbus pointed out to Palma de Mallorca (or was it to America?). Rejoining the coach, we would make our way back to L'Estartit with most of the clients exhausted after a full day.

The barbecue excursion was also a good night. On these nights, our clients would be taken to a massive *finca* or farmhouse in the country village of Saldet, on the way to Rosas. It was a very popular event, offered by all the holiday companies, with up to 300 guests in attendance. Les and I would sometimes have six coaches to look after. If this happened, I would guide two, Les would guide two and if my sister Margaret and Les's friend Trevor Butterfield happened to be visiting, as they often did, we would rope them into guiding one each. Trevor was one of Les's oldest friends from Leeds, who worked at Heathrow airport for Lufthansa Airlines, so he was already very familiar with the travel industry.

At Verges crossroads, Les and I would change coaches to begin our commentary all over again for the second group of tourists, while Margaret and Trevor would read out a script we had prepared for them, which they would have practised that afternoon on the terrace of the villa.

Large jugs of sangria would greet us on arrival, followed by photos posed with a sombrero, a baby monkey or an animal-skin pouch filled with wine that you had to pour into your mouth. The photos would be developed within the hour and sold to the clients, who by this time would be quite tipsy. A piece of chicken, a *botifarra* (Catalan sausage) and a pork chop would be accompanied by jacket potatoes, salad, butter and bread – lots of bread – in baskets, which we, as guides, had to refill… along with the wine. Naturally, this flowed like water, with the *tinto* and *blanco* followed by champagne and a flaming rum punch called *cremat*, which was set alight.

Leaving the clients to dance to the live band with some of the local lads who used to fancy their chances with the female tourists, it was time for us guides to eat with our drivers and catch up with each other's news. I always ate my dinner with a lovely lady called Geddy Laboria, who was from Portsmouth. Geddy worked for Martin Rooks Holidays in Rosas and I considered her the best guide on the whole of the Costa Brava. She was married to a man called Juan and she spoke fluent Catalan. One night, while we were watching our clients at the end of our meal, I asked her to dance and from then on every week we would look forward to renewing our friendship and dancing to 'Una Paloma Blanca' and 'La Bamba'.

The hours used to pass by so quickly – well, they always do when you are enjoying yourself – and at midnight we had to round up our clients, drunk and sober, and head back to L'Estartit, singing all the way home. Today Geddy is still one of my closest friends and we call each other every Sunday. She is now teaching Catalan children English and has a very successful school in Figueres, the home of the internationally renowned Salvador Dalí Museum.

One occasion from the barbecue that I'll never forget was when a lady with false teeth had way, way too much to drink. She ended up vomiting, so I got her cleaned up and back on the bus. We'd started off again when she suddenly exclaimed that her teeth were missing! Well, I had to stop the coach and look for them, of course. All in a day's work for a travel rep.

On Sundays, I used to avoid the bullfighting trip, but I would take the El Cid nightclub excursion that night, which featured Juan Sierra and his Ballet Español. The nightclub was just outside Rosas on the Figueras road and it was champagne a-go-go. When the bottle was finished, you simply turned it upside-down in the ice bucket and it was immediately replaced with a new one.

The warm-up acts were usually singers, followed by a very clever puppet show from Belgium. Then the Ballet Español would start, featuring three male and three female dancers. The dances were from all parts of Spain: from Madrid '*La Boda de Luis Alonso*'; from Aragon '*La Jota*'; but my favourite were the flamenco pieces from Andalucía, especially the Sevillanas. The costumes were elaborate and colourful, the dancing was exceptional, and our clients would return year after year to see Juan and his troupe.

The lead dancer was a very talented man called Juan Sierra, who reminded me so much of John, and I got to know him very well during my subsequent seasons on the Costa Brava. Juan was directed by an old Spanish dancer called Luis Principe and both of them had trained at the Academy of Dance in Madrid. The finale always consisted of Juan dancing the flamenco in his tight black trousers and red-and-black polka-dot blouse. During the dance, he would spin around so fast that the sweat from his brow used to hit my clients in the front row and send the women into a frenzy of lust.

The show would end with a burst of wild applause from the rapt audience, who would then throw red carnations at Juan from the table decorations.

As a treat for the ladies, I used to ask Juan to come on the coach, still hot and sweaty from the dance, to say goodnight in his thick Spanish accent, which seemed to be appreciated by all the females whether married or otherwise. Often the frenzy would start again while their male partners would sink back into their seats, embarrassed.

Some years later, I met Juan and Luis again when they were in Tenerife, dancing with their troupe in the Botanico Hotel. It was there that Juan had a dreadful accident, injuring his right foot. He was flown to Geneva in Switzerland to see a top surgeon, such was his will to find a cure, but the diagnosis was horrendous: Juan would never dance again. Afterwards, he attempted to work as a choreographer but, unable to live without dancing himself, he later hung himself in his hotel room. He was found by his friend and guitarist Pepe, who had accompanied him so many times over the years. The whole of Rosas went into mourning when the news broke about his death. Although he is gone, he will never be forgotten.

As a travel rep, you have to be able to deal with the good and the bad. I worked very hard to make sure everyone had a good time and generally most people did. However, on the odd occasion it did go terribly wrong. In S'Arenal, Mallorca, a group of tourists once asked to meet me in their hotel to complain about the food. This four-star hotel was the pride of the resort and I could not believe what they were claiming. I therefore agreed to have lunch there and tried most of the major dishes on the menu, including the extremely garlicky meatballs. That evening, at about midnight, I was woken by the most violent pain in my stomach and as I rushed to the loo, I had to agree with the clients that the food was definitely suspicious.

The next day, I was met by more complaints and, adding my own evidence to the list, I contacted my head office in Palma and got the whole group moved out to an exclusive five-star resort for the rest of their stay at no extra charge. My tips that week doubled – but I have avoided meatballs ever since.

Any complaints I had were always reported immediately, and I would always check again later to make sure the problems had been sorted out, as I never did trust receptionists or agents, who would sometimes bluff you just to get you off their backs. I became quite a pain for them, but they soon learned not to mess me about. It sounds quite tough, but my philosophy was that my clients had paid for their holiday as described in the brochure and if it was not up to standard, then it was my job to make sure any wrinkles or problems were ironed out. After all, many families had saved up all year to come to Spain and we had a lot of repeat bookings from clients who loved the resort.

I did have some terrible tragedies too. My first death was an eleven-month-old baby girl called Lucy Mallaban, whose name I shall remember for as long as I live. I was summoned by the Guardia Civil at 4 a.m. to go to Rosas. Arriving at the holiday centre there, I found out that she had died because her cot had not been erected properly. The judge who released her body said it was a tragic accident.

Consequently, this case was taken up by *That's Life* presenter Esther Rantzen and her team. New legislation was introduced and all tour operators thereafter had to have British Safety Standard cots in all their resorts. It was an important lesson learned, although obviously far too late for poor Lucy's family.

I had one very nice gentleman who had a heart attack on the beach at L'Estartit. He had been staying at the Villa Theresa with his lovely family: his wife and two sons who were there with their respective girlfriends. Jackie from the Fisherman's Bar ran to our office to let me know and I jumped into my Seat 850 and sped out onto the Gerona Road after the ambulance at such speed that I managed to catch up with it by the time we got to Torroella, on its way to Gerona hospital, which was an hour away. The ambulance had its lights flashing and I thought he was going to be OK, but at the Verges crossroads the ambulance stopped and the light was turned off. I had to calm his grief-stricken wife and accompany her back to the resort to tell his waiting children the awful news.

I also had a young woman of about eighteen who was admitted to Gerona hospital during the night with stomach pains. When I got there, she was just about to be examined by several gynaecologists, who were waiting for my arrival. Her two friends were over the moon when they saw me approach, believing that somehow I would be able to solve all their problems. The doctors did not speak any English and so I was asked to attend the examination in order to translate the girl's symptoms. As a young man in my late teens, this was quite embarrassing for me, but the poor girl was in so much pain I had to forget my own discomfort and focus on hers.

The doctor was quite stern and not at all friendly. He asked about the girl's menstrual cycle and then about her womb; questions that made me squirm with embarrassment as they were so personal. But the girl made me feel at ease by saying she needed to tell them the truth, so I concentrated on translating to the best of my ability. Then the doctor came out with the killer question: he asked the girl how long ago had she had an abortion and where had it been performed? Now I knew why he was so stern – Spain was a Catholic country and abortion was illegal. In fact, rich Spanish girls who found themselves in that predicament flew to London away from the prying eyes of their neighbours for the operation to be done privately on Harley Street. I apologized to the girl and asked the question, and with the answer the required treatment was administered. The girl recovered and was later sent home to consult with her doctor in the UK. She and her friends thanked me no end for translating and I never again spoke about what had been said in that room.

Our life in Spain was very sociable. Some of the friends I made there I am still in touch with now, such as Andrew Wilton, a dear man whom I first met at Gerona airport. Andrew was another holiday rep based at Lloret de Mar, in the south of Spain, so he wasn't nearby to us, but we would meet every season at the airport on transfer days, or at the pre-season get-togethers that Les organized on behalf of the company. We would go to the reps' favourite restaurant Relicario, which was close to Gerona, and eat masses of roast chicken, talking nineteen to the dozen. Andrew and I just hit it off and we remain very good friends to this day.

Les and I had a constant stream of friends visiting us for the fiestas. In turn, we would stay with them, in particular regularly making the journey to Barcelona for long weekends with our friend Angel, who had an apartment there. Barcelona is a city that never sleeps so we made the most of it, working all day and dancing the night away.

Trevor Butterfield in particular used to stay with us often. He would always regale us with tales of the places he had visited during his travels with Lufthansa. His stories made us want to see more of the world ourselves – and once that desire kicked in, well, there was no stopping us…

CHAPTER 11

...Tomorrow the World

IN JANUARY 1979, Les and I bought an Eastern Airlines ticket for $200, which enabled us to fly all along the eastern seaboard of America, including the Caribbean – from New York right down to Miami, in and out of Puerto Rico, and visiting most of the islands like Martinique, Jamaica, Trinidad and Tobago, and Dutch-owned Saint Martin as well. It was an amazing itinerary at an unbelievable price. We were also allowed to have one flight across to Los Angeles, where we stayed with some very old family friends of Les called the Mills, in a place just outside the city called Riverside. They were lovely and made us feel part of the family.

We had a wonderful holiday. I turned twenty while I was there and I remember standing in an ice-cream parlour being serenaded by these American guys, all singing 'Happy Birthday'. It was heaven.

While we were in LA, we met up with one of Les's friends called Harold, who was working at the time for a top Hollywood family that had made its money through the glamorous studio system of the 1930s, during the Golden Age of Hollywood. Harold had been in royal service and had worked for The Queen, Princess Margaret and Queen Elizabeth the Queen Mother, so when he decided to go to America, he took his CV down to Hollywood Boulevard and into a couple of domestic staff agencies – and unsurprisingly within five minutes he had got himself a new job.

The mansion where he worked was in Bel Air, a very posh area of Hollywood. Barbra Streisand and Mantovani were neighbours. Harold lived in a little gatehouse cottage on site and he told us we had to come in by the tradesman's entrance, not the main driveway. Well, the tradesman's entrance had gates the size of Buckingham Palace's. We pulled into a garage with our Avis hire car looking rather lost between four Cadillacs, three Rolls-Royces and numerous sports cars. There must have been at least fifteen beautiful cars all told; my mouth was open in shock at the sight of it all.

Harold met us and took us to the greenhouse – acres of glass stuffed with orchids and tended by two Polish gardeners. Afterwards, he showed us the swimming pool, at the end of which was a little pavilion that contained every size swimsuit Bloomingdales could supply, as well as bathing caps. It was clear that when his employers had guests in the house, they made sure their friends didn't want for anything. And of course the guests were people like Yul Brynner, Stefanie Powers and Frank Sinatra – as I saw from the photographs of these people on the piano, in the lounge. The family had an original Rodin sculpture of a ballet dancer there too, like the one in the Louvre, and a collection of extraordinary Ming Dynasty china. Harold also showed us the beautiful cut-glass cigarette holders that held three different packs of cigarettes in each one, all different brands. Apparently, the staff were instructed that once a pack had been opened and a cigarette taken out, the whole pack had to be replaced, so a guest would always have the pleasure of taking the first one from the pack. Of course, this meant that if you smoked in that household you were in heaven because you would get all the spare cigarettes.

As if all this wasn't enough, Harold then pressed a button and the curtains closed in the lounge and down from the ceiling came a full-sized cinema screen. Meanwhile, at the other end of the room, the pictures on the wall moved and a cinema projector popped out. We were told that when guests had finished dinner, a projectionist would come straight from the studio with a brand-new film and he would play them a movie.

I absolutely loved the house, especially the sweeping staircase in the grand hall, which reminded me of the one in *The Sound of Music* which the children come marching down to meet Maria and Captain von Trapp. Harold also showed us the butler's pantry, which was a treasure trove of English bone china and teardrop crystal glasses from Waterford in Ireland. But the best thing of all was the ladies' powder room, which was all done out in pink with a beautiful Parisian gilded mirror and gilded chairs. On the counter stood six two-foot-tall exquisite crystal decanters full of Chanel No. 5. They had a gold dispenser tap, so ladies who came to dinner could have a little dab of perfume. I had never seen anything like it.

However, despite all the riches, Harold told us later that his boss was very lonely, and somewhat estranged from her daughter and grandchildren. And I suppose in a way it proved to me that no matter how much money you have, if you don't have your family around you, then you have nothing. I also realized that the house was all for show, as Harold's employer actually lived in a suite of apartments upstairs and only used the house when she entertained. So all in all I ended up feeling rather sorry for her.

Anyway, we had a wonderful time in LA and Malibu, and one day we flew up to San Francisco, which for a gay man of twenty was absolutely amazing. We did all the tourist things: we went down the crooked street, walked along the piers, ate chowder and rode the cable cars from Market Street all the way down to the port. But we also went to Castro, which in those days was a big gay ghetto. There were gay policemen, gay chemists, gay bars, gay discos, gay shops, gay supermarkets – everything was gay. I couldn't believe that people had so much freedom. We ended up going over the Golden Gate Bridge and staying in the YMCA in Sausalito – a wonderful end to a wonderful holiday.

But, still, Les and I wanted to see even more of the world. So, at the end of the 1980 season, we decided to have the winter off and go on a world cruise together, for a real once-in-a-lifetime experience. That summer the *Canberra* – a gleaming white P&O ship of just over 45,000 tonnes – had sailed into Palamós and Les and I, Gil Brookes Parry, Betty Wilson and Trevor boarded the ship for the day. We had been invited on by the purser's office as a surprise to show Les and me the cabin we had booked for the round-the-world voyage, which would leave Southampton on 6 January 1981. We were given a guided tour of the vessel, shown our actual cabin and all the ship's facilities. The invitation to lunch on board the *Canberra* was the highlight of our tour as we could eat from the English menu – a real treat when you lived in Spain in pre-EEC days when English food was rarely available.

Flying home to England, we went to have our tuxedos made (one black and one white each) at Richmond's the tailors at the bottom of Briggate, then returned to L'Estartit to pack up the villa for the winter and to drive our Spanish car to the UK with our luggage, in readiness for the voyage of a lifetime. I was only twenty-one when we set sail.

Trevor came on board that January morning and saw us to our cabin. The *Canberra* was a huge liner, boasting eleven decks, a laundry, cinema, dance hall, casino, two swimming pools and a host of bars – the Cricketers', the Crow's Nest and the Alice Springs are the ones I particularly remember. It was a quarter-of-a-mile walk round the promenade deck. It would be home to Les and me for the next ninety days. We practically had to shove Trevor off the ship as he did not want to leave us at all. As he bade us farewell from the quayside, I could see he was wiping his face with a handkerchief while the ship's loudspeaker played Rod Stewart's 'We Are Sailing' and everyone threw streamers.

Les and I quickly made ourselves at home. Every day the *Canberra* would print its own newspaper, which listed the daily activities ranging from deck quoits to painting classes to piano concerts by Vincent Billington to bingo to bridge to whatever was on at the cinema. It also gave you the dress code for the evening. If it was a Captain's cocktail party, it would advise that a tuxedo was necessary; or if it was an informal evening, it might suggest a lounge suit. Occasionally, it was fancy dress: one time I went as Hotlips from Honolulu from *M*A*S*H* and Les went as Dame Edna Everage. Needless to say, we both won prizes! Luckily our berth had two huge wardrobes – one each – to hold all our clothes. Every day we would go to the Alice Springs bar and the swimming pool at the stern, which rapidly became our 'base'. There we met several lovely people, some of whom became lifelong friends.

Our first port of call was the beautiful tropical island of Madeira, where we met up with Patrick, the manager of the local OSL office, and his staff, as they knew that we were coming. In those days, you could invite guests back on board the ship, so after we had been to dinner with them on the island, they came on board for drinks so we could show off the marvellous facilities. At midnight, they had to disembark and stand at the quayside and watch us sail away, while we waved madly at them.

We then crossed the Atlantic to Port Everglades in Florida, where we toured the mango swamps on flying boats, looking out for the birds and the alligators. Our ship docked near Ford Lauderdale, so we went there to a tea dance, which was held in a gay bar. Well, we walked in and ordered a drink and heard this 'Oh hello!' – and spun round to see Michael our sommelier and John our table waiter from the ship! And then who did we see but Phil, one of the ship's photographers, and Peter, a barman... There must have been eight or nine members of staff from the *Canberra* at this gay bar, having a dance and drinking on their day off in port, so we made friends with all of them too. It was starting to dawn on me by then that gay men are very good in professions that involve dealing with the public, whether it's the tourist industry or customer relations or teaching. We seem to have a talent for it!

From Fort Lauderdale we headed south towards the mouth of the Panama Canal, which joins the Atlantic to the Pacific. Actually, Les and I got off at the docks just before the canal, because we had decided to take a train into Panama City. It was rather a rickety old train so I was glad to get off by the time we reached the city – though, as luck would have it, when we got there the station was ringed with police and we were told to get back on the train and go all the way back to where the ship was docked. So the only thing we saw was the jungle at the side of the canal.

It was quite a feat going up the Panama Canal – it's 48 miles long and the *Canberra* had to be pulled by tugs the whole way because she was such a big ship. There are actually three canals and you have to negotiate your way through three locks, which for a vessel that size is no mean feat. We started at nine in the morning and by about six in the evening we were passing under the Bridge of the Americas, which leads into the Pacific Ocean. It was a phenomenal experience – what a feat of engineering.

Our next port of call was Acapulco: my first taste of Mexico, as the *Canberra* pulled into Acapulco Bay. This used to be where the Hollywood greats vacationed in the 1950s, hence it becoming famous all around the world. We went to see the amazing cliff divers of La Quebrada and then spent some time on the glorious beach. We also ventured into the backstreets and saw the poverty that some of the Mexicans lived in, only metres away from the big plush hotels on the front. Les and I returned to the ship feeling very grateful for the luxury in our lives.

After Mexico came a day in San Francisco. We'd been there before, of course, so simply revisited our favourite places. However, we were back so late from our sightseeing that we missed dinner. Naturally, this was no problem on the *Canberra*. The beauty of having our own steward on the ship was that we could ring for room service, and within half an hour some tea and cake would be delivered to our cabin. It was all part of the service.

In the Hawaiian Islands, we chartered a small plane and flew over the active volcanoes that I remembered learning about in Mr Lucas's Geology lessons. Papua New Guinea, meanwhile, was a beautiful tropical island where we were greeted by the Royal Marines' Band. We visited a local cultural centre, where the natives dressed in feathers and performed several folkloric dances about birds, rainforests and mountains. They also served a drink called cava, which was pretty potent, which we were asked to try. It was made from a root similar to a yam and had quite a kick to it. It was beaten to a pulp with water added and then strained through a sieve before drinking.

Christchurch marked my first visit to New Zealand. I was really impressed with the city. I was also amazed by how English it looked, especially the cathedral and, bizarrely, people's gardens, which had roses in them and were impeccably neat and tidy. The hospitality of the New Zealanders was outstanding and we were made to feel very welcome as we went off on our own adventure into the city, wandering around and exploring.

After Christchurch, we spent three days in what has become one of my favourite cities, Sydney. Sailing into Sydney harbour and seeing the famous bridge and opera house was quite something. The fashion sense in Australia still seemed very colonial at that time – people wore long socks and shorts, and panama hats against the hot sun. We went to the botanical gardens to take in the exotic plants, and also the zoo, which was incredible, with creatures we'd never seen in the flesh before, like kangaroos and koalas.

From there, it was straight on to Hong Kong, where everyone immediately ran off the ship to get their tailoring done, as it was so absurdly cheap. Les and I had some lovely safari suits made for us – we looked like Stewart Granger gone wrong! We also found ourselves going round Hong Kong harbour on a car ferry – the Su Dong Rong Ferry, if memory serves – which boasted a restaurant and a nightclub on top. We were the only Englishmen in a room full of Chinese people, which became rather interesting as the karaoke started, as all the lyrics were in Chinese. It was a very funny night, and it was so refreshing to be somewhere where there were no Europeans, and not an English voice to be heard, other than our own. The food was sublime.

From Hong Kong we went to see Singapore – and the famous 'lady boys' – then we took a flight to Bangkok in Thailand. The Land of Smiles did not disappoint me at all. Bangkok is amazingly busy, but if you get away from the city itself, the countryside is fabulous. We visited the temples with the Reclining Buddha, and the Emerald Buddha. The Grand Palace Complex was next on our list and on cue Les and I started singing songs from *The King and I*. I purchased a carved elephant from a street vendor, which I have to this day. The floating market at Damnoen Saduak was the highlight of the visit, however: all those vegetables and different goods – even a floating takeaway offering beautiful Thai food – and such a wonderful chatty atmosphere, with bargaining and price-fixing going on at nineteen to the dozen. Tremendous.

By this stage of the cruise, we had palled up with a lovely couple called Jeannie and Gus from Jersey in the Channel Islands, who were travelling round the whole world as we were. So when we got to Colombo in Sri Lanka, we hired a car and toured the island with them. The man from Avis had got up at four in the morning to drive down from his village to chauffeur us about, but we told him we wanted to do the driving. This horrified the man, who thought we were doing him out of a job. He was only charging five pounds for the whole day – roughly twelve hours – so when we tipped him an additional fifteen pounds the poor man was practically kissing our feet with gratitude. It did bring it home to us how impoverished many people are. Mr Ali took us first to a tea plantation where we saw the tea being picked and processed. We then went to the Temple of the Tooth in Kandy, before making our way to an elephant farm, to see how they worked the animals, using them like tractors and cranes. While there, we stripped down to our underwear and washed the baby elephants in the river with coconut shells, while Jeannie took lots of photos of us. It was an unforgettable trip.

From Colombo we sailed to Mauritius, which is definitely a paradise island. The architecture reflected the mixture of French and English colonization and the beautiful white beaches were absolutely pristine. They reminded me of the Bounty bar advert on TV. From there we headed to Durban in South Africa. As this was 1981, the whole country was still under the apartheid regime, and Nelson Mandela was languishing in prison. It was a horrific shock to find separate post offices, toilets, buses and so on for blacks and whites when we disembarked.

Again we decided to hire a car with Jeannie and Gus, this time to see some game. We went up to a little place called Shashui Game Reserve, and ended up staying in a compound run by some Portuguese people who had been run out of Mozambique during the revolution. There was a large round hut made of mud and straw in the middle, where you ate and socialized, and smaller huts round the outside, where you slept. We were greeted at the gate by a Zulu warrior with half an ostrich eggshell covering his private parts, held together by string.

Gus and I ended up on a rather terrifying night safari with these Portuguese guys looking for nyala – a type of South African antelope – that the Portuguese wanted to capture to trade for a rhino from a different reserve. Yet another experience I will never forget. We were in the middle of the jungle in the dead of night, no street lights of course and it was absolutely pitch black – you couldn't even see your hand in front of you. We set off across the terrain as silently as we could, when suddenly the Zulus shouted loudly to the driver to stop. It turned out we were inches from a sheer drop into a gully, and only their intimate knowledge of the area had saved us.

The following day, after another safari expedition, we went into town for a drink. We found a bar, and without thinking went into the black side of the room by mistake. The poor lady who worked there was screaming at us, 'Please, don't come in this side! You've got to go round to the white side!' It was essentially the same room, just separated by a grille, but of course what we hadn't realized was that the owner could get fined a terrific amount of money for letting us drink on the 'wrong' side. I just couldn't understand it, but that was apartheid in those days. Even when we were driving back down the coast towards Durban, we noticed that the beaches were segregated. Thank goodness such a disgraceful system does not exist any more.

On the last leg of our trip, we caught a South African Airlines plane to Cape Town, where we caught up with the *Canberra* again to make a stop in Dakar, Senegal. This visit was really interesting for me, and I had been looking forward to it very much, simply because this was West Africa – a complete unknown. Dakar was the capital and it was very vibrant indeed. The costumes of the ladies were bright and vivid with all the colours of the rainbow represented – and some others thrown in for good measure. They all wore a matching colourful turban too. When we visited the market, I could not help but notice that it was all women who were shopping and that all the stallholders were female too. The men could be seen in makeshift bars or standing around in groups, but not shopping – that was definitely the ladies' domain.

The second thing that struck me was the infrastructure of the roads and pathways, which was pretty awful. This surprised me as Senegal is an ex-French colony, and usually if the French were in charge, they left a good impression, especially where basic infrastructure is concerned. I just think it had all been left to crumble after the French had moved away.

As we ventured further into the city, where people dwelt, we were taken aback by the poverty in which the Senegalese lived. The houses were mere shacks and the floors were just earth, but everything appeared clean and the population looked well. It is at times like this that I feel very grateful indeed about where I live and the conditions I live in.

Everyone seemed to be quite happy, however, and no one shied away from us. They were very interested in where we came from and where we were going to next. The sight of the *Canberra*, the big white ship, caused a lot of interest. The Senegalese also savvy, and they realized that a lot of money could be spent by us tourists as visitors to their city, so those who owned businesses welcomed us with open arms.

After Senegal, we made a final stop in Tenerife – which, unbeknownst to me, was soon to be my home – before eventually returning to Southampton. It really had been the holiday of a lifetime.

CHAPTER 12

From One Coast To Another

I N THE EARLY eighties, Les and I were asked to go and work in Tenerife for a few months during the winter. We used to fill in for the managers or head reps at all-year-round resorts so that they could have a holiday. It was great for us as we got a chance to see other parts of the world, then return to our home in the Costa Brava for the summer.

Tenerife is a beautiful island, dominated by the Teide volcano in the north. Around Puerto de la Cruz, which is in the lee of the volcano, it's very lush and tropical, with lots of vegetation, whereas the south of the island is like a desert, arid and dry and covered in volcanic rocks. The south is mainly given over to the cultivation of tomatoes and flowers, usually in greenhouses, and also hundreds of banana plantations. You used to have to be very careful if you saw a lorry coming towards you harvesting the bananas, as the roads were made out of volcanic ash and you would get absolutely covered head to foot in dust if a lorry went past. I'd always dash into the banana plantation and hide if I saw one.

Les and I were given an apartment in Los Cristianos, which at that time was a very small village with a little church square in its centre, a small port and a new marina for yachts and boats. You would see children running around in bare feet, such was the relaxed lifestyle there. Las Americas was a resort that was just being developed further down the coast. To get from one to the other, you had to leave Los Cristianos, then join the main Puerto de la Cruz road that ran down to Los Gigantes, and then drive south down into Las Americas. These days both resorts are joined up into one massive development, but back in the early eighties they were two separate towns. I used to do this journey every day to go into the main office.

By this time, OSL had bought a hotel company called Wings; I looked after villas and apartments for OSL, with the hotel operation coming under the Wings brand, splitting my time between the two. The hotel I was working in was called the Bouganville Playa in Las Americas, which had only just been built, so everything was brand new. No one ever complained. The guests were very nice, mainly English and quite well-heeled. After all, for most of them this was their second holiday, as this was the winter. I also had to look after some apartments in Los Cristianos.

I worked there with a lovely guy called David, who had a boyfriend called Franklin, from South America, and it was really nice to meet another gay couple who lived together, like Les and me. We became very good friends.

It was also in Tenerife that I met Maria Gonzalez, who owned a fruit shop in Los Cristianos and became another very dear friend. I remember going into her shop and seeing an avocado for the first time, which completely amazed me. She had to give me a recipe for guacamole as I had no idea what you were meant to do with it. Initially, Maria thought I was from Catalonia. I told her I was from England, to which she replied, 'No, no, I can tell by your accent.' I'd been living on the Costa Brava for so long that I'd picked up the dialect. It took her quite a while to believe that I wasn't from Catalonia and was actually from Yorkshire.

During the winter months in February, there always used to be a carnival in Tenerife, a celebration before the austere weeks of Lent arrived. The music and the drums would start at about midday, throughout the whole town, and everyone would get into samba mode with the swinging of hips and the clicking of fingers. Everybody would shout, '*CARNIVALE! CARNIVALE!*'

The whole of Puerto de la Cruz would dress up for the day, and a lot of the men would cross-dress. You would see a butch waiter serving in your restaurant one evening, and the next day he'd be stealing his wife's clothes and calling himself Carmen. The guys would dress as Spanish ladies in colourful flamenco outfits or black widow's dress. I was always surprised by how detailed their costumes were, with hands adorned with rings and nails covered in bright red varnish, some holding fans and all wearing sets of pearls or beads. They looked very fetching indeed. I'd never seen straight guys dressing up in ladies' clothes before, and it was hilarious. But of course, everyone dresses up in a carnival!

At 2.00 p.m., the floats would start to line up for the main procession through town. The floats represented different districts of the area, including the Orotava Valley, which is lush with vegetation. Therefore a lot of the floats were decorated with large palm trees, rich giant tropical plants, birds of paradise, and lots and lots of bananas. Some had Cuban themes, some Mexican and others South American.

The costumes were always bright reds, yellows and greens, with lots of glitter to sparkle in the Tenerife sunshine, and everyone had matching shoes and hats – some even had matching gloves – and all the participants would dance either in front of or on top of their floats.

One carnival, my bosses in Puerto de la Cruz were very sweet because they loaned me an apartment on the seafront for the weekend, so that I could celebrate my birthday in some style. I invited David and Franklin, Les's old friend Trevor Butterfield, and Aileen and Sandy, friends from Scotland who were staying with us, to a special buffet in the apartment. We all watched the carnival come down the boulevard and along the promenade. It was right in front of our balcony, so we had a spectacular bird's-eye view.

The Queen of the Carnival and her entourage came past and we all cheered. They wore pure white glittering costumes and high white heels. All of them were adorned with white ostrich feathers of differing lengths and styles. The Queen outshone everyone, however, with an enormous singular black feather on her headdress, surrounded by white; it was very effective and she looked so striking as her costume enhanced her stunning natural beauty.

The whole atmosphere was smiles, music, drums and dancing in the streets, and everyone was partying, from our balcony down to the open streets and all along the seafront. Inhibitions were swept away and everybody was having a great time.

It felt amazing to celebrate my birthday that day. I've never felt so happy in all my life. My family phoned from the UK to wish me a happy birthday and I was surrounded by friends and loved ones.

Later, Les took me out on my own to a beautiful spot just north of Puerto de la Cruz in the Orotava Valley. Here we had a fillet steak, with avocado to start – obviously! It was one of those perfect days. Looking back, it was as if I was floating on a bubble of happiness at that time. But, as we all know, all bubbles eventually have to burst.

* * *

It was one day in March 1986 that Les became terribly ill. He was sick in bed at home with a virus, feverish and in pain, and as his condition swiftly worsened I realized that he needed urgent medical care. He was transferred to the renal unit at the Santa Cruz Hospital in Tenerife. Once he'd been stabilized, I was able to go in and see him, and there I learned more about the illness that would change everything for us.

Les had told me before that he had been born with polycystic kidneys, a condition whereby small cysts present on the kidneys grow with age, causing problems as you get older. But I'd never seen any signs of his illness before; on the contrary, he'd always seemed so full of life. As I sat on the side of his bed, Les took my hand and explained gently that the prognosis did not look good: eventually the cysts would take over his whole kidney function and dialysis would be needed to keep him alive. Beyond that, it seemed a kidney transplant would become a necessity.

It was a huge shock. This was the man with whom I had shared my fears, my hopes, my dreams, my whole life – and suddenly I was hearing that he was likely to live only ten more years. Soon, it seemed, our happy world of travel and tourism and living the high life abroad would change to one of dialysis, hospitals and the encroaching possibility of death. I was left reeling at the prospect.

We discussed it all at length that night in the hospital, and afterwards I walked along the front of Puerto de la Cruz and came to the Catholic church. I went in, lit some candles and knelt down, recalling from my childhood the prayers of devotion to the Mother of God. I asked for acceptance, courage and hope for both of us, and before long the tears started to flow down my cheeks. I must have been there for about an hour and it helped to give me strength. I knew I wouldn't find all the answers to my problems there, but it did enable me to find some peace to stop my racing mind from worrying and fearing for the future.

When Les was discharged, we started to prepare for coming back to England from Tenerife. We'd been told the nearest dialysis unit at that time was in Malaga, in the south of Spain on the mainland. It would have meant a four-and-a-half-hour journey to Malaga via Madrid – there were no direct flights in those days – to get his regular kidney dialysis. So since Les was English and had kept up his taxes in England while he'd been away, we decided we needed to come home. We also realized it was important to be near the people we loved and to start preparing for the changes that his illness was going to bring into our lives. It was clear his health was only going to get worse.

As it happened, a dear friend of ours named Marie Hogg, who works for Saga Holidays, called as we were making our plans to move home. She told Les that Saga Holidays were looking for a person to work in their overseas department, which was based in Folkestone in the UK. They had asked if Les would be interested in the job. We knew several reps who were already working there, so we knew they were a good company. And even though we joked about Saga –'Send A Granny Abroad' or 'Sex And Games for the Aged' were two popular gags – we had both heard that it was a caring and considerate place to work.

So we set off for Folkestone. Les went before me and he stayed in a bed and breakfast for about a month while I was still in Tenerife tying up loose ends, before he found a flat in Augusta Gardens, which became our home. It was one street back from the seafront, and I worked hard to make it look cosy, tiling the bathroom and the kitchen and generally turning it into a home. After I'd settled in, I also got a job at Saga, in the reservations department.

Les found that his job required him to be away a lot visiting foreign resorts. He only had to make fleeting visits, but he was often abroad nonetheless. Luckily he hadn't had to start dialysis yet, so he was able to travel, but it was a tiring job for him. While he was away, I busied myself making friends with my new colleagues to help me settle in and to keep me company. A guy named Peter Bentley ran my department, along with two supervisors called Richard Pickering and Julie Moore, and two deputies, Anne Spratling and Sarah Hicks, who were in charge of hotel bookings and overbookings, of which there were many in those days. I also got to know other members of staff, such as John Ayris from Dover, and Liz from Deal – who was the first Goth that I had ever known – both of whom became great friends.

Saga was a fantastic company for overtime as it was offered every night from five till seven. Most of us agreed it was a good way to top up your wages, so the office was always busy then. There was also a canteen and a social club, where I met Suzanne Dowle, Mark Seymour, Kay Thompson and Mandy James, all of whom also became friends. The Saga Social Club was the place to be on a Friday night and we all partied together: we had fancy-dress dos and discos and other social events organized for us by the committee. John Ayris would stay over with me at our flat: we would do overtime and then attend the many functions held at the Social Club afterwards.

It was a magical time for me: all these new friends and colleagues really helped me to face my future and also helped me to settle into the town. And of course the job itself was perfect. As I had worked in so many resorts abroad, I had first-hand knowledge of the towns and the hotels, which was hugely useful when I was selling the holidays. It meant I could talk to people over the phone about the places they were going and make sure they got the holiday that was right for them. It worked well for everyone.

Les, however, was not really enjoying his time back in the UK, nor his job at Saga, as he found the overseas department rather frustrating, so he decided to set up a little self-catering agency in Los Gigantes, Tenerife. Although he had been diagnosed with his worsening kidney problem, he was still outwardly in good health most of the time. So for around two years he commuted to and from Tenerife, sometimes staying there for months at a time. We would take it in turns to visit each other, with Les coming back to England if his business was quiet, or me popping out to Tenerife for a holiday if he was busy. Although we lived together as often as we could, we would often go two or three months without seeing each other, which was very hard.

While he was away, I was more or less adopted by Anne Spratling and her parents, Gill and Ernie, who lived in Cheriton in Folkestone. They were so kind to me and always used to ask me round for dinner and to play Trivial Pursuit. John Ayris's family were also ever so good to me and they often invited me to meals at their house in Dover. I actually played matchmaker between John and Anne, and after a year or so they went off travelling and, on their return, set up a company called East of India – which sells artisan-made gifts from around the world and is still a tremendous success today. I also used to have leisurely Sunday breakfasts with my friend Richard Pickering, who was courting Debbie from Personnel at the time (they are now married with two beautiful daughters).

Eventually, I became a member of Saga's Social Club committee myself and I would organize theatre and ballet trips up to London. One night, we went to see *The Nutcracker* and I had some spare tickets left over because some of the ladies were ill and couldn't come. When I went into the theatre, I couldn't believe it. The whole foyer was filled with gentlemen in tuxedos, looking very obviously like bodyguards. I knew somebody of some importance must be coming, so I took the spare tickets to the box office and the lady practically snapped my hand off in her haste to take the tickets back. I asked what was going on and was told that Princess Margaret, the Queen's sister, was actually coming to the theatre that night. So I raced back onto the coach and hissed at everyone to get off but to stay in the foyer so that we could watch the arrival of the VIPs. First the police out-riders arrived, then a Daimler with a flashing blue light on top turned up... and then out stepped Princess Margaret in a beautiful pink Christian Dior dress, with a lovely little fur coat and a sparkling tiara. Well, we ran up to our boxes while she went into a private room, and then when she came out we had to stand up for the national anthem. It was quite something to have a real princess in the theatre and the whole audience was buzzing with excitement.

Me (left), aged about a year, with my big brother Patrick.

Left: Me with Patrick again. I idolized him when I was small, and followed in his footsteps throughout my early childhood – even onto the football field!

The family grows: now I'm the big brother (centre), hugging my little brothers Martin (right) and Terence.

My mum and dad on their wedding day in 1955.

Me with my beloved Auntie Dolly.

All grown up: (from left to right) me, my sister Margaret, and my brothers Terence and Martin.

I was an altar boy and the Catholic Church became a huge part of my life – so much so that I nearly became a priest. This is me at my First Holy Communion at St Francis's.

Even at an early age, there was a showman inside me. Here I am demonstrating my Irish dancing skills, aged eight.

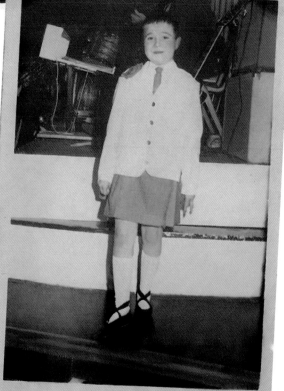

Once a tour guide, always a tour guide. The travel bug bit me in my teens. Here I am at work at Gerona airport in the late 1970s.

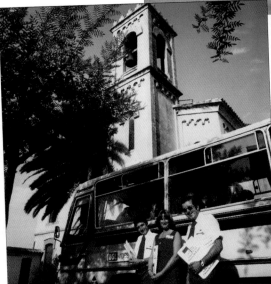

Left: Travel not only widened my horizons – it also brought me love. Enter Les (far right), with me and another OSL colleague in Spain.

The love of my life: me and Les in the Cape Verde islands in February 1994.

Coach Trip begins: day one, series one. The adventure continues to this day.

Left: I always do a lot of research about our destinations, so that I can inform the tourists with authority about the wonderful places we visit.

The vote is the worst part of the job. This shot was taken just before a vote on series two.

Coach Trip has not only taken me to some amazing destinations – I've participated in plenty of incredible activities too. Here I am as a gladiator in Rome (top left), as a Wild West cowboy (top right), demonstrating my riding skills (below left), and post-mud bath in Xanthi, Greece (below right).

Left: My new job has introduced me to lots of celebrities. This is me with David Ginola during series two.

Below: The first *Celebrity Coach Trip* in 2010. At least two more celebrity series are planned for the future.

Left: I was honoured to be given an exclusive tour of the *Coronation Street* set in March 2011.

Right: The stardust has sprinkled me too. Here I am in my dressing room for the Southport pantomime *Aladdin* in December 2010.

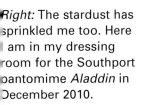

Sit back, relax, and enjoy the ride of your life.

While in Folkestone I also made friends with several men from the local gay community. There were plenty of discos and trips up to Chatham, the closest big town, and I would often go and dance the night away on my own. I used to love dancing to a song called 'Ride on Time' by Black Box, which was number one at the time. So although I missed Les while he was away, I had made lots of friends and never felt lonely. By this time, 1989, I had made a natural transition over to the cruise department at Saga Holidays, having done a round-the-world cruise myself, and I was really having a whale of a time with my career.

Unfortunately, Les was not happy. He never felt settled in Folkestone, so spent a great deal of time in Tenerife, and we started to grow apart, which worried me. I used to visit Tenerife for holidays and Les and I would talk endlessly and share our lives together again, but it was not enough. We were simply living too far away from each other. We needed to be building our future in the same place, and enjoying what time we had left together.

In January 1990, something happened that made me surer than ever that I didn't want to waste a single second apart from Les. On Monday 15 January 1990, I received a phone call at work from my brother Patrick, who said he was really sorry; he had to tell me that my dad, our dad, had passed away that morning of a massive heart attack. I was stunned at the news. I think I was still in shock when he said, 'Come home, Brendan, as soon as you can.' He told me that Mum had requested that I get the train and not drive from Folkestone to Yorkshire, and then the call ended. I put the phone down slowly and began to cry. I had only just been home for a lovely family Christmas, and now I was returning to Leeds to bury my father.

Saga Holidays were extremely kind to me and many colleagues, including Mandy James and Kay Thompson, comforted me in the office until a taxi arrived to take me to Augusta Gardens to pack my things for home. Saga organized a flight from Gatwick to Leeds-

Bradford airport for me that same evening and a dear neighbour, Brian, accompanied me to Gatwick and sat with me till I departed.

My sister Margaret and her boyfriend Patrick were waiting for me at Leeds-Bradford airport and we hugged each other and drove home in silence. The whole house was in mourning and as I embraced my mum she started to cry, which upset us all.

We had a few days to wait for the funeral, but this enabled my father's sisters – all six of them, Auntie Mary having passed away – to travel from Ireland to attend. It also gave us time to arrange everything with Father Corbally, who had been our parish priest for over twenty-five years now and who had of course known my father personally.

The funeral was a massive affair. My father was well known within the Irish community, and also well thought of. I remember when we took him into church the evening before his Requiem Mass: as the procession of cars turned the corner, we could see that the whole street and the car park at St Francis's were absolutely packed with people, all dressed in their suits. Many were family friends, relations and close neighbours, some were work colleagues of my dad's, and others were friends who remembered my dad from the Irish dances at St Francis's or the Green Rooms. It is hard to carry your own father into church and the sense of loss and grief was a heavy burden to bear, but carry him we did, with pride and respect for a lovely gentleman who was *my dad*.

The next day, Father Corbally gave my father an amazing eulogy – during which the sunlight cascaded through the windows of the church and illuminated the coffin. He spoke of my father who would help the church all he could, but whenever it came time to thank him for his help, Tom Sheerin would have disappeared and gone back to be with his wife Maureen and his children at home, whom he idolized.

My dad's sisters Frances, Theresa, Pauline, Bernadette, Kathleen and Dymphna, along with his brother John, helped us to bury him in Cottingley Cemetery, Leeds. Every time I visit my home town, I always go and visit my father: Thomas Joseph Sheerin RIP.

My father's death made me realize that you have to make every moment count in this life. Les and I decided that he would sell his business in Tenerife as soon as he could and come back to live in England, where we would embark on a fresh project together somewhere new. Les had learned that he would soon need dialysis, and it was the perfect time to put down roots elsewhere.

It seemed natural to look to the north of England for our new home, so that we could be close to our respective families. In a way, we were both northerners: Les was born in Birmingham but had lived in Leeds ever since he was a young boy, so really he was an honorary Yorkshireman; and of course I had been born in Leeds.

Les sold the business in Tenerife very quickly and in a very short space of time we decided to buy a fish-and-chip shop, with a sixty-seat restaurant attached, up in Scarborough.

We had been in Folkestone for four years. Now the next phase of our adventure together was to begin…

CHAPTER 13

Mushy Peas and Other Adventures

WE HAD CHOSEN to look for a fish-and-chip shop because we wanted to find a seasonal business, where we could work hard during the summer months and then have the winter off, as we had been used to in the travel industry. So without further ado, I went back to Leeds to enroll on a fish-fryer course at the Thomas Danby Catering College.

My course covered everything from buying fish to preparing it and – most importantly – which fish was which, as I did not have a clue. The course also covered which potatoes made good chips and which didn't, and how mushy peas, beans, curry sauce and gravy could improve your profits no end.

I was then farmed out to a lovely couple on an industrial estate near Pudsey for my apprenticeship. I would help the gentleman 'rumble' the potatoes (peel them in a machine), rinse them, then put them through the chipper into large barrels of water. There they were 'drywhited' (immersed in a chemical to prevent discolouration) and left for twenty minutes before the stoppers were removed and the chips drained. We also used to 'eye' the potatoes so there would never be any black bits in the chips.

By the time my training was completed, Les had found a fish-and-chip takeaway and restaurant for sale in Scarborough on Eastborough, which was the main route down to the beach. It had a four-bedroomed flat above the shop and it was perfect for us. We met the couple selling it and it was agreed that for an interim period I would work alongside Darren, the son of the owner, so that I could see the operational side of the business at first hand.

Making batter was my first job. Oh, the amount of buckets of batter we had to make before the shop opened... I had learned to fry in Pudsey, but Darren's technique was much better, so I adopted his. In just two weeks, I received an intensive course in how to run a takeaway from the fryer's position. Portion control was the secret, I was told. Apparently, if you got that right, everything else would fall into place.

We took over Clays Fisheries in July 1990 and immediately started working ourselves to the bone. But we seemed to get the hang of it and by the winter, when it had calmed down, it was manageable with just myself and one other member of staff.

Les did the accounts, the ordering and the staff wages. The restaurant could hold forty-eight people, so in the height of the summer we had to have waitresses and washers-up and cellar boys for the chips.

Our mushy peas were very popular and we sold panloads, but they were horrendous to make as they had a life of their own. After being soaked overnight, they were rinsed, then sugar and bicarbonate of soda were added, and then they were brought to the boil to simmer. It was this time that was the most dangerous, because if you forgot them or turned away for a second, they would boil over like Vesuvius and start flowing like lava all over the kitchen floor.

I loved the work and thrived on meeting customers and enjoying the banter with them. Most of the fish came from Deighton's, which was down on Scarborough harbour, and it could not have been any fresher. I also used to go to Hull for supplies, which was only 40 minutes from Scarborough and a great place to visit, especially for shopping. I used to be at the docks for 5 a.m. to buy from the fishermen on their return from the sea.

It was at Hull docks that I first met my friend Robert Chatterton, whose parents ran a fish-and-chip shop in Hull. Robert and I would meet every week on the seafront and a strong friendship developed which has lasted to this day. I also met my friend Gary there, who worked in fish as well; he would later come to wave me off on the *Coach Trip* bus when the programme was filmed in Hull.

Word soon got round about Clays Fisheries and our little fish-and-chip shop became a popular destination, doing a roaring trade in the summer. Many a night, just when we were closing, a coach would pull up and I would have to turn the pans back on as I would get an order for forty-eight haddock and chips for the lads on the coach (the driver would get his for free). The shop was so busy that we could only close in the depths of winter, in January and February, and then we would have to reopen in March in time for Easter when the Scarborough season would begin all over again.

Les and I also threw ourselves into a social life, as all work and no play was getting us down. We went to every performance at the YMCA Theatre, and we attended all the plays at the Stephen Joseph Theatre. We dined out at the Kam Sang Chinese or at Florio's, the Italian restaurant on Aberdeen Walk. We always left the mobiles at home and if the fish-and-chip shop burned down while we were out, well, so be it. We had learned from our time in Folkestone that it was important to maintain our own relationship first and foremost.

We made friends – a wonderful group of friends – with whom I remain close today. There was Janey and Stewart Walker, who lived nearby in the parish of Hutton Buscel (Stewart was my dentist, as a matter of fact); Barry Sykes and Michael from Princess Street; Angie Sellers; Reg Price; Dave and Sue Young, who had the Post Office on Newlands Parade; Brenda and her beautiful girls from Northfield Way; John and June Hoy; and Kev and Diane, who lived on the north side of town. These were the nucleus of our group of friends, many of whom started out as customers, and we dined at each other's houses countless times, spending bonfire nights together and enjoying the summer concerts at Castle Howard, where we picnicked on smoked salmon and salad as the *1812 Overture* rang out over the wonderful Yorkshire countryside.

But although we enjoyed running the chippy, it was not always easy. There was a public house just a few doors away and we did a roaring trade with its customers. The clientele was a bit rough to say the least, but we never judged them and were happy to have the business. One night, however, things got a bit nasty with a young man called Paul, who had been drinking at the pub. He and his friend had come in and bought some chips. While he was there, he commented to his friend that this particular chippy was a gay establishment, saying it so loudly that my other customers in the restaurant heard him. He started calling me names but I took it all in my stride, just thanking the pair of them for their custom and telling them not to come back as we could manage from now on without their trade. In effect, I barred them.

An hour later, they both returned and Paul made some more comments about my sexuality. I felt rather sorry for him as usually anyone who is that prejudiced is struggling to accept part of himself, though at the same time I was furious that he should dare to say such things in my own shop. Clearly, I could not tolerate that kind of behaviour on my premises, so I asked them quite firmly to leave. They started getting aggressive so I threatened to call the police if they did not get out of my shop immediately. Paul jeered at me, thinking I would cave in, but I stood my ground and picked up the phone and they went back into the pub.

The police van arrived within minutes and two handsome policemen came into the restaurant and I told them what had happened. They were very kind and understanding and said I had two choices: to follow it through and have them arrested or to forget the incident and hope it would blow over. But by then I was livid. Not only was this my place of work, but it was also our home over the shop – and I was not going to let anyone get away with that sort of prejudice. So I asked the policemen to follow me and, still in my apron and frying jacket, I walked into the pub.

Immediately, the room fell silent. It made me want to laugh – everyone looked so worried when they saw the two policemen. The look on Paul's face as I identified him was one of utter shock. He was arrested and taken away in front of the whole pub, and was later charged with breach of the peace. I thought I was going to have a lot of trouble from the patrons of the pub later that night, but after I had closed not a sound could be heard in all of Eastborough.

Paul was bound over to keep the peace for nine months the following February, while I was away on holiday in Australia.

While travelling in Oz, I learned the sad news that my beloved Auntie Dolly had passed away. We had remained close even after I'd grown up, and just before I had left for Australia I'd visited her in the hospital in Leeds, where she was being treated for cancer. I took Les with me for the first time: this man whom she had heard so much about, but whom she had never met for one reason or another. I could tell she liked him. She was looking meaningfully at me and I knew she wanted to voice her approval, but of course she couldn't because Les was sitting right there.

She told me not to cancel my trip to Australia, and so I was in Alice Springs when I heard the news. Later that day, we visited Ayers Rock, and I climbed right to the top and cried my eyes out. Auntie Dolly was so proud of me – she would always tell everyone where I was in the world and what I was doing – a real champion of my life. She was a wonderful, warm, generous woman and I still miss her to this day.

It was some time after we got back from Australia that Les's health started to fail. He desperately needed a transplant. At the time, he was having his dialysis at home upstairs, which helped to extend his life significantly, but he was very tired. He had been on renal dialysis for about three or four years at this point and was being treated by Dr Turney of Leeds General Infirmary. He also had visits from Mavis Wilde, who was his renal nurse in Scarborough. He was on the transplant list for a new kidney, but as time went on and no call came, the chance of Les receiving one of those precious organs seemed slimmer than ever.

We never gave up hope for a transplant for Les, though; it was something you could never give up on. The chance of a new life, the chance to enjoy simple pleasures: to drink a full glass of cold milk; to walk around Peasholm Park hand in hand again, or along the seafront at Scarborough; or even, most of all, the chance for us to travel once more to faraway places and destinations.

One evening, we closed the fish-and-chip shop early and used the restaurant part to entertain our friends the Mills, who were visiting from the US, with a delicious roast beef dinner. Pat, Les's sister, was over from Leeds that night too, along with his nephew Andrew. I had just served dessert when the phone rang. I answered it. Dr Turney wished me a good evening and then he asked for Les. I immediately summoned him to the phone with some urgency: this was *the* call. My eyes started to fill with tears. This was what we had been waiting for, for over two years; this was a chance of a better life for Les; this was the gift of a kidney.

All I knew was that a lady had died on the motorway and she had expressly wished that all of her organs be used to help others in need. Her kidneys were rushing as we spoke to St James's Hospital in Leeds and there was a possibility that Les could be a recipient of one of those kidneys if all the bloods and tissues matched. He had to get to Leeds as soon as possible. After he put the phone down, there was a minute or two of hugging, of excitement, of thanking God, of hoping against hope, of wishing all would be well. Les quickly went upstairs to fetch his pre-packed bag, while Pat got the car ready for their departure. I had to run the business so could not accompany him, but as we embraced tightly I wished him well and asked him to call me first thing in the morning with the news of whether or not he would receive the kidney.

I remember when I got into bed that night I looked at his dialysis machine on the other side of the room and I started talking to it. 'And you won't be staying here much longer with your time restrictions and your timetable with your pinging and ponging sounds… No, *out* you will be going and as soon as it can be arranged!' Feeling much relief after saying all that, I drifted off to sleep.

When I woke up the next morning and recalled what I had said, I thought, 'I am not going to repeat that to anyone as they will be locking me away,' but I didn't take a word of it back. The machine had been so much a part of our life, it was like an unwelcome family member.

After Les arrived at the hospital, his bloods and tissues were tested during the night to see if he was the nearest match. Another gentleman went through the same procedure, and so when Les called me at 5.30 a.m. after a restless night to say he was the nearest match I was so, so pleased for him, but I also felt sorry for the other man.

Les's kidney transplant operation, which took place at 9.00 a.m. that same day, was a great success. Les was very poorly afterwards, but he slowly made a good recovery. Mavis, his renal nurse, visited practically daily when he returned to Scarborough, and with the anti-rejection drugs his health improved in leaps and bounds. Les had been given the gift of life and he was so thankful. Through Mavis, he wrote anonymously to the donor's family to express his gratitude and to tell them how much it meant to him. Mavis ensured the letter reached them. Les felt it was very important to thank them in this way.

Mavis and Les also founded the Scarborough Kidney Transplant Support Group to help those still waiting for that special phone call, and their families too. Les loved attending their meetings and helping those who were either waiting for transplants or who had already had them. I always tried to attend these dinners and meetings too, when my work allowed, and the group was such a lovely collection of people, who all genuinely cared for each other.

Les's passion had always been travel, but buses in particular (he had in fact started his career as a bus conductor, then a driver, before he became a courier). After he received his transplant, I encouraged him to buy a restored Routemaster bus as a hobby, thinking it would give him focus and also get him out of the house to enjoy life more. He took my advice, and bought an old blue bus from Lancashire, complete with the traditional rear open platform. He would attend bus rallies all over the country, sometimes with friends, but also with my younger brothers Martin and Terence. He loved driving that bus and it was his pride and joy. He even took the Scarborough Kidney Transplant Support Group out one December to see the Christmas lights at Thornton-le-Dale.

With Les's health vastly improved, for the time being at least, we embarked on a vacation that marked the pinnacle of our travelling dreams: flying on Concorde. As we checked in early, we were given seats 1A and 1B, which the stewardess informed us were usually reserved for royalty or film stars! The Concorde departure lounge was first class in every way, decorated with beautifully coloured stained glass and serving only the best drinks and canapés.

Concorde had its own call sign, Speedbird 1, and it was given priority over all the other airlines, so we taxied straight to the front of the queue upon departure. The twin-spool Rolls-Royce engines roared for take-off with phenomenal power. I listened to those engines with particular interest, as my dad had worked for Monkbridge Forge, whose biggest customer was Rolls-Royce. It was a great possibility that my father had manufactured the very engine blades that were about to send us rocketing skywards.

We flew over Devon as British Airways' finest stewardesses served us lobster salad, fillet mignon and crème brûlée, all washed down with the very best of French burgundys. The captain kept us informed of our speed and when we reached Mach 2.04 a resounding cheer went through the cabin – we were travelling at twice the speed of sound. Normally, it would have taken a jumbo jet 8–11 hours to fly to the Bahamas, our destination, but for us it was to be just 3 hours. We also gained height rapidly and soon reached our cruising altitude of 60,000 feet, which is double that of a normal aeroplane. We could see the curvature of the Earth, we were so high. What a view.

With our dream of flying supersonic realized, we decided to sell the shop and move to a little village called Flixton, which became our home in the country in 1995.

During my final week in the shop, the new owner of Clays Fisheries was working alongside me, learning the art of frying fish, when Paul, the young man from the pub all those years ago, walked in. I had not seen him since that evening when he had been arrested.

He ordered chicken and chips and at first I wondered whether I should turn him away, but it had been years since the incident and he looked very sheepish indeed. Then he asked if he could talk to me privately at the other end of the shop, and I agreed. It seemed that he had heard we were selling up. He said he wanted to apologize for that awful night and wish me luck for the future, and could I forgive him for the things he had said? Well, I thought the ground was going to open up and swallow me whole, such was the effect of his words. I accepted his apology and told him to forget what had happened and move on, and hopefully he would find closure to the entire affair. I treated him to his supper as a gesture of goodwill and he left the shop looking a lot happier than when he had come in.

I have never had such an incident before or since, but I was prepared to stand up for what I thought was right for myself and for Les. I was always taught that if you face your fears you can be stronger than them. It was a lesson I was to learn again the hard way over the next few years.

CHAPTER 14

Stop All the Clocks

OUR NEW HOME, Hawthorne Cottage, was a beautiful detached three-bedroomed house that looked like something a child would draw. With a stable block and garage at the back, it looked out onto the Yorkshire Wolds, rolling hills that lead from Scarborough down to Driffield. It became a very special place for both of us and we took great delight in entertaining our many friends there. We had a lovely big conservatory which looked out onto the garden and was perfect for entertaining, and our families would often come over for our legendary Sunday lunches. We would also host Christmas and one year we had fourteen of us crammed into our little cottage. We had many happy times in that gorgeous house.

Les retired due to his ill health, so to give him a wonderful setting in which to enjoy his slower pace of life, I set about creating an old-fashioned cottage garden with a vegetable patch and plenty of roses – the latter reminding me of my Irish grandmother in Carrandine, who had maintained a beautiful rose garden at the back of her house, with blooms all the colours of the rainbow. To complete the bucolic fantasy, I built a hen run and a duck pond, then went off to a nearby market town called Malton and came back with thirty hens and a cockerel in the back of my Ford Fiesta. The poor cockerel was exhausted with thirty girlfriends to service, and Les wasn't too happy to have quite so many hens running about, so I managed to palm ten of them off on a friend called Ron who lived down the lane, and life began to settle down into something resembling normality.

The people in Flixton were lovely. We made friends with many of our neighbours, including Sandra, Jenny and Georgina, and they welcomed us to the area with such warmth that we knew instinctively it was the right place for us.

Les looked after the house and the bills, while I maintained the garden and the menageries of fowl we possessed. We worked as a team in other ways, too: I would grow vegetables such as aubergines so that Les could cook us a tasty Greek moussaka. He was a great cook and I only had to mention that we had not had Mexican food for a while and within three days we were eating it.

Eating was quite an important pastime for both of us. I think we adopted this from our lifestyle in Spain. Each night we always ate in the conservatory together. We would tell each other about the day we had had, what we had done and who we had met and talked to, and the general titbits in our daily lives. After dinner, we either read or watched a programme on TV. We would always hold hands while watching TV – just holding hands, as simple as that, and it was automatic too, the way we reached for each other. We had also mastered that old-married-couple skill where I might think of something and then he would say it five minutes later, or vice versa: such was our bond with each other.

Les and I loved the peace and tranquillity of living in the country. Around this time I was helping our friends from Folkestone, John Ayris and Anne Spratling, with their East of India business, selling their goods at trade shows around the country. But I needed a proper job. Les had saved up enough money to retire but I was still young, only thirty-six, and I needed to work.

Then one day I saw an advert for a job at the Tourist Information Centre in Scarborough, working for the Borough Council. It appealed to me as the job involved working closely with members of the public – something I've done in all my roles – and of course it was an opportunity to get back into tourism as well. I was interviewed by a lady called Janet Deacon, who was to be my boss, and Diane Peacock, her assistant manager. Janet was impressed with my experience working in tourism abroad, and even more impressed with my fluent Spanish and French.

So I was soon behind the desk at the Tourist Information Centre, serving customers, booking hotels, advising foreign tourists, and helping the many Spanish students who were working in Scarborough over the summer to improve their English. A lady called Denise Whitelaw was the supervisor and she and I hit it off straight away, perhaps partly because we both came from Leeds. But we also shared the same mischievous sense of humour – I would see a lady walking towards us with a funny lampshade hat and I would whisper in Denise's ear, 'You can serve this lady with the wonderful hat,' and poor Denise would look up from her paperwork and see this woman in front of her and collapse in giggles.

After three years at the Tourist Information Centre, I was asked to join the Spa complex, which is also run by Scarborough Borough Council. The Spa complex is a beautiful Victorian theatre and conference complex on the Scarborough seafront. It is a huge venue – the theatre seats 600, the concert hall seats nearly 2,000, and there is a lovely outdoor sun lounge that serves as an orchestral venue during the summer. But although there was a lot to do, I loved it. My boss was a kind, gentle man called Keith Norton and we worked as a team with a girl called Karen Mills. My work would include running talent contests such as Scarborough's 'Search for a Star', which I managed with a lovely choreographer and dancer called Nikki Sweeney, and all in all we were a happy band.

Due to the nature of the job, I would often have to work weekends, so Les would use those occasions as an opportunity to see his sister Pat and his nephew Andrew, who lived in Leeds, which is about an hour's drive from Flixton. He would also go away cruising to the Caribbean and Mediterranean with Pat, while I worked. Pat and Les were very close so I never resented this; in any case, Les and I were both firm believers in taking every opportunity that came our way, especially because Les's health was in an increasingly steep decline. The years of dialysis and kidney failure had forced his other organs to work harder and his heart had become very weak. In addition, the anti-rejection drugs he was on following the transplant meant that his immune system was very low indeed, and he was susceptible to every passing cold and virus. He had to have several further operations while we lived at Hawthorne Cottage, including a triple heart bypass. Throughout it all, Les was patient and brave. He bore the pain of his illnesses with great courage and fortitude and rarely complained. If he did suffer a low period, it was up to me to support him and to try to cheer him up and pull him out of the doldrums, and the holidays with Pat were a real highlight of those years.

So if there was a chance to go on holiday, he would always take it, with my blessing, as we never knew what the future would hold. A funny thing about Les was that he had no dress sense; it was always my job to advise what to wear with what if we were going out. He trusted my judgment implicitly, and so if he was going on a cruise with Pat, he would lay all his clothes out on the bed for me before he packed them, and I would advise him what to wear and for which occasion.

In December 2001, Les had to have a heart valve replaced at Leeds General Infirmary. It was a tricky operation, but Les and I always faced his health problems honestly and we always said that whatever happened, we'd have no regrets.

As we waited for the date of the surgery, Les took his will out of the filing cabinet and put it on the desk, just in case. As unmarried gay men, we had watertight wills to make sure our property was protected if one of us should die first. Of course, Les was right to be practical, but I could hardly bring myself to look at it every time I went past the desk as we counted down the days till the date of the operation.

Eventually, the day came and I sat on the hospital bed holding Les's hand while the anaesthetist talked us through the risks. At five o'clock that evening, they took him down to the operating theatre, and I left the hospital and started wandering aimlessly round the streets, into what is now the Millennium Square, in front of the Civic Centre, round George Street and ending up in St Anne's Cathedral, where years and years earlier Les and I had dipped our rings into holy water and given them to each other, along with a promise. It was nearly Christmas, and as I entered the cathedral I noticed that the decorations were up and the crib was being prepared for Christmas Eve Mass. I found a statue of Our Lady and I lit six candles and said my prayers, just as I had done as a little child. I asked God not to take Les away from me and to give me the strength and courage to face whatever was meant to be.

I stayed with my mother that night in Leeds, and the next day I went to see Les. My prayers had been answered: Les had survived the operation. On 19 December, I picked him up and took him back home to Hawthorne Cottage. It was the best Christmas present I had ever had. His sister Pat, nephew Andrew and brother-in-law Mick all came for the holiday, and we also had a dear friend staying with us, Nadir Akbari, who had flown in from Ibiza to spend the festive season with us.

Les was obviously still weak from the operation but we all took turns to care for him, and I made sure he had everything he needed. He and I were coming up to twenty-five years of being together, so our plan was to have a holiday in the New Year when he had recovered, perhaps visiting Nadir in Ibiza first, then going off to Australia or Florida to celebrate our anniversary. We were full of plans for the future.

On Christmas Eve, I went to Midnight Mass at St Joseph's in Green Lane in Scarborough, as I had done for several years, and then the following morning I was up early to prepare the Christmas dinner for all of us. Les's family played a part in setting the table while Nadir kept Les company. I enjoy cooking for large groups of people so it was a happy, busy morning. When the food was ready, we all sat down to eat in the conservatory. I carved some turkey for Les – he only wanted a small piece – and as I passed it to him I looked at his face and suddenly this awful premonition came over me that Les was going to die. It hit me like a ton of bricks. I looked into his eyes and he said, 'Thank you so much for all of this.' And of course he meant cooking the Christmas dinner for everyone, but I also knew it meant something more. I felt sick with worry and had to put on an act for the whole of that Christmas luncheon, which seemed to go on for ever.

Eventually – after the pudding, the cheese, the coffee and the washing-up – I managed to escape upstairs to the bedroom where I called a dear friend of mine, Barry Sykes, who lived in Scarborough. Barely able to hold back the tears, I confided my fears that Les was going to die.

'Don't be so silly,' he said. 'Les has always come out of these operations and he's always survived them. He's a fighter.'

But he couldn't reassure me and, sensing my distress, he offered to meet up with me that evening to talk it over. So that Christmas night, I slipped out of the house and Barry and I walked along the seafront together, while I sobbed at the thought of losing Les. I just couldn't shake off this awful premonition and however much Barry tried to reassure me, I knew something was wrong.

Pat, Mick and Andrew left after Boxing Day, but Nadir stayed on to keep Les company while I went to work at the Spa – there was a pantomime on over the whole Christmas period, so I couldn't take the time off. On 28 December, Les had an appointment scheduled at

9 a.m. with Dr Hughes, just to make sure everything was all right after his operation. The evening before, Les, Nadir and I all had dinner together, we watched a bit of TV and discussed our twenty-fifth anniversary plans again. Then, still quite early, I made a move to go to bed, reminding Les that he needed to be up early the next day to get to his appointment. I said goodnight to Nadir and I leaned over Les in his chair and kissed him, telling him that I loved him.

On the morning of 28 December, at about seven o'clock, I walked into Les's room with a cup of tea, as I always did. He was still fast asleep, looking very peaceful. I put the tea down on his bedside cabinet, saying loudly, 'Les, wake up, you're going to be late for your doctor's appointment, have you forgotten?' I went over to the window to open the curtains and as the light flooded into the room, the realization suddenly dawned on me. He was dead. I went over to touch Les's face and he was cold. Involuntarily, I let out a scream, from the very depths of my soul.

Nadir was nearby in the guest bedroom, and he immediately came running out in his pyjamas, saying, 'What's wrong?' Wild with grief, I shouted, 'Get an ambulance, just get an ambulance, just get me the phone, get me the phone...' I took the pillows from under Les's head and quickly but gently laid him down flat – I was conscious that I didn't want to hurt him, as he had just had his operation. My cheeks were so hot with tears that my glasses started to steam up, so I had to throw them off. I knew first aid so I started blowing into his mouth as hard as I could and giving him heart massage. Meanwhile Nadir had phoned 999, and the lady in the control room asked him if someone was trying to breathe for him. Nadir held the phone to my ear and through tears I sobbed, 'I am, but he's gone, he's already gone...' She told me, 'Don't worry, there's an ambulance two minutes away, so please keep breathing for him.' I replied that I'd seen dead bodies before and I was sure he'd gone, but she said, 'Don't give up hope. They'll have a defibrillator in the ambulance.' So I carried on with my manual resuscitation until the ambulance arrived.

Nadir showed the men upstairs and they asked me to leave the room while they tried to revive Les. Sadly, though, a few minutes later they came down and confirmed that he was gone. He was only fifty-nine.

As it was a sudden death at home, the ambulance men told me they would have to send for the police, so not long afterwards two very kind and sympathetic policemen duly arrived, as did some friends of mine, John and June Hoy, who had dropped everything to come over when I phoned. The policemen came down and we sat in the conservatory while they took some details from me. I was in such a state that when they asked me his date of birth, I couldn't even remember the year – it was a complete blank. The stouter policeman, named Shaun, then suggested that I come back upstairs to take Les's gold wedding ring from his finger, in case it went missing in transit to the hospital or the undertaker. I had told him about the significance of the ring so he knew how important it was to me. So I went up with this policeman to the room where Les was laid and he stopped at the doorway, saying to me, 'No, Brendan, I don't think I can come in to the room with you. This is something that you have got to do for yourself. I think you should take that ring off his finger and put it on your own, on the same finger that you have the ring that he gave to you, and then your love will continue, even though he is not on this earth.' I thought that this was the most wonderful thing that a policeman could ever say to a human being, and I am very grateful to that man, as since that day I have never had Les's ring off my finger. In fact, his ring is always on the inside, and mine is on the outside, so it is as if I am protecting him somehow.

Removing that ring was the hardest thing I have ever had to do. Downstairs, I could hear the police leaving, making practical arrangements with Nadir, John and June. Meanwhile I sat quietly with Les upstairs, holding him in my arms, as even though his body was dead, I knew his spirit would be somewhere in and around Hawthorne Cottage. My mother had given me some holy water from Knock, which is a shrine in Ireland dedicated to Our Lady, so I blessed his body with the holy water, thanking God for the wonderful twenty-five years of happiness that we had enjoyed together, and saying that I understood it was now time for him to go. I must have stayed with him in my arms for about forty-five minutes, until Nadir knocked on the door and told me the undertakers had arrived. So I had to leave my dear friend, come downstairs and sit in the lounge, and they shut the door so that I wouldn't see Les actually leave our beautiful home, and I wouldn't see him leave me.

The undertakers were very good. They took him away, to the hospital first and then to the mortuary. Nadir also had to leave the following morning, so the next few days were a blur of formalities, registering the death and making the funeral arrangements and so on. But one thing I remember was that people were extremely kind to me. The lady at the registry office was one example. She told me, 'I can't register that you were his partner on the death certificate, but what I can do is note in a special section that you found him dead at your home, and that will help when you have to talk to banks, funeral directors, probate lawyers or anyone that needs a death certificate. All I can say is that I am so sorry.' In two or three years' time, the law was to change in England and Les and I could have registered as a civil partnership. But it didn't matter to me – I knew we had been together for a good deal longer than many legal marriages.

Of course, I then had to start ringing people and telling them what had happened, which was very painful. I was so glad of answering machines, because every time I tried to talk to anybody I just filled up and couldn't speak. My heart was slowly breaking; it was as simple as that. But I knew I had to be strong, as I still had to make all the funeral arrangements.

The first thing I needed to do was to find a vicar, because I didn't want to use one of these rent-an-hour vicars who didn't know Les or me. Les wasn't a Catholic, but it seemed right that I should ask Father Bill, who was the priest at St Joseph's in Scarborough. Les always used to pick me up from Mass on Sunday mornings, so Father Bill had got to know him when he would see him waiting for me at the back of the church. When Les was in hospital, Father Bill sent him a card and put Les on the 'sick list' so that he would be prayed for by the parish. He was a lovely, kind man. Despite the Catholic Church's views on homosexuality, when I asked him if he would officiate at Les's funeral he immediately said yes. So when it came to the crunch, the God of my understanding, and my church, were both there for me when I needed them, and I will never forget that.

I asked Father about a certain piece of music that I wished to use in the service, because I wanted Les's funeral to be full of music that we both loved together. One of the hymns that the boys sing in Montserrat, just the other side of Barcelona, is called 'The Lorelei'. It's a Catalan hymn and Les loved it, and we often used to sing along to it in the car. So I asked Father if I could play my old tape of 'The Lorelei', and he immediately said, 'Brendan, I have a pristine copy of it on CD, so we'll use that. I will help you in any way that I can with the music.' I knew then that I had made the right choice of priest.

Slowly, the plans for the funeral fell into place. As well as 'The Lorelei', I wanted Edith Piaf singing 'Je Ne Regrette Rien', Roy Orbison's 'Anything You Want', and Elvis Presley's 'The Wonder of You', which really encapsulated how Les and I felt about each other. Les's renal nurse, Mavis Wilde, agreed to say a prayer, and another friend of ours, Angie Sellers, was to say another prayer on behalf of our friends and families. My brother Terence was to read the famous W. H. Auden poem, 'Funeral Blues' ('Stop all the clocks...'). And the secretary and the president of the Samaritans also agreed to say a prayer to represent Les's charitable work. After Les's kidney transplant, he had become a Samaritan in his spare time, as his way of giving something back to the community after he'd been given a second chance of life. He'd manned the telephones and even though his health was not that good, he always came away the better for it, hoping that he had made a difference.

I also needed to sort out the flowers for the funeral, so I went to see a florist called Melanie, a lovely girl who lived in our village, whose family had owned Hawthorne Cottage before us. She showed me the catalogue of flowers to choose from but I couldn't focus; it felt like an impossible decision. So she gave me a card to write instead, but that was even worse – my eyes filled with tears and my glasses steamed up so I couldn't see. Realizing my predicament, Melanie gently said, 'Brendan, I think that you should go back home, make yourself a cup of tea, and think about what you want to put on Les's card in your own home. Please look after yourself. All my family send their condolences and we are so sorry.'

So I went back home and had a cup of tea, which was all I was living on really, just gallons and gallons of tea. I must have lost two or three stone in that period. Later that evening, I decided to put the answer machine on as I didn't want to answer the phone that night; I'd had enough. But then the doorbell went, and there was Melanie, the lovely girl from the florists, holding a beautiful white jasmine plant. 'This is for you, Brendan, not for Les,' she said, handing it to me. 'I know you are in a lot of pain, and I know it's awful what's happened, but this is for you, because we all love you as well. It's from all of my family. I've been so worried about you all afternoon since you left the shop.' That was just one of the acts of love people showed me after Les's death.

I had to go to church on the Sunday and I didn't really want to go, so Angie Sellers came to meet me and took me to Mass with her mother, Margaret. Margaret was a dear old lady, an ex-diplomat's wife. I promised myself that I wouldn't cry in church, and I somehow managed to hold myself together as we were saying hello to people and sitting down, but when the organ and the music started and the priest came out, I started to cry and I just couldn't stop. I cried through Communion, and I could feel people putting their hands on my shoulders and giving me a squeeze. I was in such a daze I didn't even know who they were, but I knew they were acts of love and acts of solidarity. That message of acceptance and love within the congregation of my church was one that will stay with me for ever.

I was lucky to be surrounded by my dearest friends, all of whom came to the house and looked after me in the run-up to the funeral. I also had lots of visits from the old ladies of the village, who probably didn't quite understand the idea of two men living together, but who nonetheless offered me cards and asked if they could attend the funeral, which of course they could. My brothers came over from Leeds too so I felt surrounded by love and good wishes.

I'd arranged for the funeral to take place at Octon Crematorium. Octon is a hamlet high up on the hills in the middle of the Wolds, surrounded by fields and countryside, with a beautiful chapel and a lovely area for a tea afterwards. I had chosen it because I wanted Les to rest on the Wolds where the beautiful fields were, where the wild poppies grew.

We all met at our house first and waited for the coffin to arrive. Seeing it was a jolt: it hit me all over again that this was the last time that Les would be outside our home. On my way up to the crematorium, I wept like a baby, because I knew that he would never come back to Hawthorne Cottage, and that this was his last journey on this Earth.

Six of us carried the coffin into the chapel: me, his nephew Andrew, his brother-in-law Mick, my brother Terence, his old friend Trevor, and my brother Patrick. Inside, the chapel was packed. Father Bill did us proud and the service was perfect: everybody said their prayers and listened to the music that I had chosen and the whole thing was hugely moving and beautiful. Somehow, it felt like it was the last thing that I could do for Les, to make sure his funeral went off well, and so when I look back now I am proud that I managed to do that for him successfully. It was my final act of love for him.

But the aftermath was horrendous. Living alone in Hawthorne Cottage, having only myself to think about: these were new concepts that I'd never had to deal with in my whole life. I'd always had somebody by my side or to talk to when I got home; someone to eat my dinner or watch TV with; someone to read with; someone to drive out in the car with; someone to go shopping with; someone to do the washing with. It was awful. Les and I used to hold hands all the time and I would find myself sitting on my own and unconsciously putting my hand out to be taken in Les's, which was sometimes just too much to bear. I lost count of the times I broke down and cried at a piece of music I heard that we had both loved, or a film I saw that we'd both watched. The grief could take your breath away. You think you can't cry any more, but you can and you can go on crying. That's what it was like. The pain in my heart was horrendous, it was as if somebody had stabbed me with a carving knife and was turning it in my heart. There were times when I would go to make a cup of tea and I would be stood by the kettle and go dizzy and have to hold myself until it subsided. Waves of despair and grief would just flood over me like a tsunami. But I had to keep functioning somehow, even though it felt almost impossible.

I remember my friend Reg Price told me, 'The pain and the suffering that you're going through now is the price you have to pay for twenty-five years of love, devotion, companionship and friend-ship, of being together and sharing the pain and the joys of life.' I knew it was a price worth paying, but that didn't make it any easier. Even now, after over ten years, I still miss him, and still feel pain and heartache when I think of him. To be honest, I don't think that you ever get over losing someone you love, but you do learn to deal with that pain better on a daily basis and you develop strategies on how to cope.

Les's plaque is up at Octon and his ashes were scattered there too, near to a beautiful tree that I sometimes go and stand by, so I can talk to him. As far as I know, he is still with me. On two occasions, I have had dreams in which he came to me in my sleep to say that he loved me and that everything would be OK, and assured me my grief would end. I suppose psychoanalysts or psychiatrists might say that it's poppycock and that it was simply the grief-stricken imaginings of a bereaved person. But I know in my heart of hearts that Les's spirit came to me on those two occasions, and I believe he stayed with me for a while before he went to heaven. In Hawthorne Cottage, I would hear noises sometimes and I would think, 'Yes, Les, I know it's you. I'm fine, I'm getting through it.' It was a comfort to me.

I was also lucky enough to have lots of support from friends and people who love me: Janey and Stewart Walker, June and John Hoy, Reg Price, Sue and David Young, Angie Sellers and dear Barry Sykes. All these people who loved me helped me to cope with my life. Because there were times when I really didn't want to go on, I was in such a state. I felt very angry with God for a long time, but gradually my faith was restored to me and I began to attend Mass at St Joseph's Church again.

It also helped when I went back to work at the Spa complex. Every morning I would approach the B&Q roundabout on the Seamer Road on my way to work and have an internal struggle with myself: would I turn left and start my day's work at the Spa – or would I turn the car around and go back to bed to hide under the covers? Every day it was a fresh challenge, but I always managed to turn left, even on those days when I just wanted to go back home and cry. I kept myself busy, booking events, looking after the conferences, overseeing the dances and drama festivals, taking care of all the actors and actresses who used to come through to play in the theatre, sorting out the summer shows we used to have, looking after Simon Kenworthy and the Scarborough Spa Orchestra when they held their concerts in the grand hall or in the sun lounge during the summer months.

I threw myself back into my work really, and I think it helped me to get over my loss. My colleagues were very kind. I needed reasons to keep going: a job to do, a house to run, a garden to look after and hens waiting for me to feed them. All this gave me a focus over the next two years, even though it felt like I was on autopilot for a lot of the time.

Then one day, in May 2004, I got a call from my old boss, Janet Deacon, with whom I used to work at the Tourist Information Centre. She said, 'I've had an email from a television company, and they are looking for ex-tour reps and ex-coach couriers like yourself. I think you should apply for it, because you'd be good at television.'

It was a call that would change my life.

CHAPTER 15

My Coach Trip Discovery

THE TELEVISION COMPANY that had contacted Janet was called 12 Yard Productions, based in Livonia Street, London. Janet urged me to apply for the job so, without really thinking too much about it, I emailed a young lady called Beth Davies, who worked there. I was sent a long, detailed questionnaire to fill in, which I returned with a photo of myself.

The very next day I received a phone call from an excited Beth, who went through the questionnaire at length with me. She was a lovely girl and we hit it off immediately – I made her laugh out loud at my antics as a courier. As the day went on, I received a flurry of calls from other members of the production staff: Matt Walton, Andrew Brereton, Peter Hall... I didn't really know who everyone was, but I am always happy to chat and they must have liked me because they asked if I could come down to London the next day to have an interview.

Well, I couldn't take time off work at such short notice, but the following Monday I travelled down to London to stay with my old friend Andrew Wilton, with whom I had worked on the Costa Brava during the early eighties. I told him about my interview over supper that evening, introducing the subject with a mischievous 'You'll never guess what I've done...' Andrew just gave me a look as if to say, 'Knowing you, nothing would surprise me.' He was very enthusiastic when I divulged more, telling me that this could really take off and that he could definitely see me in the role as I had described it. Only time would tell.

The following morning, I took the Tube to Oxford Circus and walked through the busy media and shopping district of Soho for my 11 a.m. interview. I was quite nervous but still fairly detached from it all – I had nothing to lose if they didn't choose me. At the appointed time, I pushed the buzzer and was shown to a top-floor office by a smiling Beth, who gave me a cup of tea while she rallied all the people who were to meet me. The tea helped to calm my nerves as I was shown into another office that contained a camera on a tripod at one end of the room. I was asked to sit down opposite the camera, as the interview was to be filmed, and I was given a release form to sign.

The office began to fill up with very young people, all casually but smartly dressed in T-shirts, sports jackets and jeans. Matt Walton and Andrew Brereton introduced themselves: Matt was the Producer/ Director and Andrew the Executive Producer. Apparently it was Andrew's idea to develop a programme along these lines after his parents had been on a coach trip. They were joined by various other people – Sarah Edwards and Gail Harman, who were part of 12 Yard's development team; the production manager, Peter Hall; and another man called Mike Beale, who looked very important (I later found out he was the part-owner of the company, along with David Young).

The interview went ahead and I tried just to be my normal self as we chatted about my experiences as a travel rep. I was a bit on edge at first, but everyone was so welcoming that they soon put me at ease. After that, I could only be myself. I didn't try too hard or beg for the job, I wasn't subservient or too eager to please – I was simply me.

Matt and Andrew explained that a pilot episode would have to be produced over a long weekend in the summer to see if the idea would work in practice, and that they would then use that to try to entice Channel 4 into commissioning the whole series. This concerned me: I had a holiday booked in Malaga around that time to see my old friend Robert Chatterton, who had moved from Hull to run a restaurant in Spain, but they quickly reassured me that if I was successful, they would simply fly me over from Malaga and back to do the pilot during my holidays. Beth then told me they had a few other people to see later that week, but that they would let me know by Friday if my application had been successful. Some of the team then took me out to an American-style burger bar for lunch and later I got a taxi back to Andrew Wilton's.

I wasn't sure how I had done. The gist I got from them at that early stage was that they were interested, and so that's what I took away with me – but I didn't get my hopes up. They still had more candidates to interview and you never knew who else might be in the running or what they could offer. I had done my best and was more than content with that.

That evening, I bought two tickets for *Les Misérables*. I had arranged to meet up with a former colleague from the Spa and local Scarborough lad, Ben James-Ellis, who had just started at the Italia Conti Academy of Theatre Arts. Afterwards, we had supper in a Chinese restaurant so I knew that, despite him being a poor student, he was at least getting one good meal that day. Ben went on to be a contestant in the BBC's *Any Dream Will Do*, as well as to star as Link Larkin in the West End production of *Hairspray* and as Norman in *Dreamboats and Petticoats*. We remain good friends today in spite of our busy schedules.

The following morning, after visiting more friends to make the most of my trip down south, I got the train back to Scarborough via York. As the 125 service left King's Cross, I reflected on my hectic stay in the capital. I always enjoy visiting London – it's a beautiful and exhilarating city – but as the train departed that morning, I was very much looking forward to arriving home in Flixton and to seeing the tranquil green countryside that surrounds the village. I wanted to have some peace and quiet before my return to work at the Spa complex the next day.

My mobile phone started to ring as the train pulled into platform five at Doncaster station, half an hour from York. Now, I am sure many things have happened at Doncaster railway station over the years: many people have met or departed from each other, some with sorrow and some full of joy to be home. But, for me, Doncaster station was the unlikely setting of the phone call that was to ensure that life as I knew it would never be the same again.

Beth Davies was on the line to inform me that they had found the person they were looking for. Swallowing my disappointment, I congratulated her and thanked her for the opportunity to be interviewed, telling her that it was lovely meeting her and asking that she should keep me in mind if anything else came up.

There was a pause, then she laughed. 'Oh no, darling, it's *you*! It's just got to be you!' she exclaimed. She said they had been so delighted with my performance the day before that they had cancelled all the other interviews as they were so sure I was the man for the job.

Well, what a feeling: flabbergasted, excited and scared, all at once. What a shock, what an opportunity. I could hardly believe my ears. I sat there holding the phone limply, staring out at these people on the platform through the window in a complete daze. A voice whispered over and over in my head: 'Oh my goodness me, what have I got myself into now?'

As I somehow managed to finish the call, the train started to move off from platform five and I was left with a churning feeling in my stomach as the fear crept in and took hold. What if the pilot went on to be commissioned and became a series? How would it change my life? I knew I would need to have a cup of tea at York station and to call my old friend Reg Price, who would advise me and calm me down. Clearly, this was the beginning of what was going to be an awfully big adventure.

* * *

The pilot of the programme was called *Summer Holiday*, which then changed to *Coach Trip* at the last minute. As promised, I was flown from Malaga to London to act as the courier/guide for the show.

The team assembled at the Rydges Kensington Plaza Hotel on Gloucester Road in London one Friday morning in June 2004. There I met my coach driver, Sam, for the first time, who was very nice. As for me, well, I was extremely nervous. We filmed various establishing shots: the coach arriving at the hotel, the doors opening and closing, me getting on and off and so on. I was asked to describe my feelings about the small tour I was about to take, so I said that I was very excited, as the experience was completely new to me and something I'd never done before, in terms of making a TV show. I also mentioned the encroaching fear that was slowly beginning to fill me as the reality of what we were about to do set in.

I then met the eleven tourists I was to be in charge of, and they were told to sit on the coach after the introductions.

They were a mixed bunch, as would be the pattern on the subsequent shows too. John was eighty years old and a retired engineer from Rossendale, Lancashire. I warmed to him when I heard his northern accent; it was something familiar to quell my nerves. Unusually, he was travelling solo; for the later series, it would be only pairs of tourists who travelled on the coach.

I next met Jaki, a feminist hippie with a guitar. I cannot help it but whenever I see a guitar in someone's hand I always think of that bit in *The Sound of Music* when Captain von Trapp starts to play his guitar and sing 'Edelweiss', and Baroness Schraeder says if she had known all this music was in the house she would have brought her harmonica! Jaki was a teacher from Brighton, who was travelling with her friend Peggy, a musician from California. After them came Jacqueline and Alan, who were a pleasant couple; he was a fraud investigator and she was also a teacher. With two teachers on board, I would clearly have to behave myself…

Gavin and Michael were the two young guys on the tour. Michael was in insurance and seemed like a nice chap, though I worried about his musical abilities having heard him mimic a guitar piece out loud. Gavin described himself as an entrepreneur. I had my reservations about him, as he was a bit too smart for my liking and a bit of a boy about town.

By contrast, Matt and Kerrie from Farnborough were a couple of young people who worked in their local Asda. They were quite innocent really; Kerrie had never even stayed in a hotel before.

The final two tourists were two cheeky ladies from the West Country, Siobhan and Nicky. Nicky was quite shy, but Siobhan had wandering hands, especially where my bottom was concerned. I soon realized I would have to watch her as she liked to be touchy-feely and free and easy. Well, not with me, darling!

My old friend Beth Davies was outside the hotel with the other members of staff from the office and everyone was very excited as the coach departed for Oxford and they waved us off. I felt sick with nerves and wondered if I had done the right thing or not. I had to take a swig from a small bottle of water before picking up the microphone and introducing myself as the guide and Sam as the driver. I then went through the health and safety briefing with them as we sped out onto the M25, all the while hoping that the butterflies churning mercilessly in my stomach would leave me.

After introducing everyone to each other, I announced that our first excursion was to Oxford for a spot of punting on the river, which the tourists were all quite happy about. The punting was a tremendous success and lots of fun, despite some people in the group having no idea how to do it. It was rather difficult to get Peggy in and out of the punts – she was a big lady with bad arthritis in her legs – but together we managed to help her.

We then found a lovely pub where I organized lunch and drinks for everyone, after asking the landlady if she could cope with such a large group, of course. We always had to remember that not only did we have the coach party, but we also had the camera and sound crew, producers, directors and runners too. It all added up.

At Coombe Abbey that evening, we attended a medieval banquet in full fancy dress. It reminded me so much of the barbecues we used to organize at Saldet. Poor Peggy missed the evening excursion, unfortunately, as she was exhausted from the punting in Oxford that day.

Matt was elected as Baron for the evening and slowly but surely started to get drunk on the wine and mead, which were freely served. It was to be the best night he had ever had. He even drank the finger-bowl water as he thought it might be alcoholic.

In fact, all in all it was a rather drunken evening. Gavin dressed as a jester and then mysteriously disappeared from the table: I later found him in the stables laid out in the straw. Alan seemed to be egging on Siobhan to drink more so that she would get touchy-feely with him. And as for Matt, he couldn't actually speak by the end of the night, much to Kerrie's disgust. Several hours later, I discovered that Gavin had emerged from the stables only to gatecrash a wedding celebration in full jester's costume, though fortunately he fled to his room before the police arrived.

At 1 a.m. I ferried my charges back to the hotel with a great deal of patience, as my role required. I just couldn't help feeling that I was back on the Costa Brava doing the same job I had done years ago and that nothing had changed.

The next day, Peggy sadly left the group and returned to London, due to ill health, and we carried on to Birdland Park in Bourton-on-the-Water, to see the birds of prey. The coach trip was enlivened by Jaki expressing herself on the guitar with a mixture of feminist and risqué songs and poems. A couple of camera guys actually filmed inside the coach as she sang, using lightweight portable cameras, so that it would give the team an idea of how the programme would look when revolving cameras were fitted inside the coach. As an alternative to Jaki's offerings, I led a sing-song of all the old favourites – 'I Belong to Glasgow', 'Cockles and Mussels', 'Pack Up Your Troubles' and so on – which I believe was preferred by many of the travellers.

Kerrie was not happy when we arrived at Birdland. She hated the birds and was clearly very frightened of them, despite Matt's assurances that they were safely chained up. She started to cry and got rather upset, so in the end everyone backed off and let her be.

Unsurprisingly, Gavin chose an eagle to hold – as ever, he was very confident and full of himself. Michael was interested too, but in less of an alpha male way. The others also enjoyed their visit, but Siobhan got terribly emotional about how majestic the birds were; it seemed to be quite overwhelming for her to be near them. As she cried, I wondered where she had been all her life, as surely down in the West Country the birdlife must be amazing? In any case, I managed to distract her by setting a quiz for the group, which took them around the park gathering ornithological information. We returned to the coach for the quiz itself. Michael rather surprised everyone with his competitiveness – when his team lost, there was no stopping the shouting and bad feeling.

At Cheltenham, we had lunch and then went on to a cider-producing farm at Much Marcle, where we had our first vote. This was a crucial part of the show, when the fellow travellers would 'vote off' one of their number, who would then immediately leave the coach for the rest of the trip. It was to be an open vote – in other words, everyone would have their say and would have to give a reason as to why they had chosen that couple or individual.

The voting part of the pilot was all new to me. I enjoyed the travelling and acting as the courier, as it was like working in Spain again, but the vote intrigued me. Would people be honest? Would they change their minds? Would there be disagreements?

The first-ever vote went ahead and Jacqueline and Alan were duly voted off, on the grounds that she was nice but he was boring. I thought they were a lovely, interesting couple, but clearly the group felt differently. After we gave them a chance to say their goodbyes, we left them by the side of the road as the coach pulled away. Amazingly enough, those who were still left on the coach showed no signs of remorse or guilt. I should add that of course the production company later ensure, off-camera, that all the contestants get home safely – but it does make great TV when the big coach pulls away, leaving the exiting duo standing forlornly by the side of the road with their luggage and not a lot else.

The next day, we toured Longleat Safari Park, driving around and admiring the wonderful wild animals. My next task for the group was for them to find their way out of the park's maze, with the winners being granted immunity from that afternoon's vote. The group were split into teams. First off were Michael and Gavin, next were Matt, Kerrie and John, and finally the last to go in were Jaki, Siobhan and Nicky. They all got incredibly lost and what should have taken them only forty minutes to work out ended up taking more than an hour and a half. John's skills helped his team to triumph, winning immunity not only for himself but also for Matt and Kerrie. Jaki, Siobhan and Nicky all worked together as a team, with Jaki eventually finding the exit. As for Michael and Gavin, they were completely lost and in the end only got out after being helped by a group of children.

The vote that followed was very interesting and really opened my eyes as to how the voting system would operate. At first, it looked like Michael and Gavin were going to be voted off, but as it was an open vote on this pilot show, they were allowed to plead for their seats on the coach. At the very last minute, Siobhan and Nicky changed their minds and decided to turn on Jaki, who with three votes had to leave the coach. What shocked and surprised me was that in spite of Jaki helping Siobhan and Nicky to get out of the maze and working as a team with them all morning, it seemed quite easy for them to switch their allegiance to Michael and Gavin when the chips were down.

Of course, fans of the show will notice that this sort of 'open vote' is not how the vote works in the actual series. As with most new television shows, the pilot was a big learning curve, and one of the things the producers realized was that allowing people to change their minds during the vote could mean that the votes could go on for hours and hours before a decision was made, and we'd never finish in time for dinner each night! So the decision was made for future series to make each couple 'lock in' their vote in private before they revealed it to the group. In addition, as the series would go on for thirty days, and not just three as in the pilot, it was also decided that it would be fairer to give people a second chance after they were first voted for, so that they could try to build bridges with other couples. This is how the famous yellow- and red-card system came about; the first yellow card is a warning, but if you don't improve your popularity, you get a second, which becomes a red card and you're off the bus!

Jaki left with a few choice words for the girls, who naturally began to feel guilty and remorseful. Nicky openly began to cry, in fact, in what seemed a clear case of delayed guilt. In any case, despite poor Jaki's betrayal, it obviously resulted in some great footage for the ever-present cameras.

We left Jaki by the roadside and returned to London that afternoon. We had all enjoyed our adventure. Matt Walton and Andrew Brereton from 12 Yard told me they were really pleased with the way things had progressed and that they had gathered lots of information to be used in the event of a series being made. Matt told me the many hours of footage would be edited during July and reduced down to a twenty-minute presentation, which would be shown to Channel 4. Then, the commissioner for daytime television there would decide if the pilot could be turned into a full series.

I was thanked by the team and said goodbye to them all before we went our separate ways. All the camera- and sound men, as well as Matt and Andrew, had been so kind to me, despite me being completely wet behind the ears when it came to TV work. The only advice given at the start was to be myself and not to look at the cameras, and hopefully I had achieved this with not too many complaints.

The next day, very early in the morning, a car was booked for me by 12 Yard to take me to Gatwick airport and to my flight back to Malaga to resume my holiday. 'This is the way to travel,' I mused to myself as we sped through the half-empty streets of London at six in the morning. I thought of the many hours I had spent travelling the world, laden with baggage, only able to afford the train or coach to the airport or being reliant on good friends to take me there. By contrast, I felt very cosy in that chauffeur-driven car while I relaxed in the back, wondering if the pilot episode would be made into a series and, if so, whether they would use me or some top presenter or famous actor instead. If it is meant to be, it will be, I told myself.

Little did I know that the die was cast and I would soon be thrown headfirst into the crazy world of television. I would not have to wait too long for that to happen.

CHAPTER 16

A New Adventure

MATT WALTON AND Andrew Brereton submitted the presentation to the commissioner of daytime television, Adam MacDonald, in July 2004 and by August a decision had been reached. The series would be made. Filming would commence on 27 September and finish on 1 November 2004. The programme would then be edited and was planned for transmission on Channel 4 in spring 2005, in a teatime slot of 5.30 p.m.

I received the call from Matt, confirming that I would be the tour manager for the new series, while I was at work at the Spa complex. After I put the phone down, I left my office and told Karen, our secretary, that I was taking the lift to the roof garden, where there were beautiful views over the bay of Scarborough. My shift had not quite finished but I just needed a quiet place at that time for the news to sink in. My heart was leaping out of my chest with excitement as I stood looking across the bay to the castle. I felt a deep sense of gratitude that I had been given this chance to have such an adventure. What an amazing opportunity for someone who hadn't even been in front of a camera before. It seemed they did not want a top presenter or a first-rate actor – they wanted a humble ex-tour guide, an amateur who had never been filmed before, a lad from Leeds, an assistant manager of the Scarborough Spa complex... I thought of Les and wondered what he would have made of my news.

I wondered if he already knew, along with my Aunt Pat who had died only a few months before he had, and if they were both looking down from heaven and smiling.

The news was greeted with amazement by my family and friends. It was a surprise for some, but for many it seemed a natural progression of my life. I had always been a bit of a comedian, had always laughed and seen the funny side of life, had always had the knack of making funny observations without being cruel. 'You will be great in front of the camera' and 'you were made for television' were the comments I received from my dearest friends.

My mother was very pleased when she heard about the series, but in a way I think she was also afraid for me. Mothers always worry about their children and I don't think that ever stops, even as we grow into adulthood. My mum now lives in the very west of Ireland in a beautiful part of the world, away from the big cities and the bright lights. I had to explain that this was only a first series and yes, of course I would be careful, and yes, I would keep her posted with developments and call her every week from wherever I was in the world to reassure her I was OK. My eldest brother Patrick thought it was some sort of joke and a good one at that. He was really surprised by the news and amazed at the prospect of his younger brother being on telly. Margaret, my sister, and my brothers Martin and Terence were thrilled that I had been given this opportunity to shine – and shine I was most certainly going to do. The news soon hit Beeston, Leeds, and I started to get congratulatory phone calls from all my cousins and aunts and uncles.

I applied to Keith Norton, my manager at the Spa complex, for a leave of absence and this was granted with the blessing of Janet Deacon. The news had spread through the Spa like wildfire and everyone was pleased for me, including the many patrons of the Spa Orchestra, whom I used to look after daily as front-of-house manager. Everyone was excited, but no one's enthusiasm could match my own. This was my time and no one could take it away from me. I felt humbled, not cocky, but I also felt extremely fearful. How would I get on?

The route of series one, for example, would take thirty days. My goodness – most tours are ten to fifteen days at the most. I would have to conserve my energy to last that long.

The plan was to head for Amsterdam and end up in Paris, via such beautiful cities as Baden-Baden, Munich, Salzburg, Vienna, Venice, Rome, Florence, Pisa/Parma, Andorra and Barcelona. The tour was in fact an extended version of the traditional 'Grand Tour' of Europe offered by standard coach tour companies. I had never really visited northern Europe before as my work had always been in the southern countries like Spain, and Les and I had tended to go on long-haul trips outside of Europe for our holidays, so I was tremendously excited about visiting new places like Germany and Austria. I couldn't wait to get to Salzburg – with my love of *The Sound of Music*, it was one of my absolute dream destinations.

I began by digging out all my old notes from my years as a guide – and some of Les's too – and sifting through information in our personal library with regards to the places we would visit on the trip. I have always done my own research without anyone else's help. I feel it is part of any courier's job to know where you are going and what you are seeing, and on *Coach Trip* it is important to me to be familiar with the many destinations featured on the programme. In terms of the regular activities we undertake, I am lucky to have an amazing team of researchers at my disposal, and they work very hard to help set up all the interesting and comical events. Yet it's still very important to me to do my own factual research about each place we visit, and I continue to do my own location research to this day.

I began to prepare my research notes at home in the evenings and at weekends, and Beth, Andrew and Matt called me to discuss several things, for example the routes, distances, maps of cities and countries, passenger lists – including passport details to enable us to pass smoothly through border controls – coffee stops and what we could and could not do in certain places.

As this was the first series, it was going to be an adventure for all of us. *Coach Trip* was a unique entity – no one had ever done this sort of programme before. We were making a series on the move, not in the comfort of a studio, through all these countries, with no one really having any previous experience at all in these matters. So it was no wonder that everyone was enormously excited and energized to be starting the trip.

The basic concept of the show is this: *Coach Trip* is a competition involving up to seven couples who travel throughout Europe with their tour guide (that's me), experiencing the sights, sounds and tastes that Europe has to offer – all for free. The camera crew on board the coach and travelling with us capture every moment on film: the wonder, the catfights, the laughter and the tears.

Every day, each couple have to cast a vote against their least favourite couple and give a reason why; and the couple with the most votes receive a yellow card. This couple can carry on travelling, but if they receive a further yellow card, this then becomes a red card and they have to leave the coach. The losing couple are then sent home. They're replaced by a new couple and the tour continues. If the group are becoming too comfortable and sharing the yellow cards amongst themselves, I always have the right to introduce an 'instant red card' day, which shakes the group up somewhat and induces an element of fear in the contestants.

On the final day of the trip, the vote is changed and the group are asked to vote for their favourite couple travelling on the coach, who are then declared the winners, receiving a voucher for a future coach trip (though not one that will be filmed!).

We make the series over a period of thirty days, and all that footage is then edited down into thirty programmes of thirty minutes' duration. These are shown on Channel 4 five days a week for six weeks, usually at 5.30 in the afternoon – perfect timing for a nice cup of tea and a sit-down!

I left Hawthorne Cottage two days before filming was due to start and travelled down by train via York. Sandra, my dearest neighbour in Flixton, was going to look after my hens and ducks while I was away. Her reward would be all the eggs produced and a bottle of perfume from me.

Arriving in London, I checked in at the Charlotte Street Hotel, which was very luxurious indeed. Beth had told me to treat myself, so in the morning I had my piping-hot English breakfast wheeled in on a trolley covered in a beautiful white linen cloth, with shining silver domes over the plates. I was amazed at the amount of fresh strawberries that made up my fruit order in their crystal glass bowl. I got straight on the phone to Barry Sykes, and Dave and Sue Young, and regaled everyone in Scarborough about how posh it all was: how my double bed was the biggest I had ever seen; how I had a TV in the bathroom as well as in the lounge; and finally how I had a whole box of chocolates on my pillow in the evening and not just the usual lonely single sliver of mint chocolate. I wanted them to share in the excitement of what was happening; believe me, it's not every day a young lad from Leeds finds himself waking up with such luxury, and it was definitely something to call home about.

At Rydges Kensington Plaza Hotel in Gloucester Road, London, I met John Graham, who was to be the production manager on series one and two. John's job was to get things done to enable our smooth passage through all these countries and all these hotels, to pay for the endless coffees, teas, lunches and dinners we had when we stopped, and to stick to our filming schedule like glue. He also solved many problems that occurred on these outings and became a dear friend and mentor to me. John had a wealth of experience from working on *This is Your Life* with Eamonn Andrews, a programme I used to watch in my pyjamas as a young boy. He had many stories about his television life, including meeting such famous people as Zsa Zsa Gabor, Bob Hope and Charlton Heston. We often had dinners together on the road and always met for breakfast, when he would tell me, using quite descriptive language, who was being problematic that day, to my great amusement.

I was to wear a microphone, which was quite a novelty. It was positioned on the front of my shirt with a lead going down and then round to my back pocket. Mr Roberto Garcia was to be my main sound man: he looked after my microphones and fitted me every morning. He also monitored me from the back of the coach and I would have a sound test most mornings with him. This was new to me too and it made me feel like a newsreader from the *News at Ten*. Jon Padley was to be the first cameraman I worked with. He has filmed practically every interview or activity that I have done since series one; he really has focused his camera on me in all sorts of situations! These two gentlemen have been with me on every series since I first started out on *Coach Trip*. They are remarkably kind and understanding and they are the founding members of the *Coach Trip* family of professionals who really and truly make the programme the success it is.

The coach was rigged out with cameras that revolve around in the front passenger section. This was a new development from the pilot and meant that the associate producers did not need to crouch down and use lightweight portable cameras any longer. Each table had microphones for sound and each tourist had to put on their own personal mic as soon as we got on the coach each day. At the back of the coach were monitors, screens and sound desks, operated by the crew under the direction of the producer and director. In the middle of the coach were a fridge and a kit storage area, from where steps led down to the loo and the emergency exit. The middle section was also where a small production office was situated. For series one and two, Matt or Andrew used to conduct interviews with both myself and the tourists in the middle section while the coach was moving; it was like a mini-studio curtained off from the rest of the coach, and they could get the footage they needed while we were on the move.

Before I met the tourists, I was to meet Chris Groombridge, who was to be our driver for the first series. He worked for Motts Travel, who provided the logo-free coach for us. Chris is experienced in touring with clients too, but on this trip he was focused solely on driving the coach, as I would do all the guiding. As it turned out, we would work together only on this first series, as afterwards Paul Donald joined the show and he has been our driver ever since the start of series two.

Finally, the day dawned when the coach was due to set off. All the preparations had been made, the passports checked, the travel documents put in order, the camera and sound equipment loaded on board. I welcomed the seven couples who would start off on the coach on this inaugural series, and together we headed for Amsterdam, where the programme would officially begin. The 12 Yard staff gathered to wave us off, and I had a special goodbye with Beth Davies, who told me she was moving on from 12 Yard as she'd got a fantastic new job at the BBC. I was thrilled for her, although I was also a little upset that we wouldn't be working together any more. People say to me that Beth 'discovered' me, and I suppose she did. I will certainly always remember her fondly. I wished her the best of luck in her new role, and then the coach doors closed with a mechanical hiss and we were off.

It was my first time visiting Amsterdam, and it was extraordinary. As I wandered the streets of this beautiful city, I couldn't help but recall its status as a gay mecca in the 1970s. It was such a progressive place, and it had had such a positive reputation in my youth, invoked by all as *the* place to go, that it was amazing finally to be there myself, after all these years. I was impressed by the canals and the flower markets, by the art galleries, and by Dam Square.

Once filming began in earnest, we soon fell into a routine. I treated every day as an adventure. I was nervous for the first few days of the trip, but after everyone had settled down I was just myself and acted accordingly.

I was always up an hour earlier than everyone else. I would review the itinerary for the day and reread my research notes to make sure the information I needed was in my head, and then I would have my breakfast with Johnny Graham. I would check everyone was down for breakfast and if not I would go and find them with a cameraman and 'knock' them up. The condition of the clients' rooms never ceased to amaze me: even if they were staying there for just one night, there would often be clothes, knickers, perfume and hairdryers all over the place, and you could always tell if they had had a party the night before as the empty wine bottles would be on the floor and a half-drunk glass of red vino would be resting, forgotten, on the bedside table.

It was my job to make sure we left on time, so I had to round up not only the tourists but also some of the crew to get them on the coach and start the ball rolling as we headed to our first activity. I would announce where we were going and give my description of the city or town or area we were visiting, just like any normal tour guide, including making any health and safety announcements that might be required about our forthcoming activities. There would always be two activities each day, with lunch in between. We might play a game on the coach, depending on the amount of time spent travelling, but otherwise the day would be left to unfold naturally. Things would be said, misunderstandings would occur and people would generally form alliances or decide they disliked each other, due to their differing personalities. This would all be captured on camera, of course. Finally, there would be a vote at the end of the day when I would have to deliver a yellow or red card to one unlucky couple to reflect the decision of the group, whether I liked it or not.

There have been many instances when I did not want to deliver the verdict, but as I have always maintained: 'I am Switzerland and therefore neutral.' I do not have any influence whatsoever with the vote, which is exactly as it should be. There have been many who have been stabbed in the back, many who have been misunderstood, and many who have left because their behaviour was unacceptable – but for whatever reason they have gone, it comes down to the fact that their fellow travellers wanted to keep the seat on that coach for themselves, to enable the experience of a lifetime to continue. I have learned that the contestants will do and say anything to stay on the coach, such is the competitive nature of some of the tourists.

As ever, travelling through Europe was fascinating, and I loved the route we took in series one. We visited many of my favourite places – Munich, for example, which is a lovely city. I was very impressed with the Marienplatz, with its glockenspiel, the cathedral and its green onion-shaped copper domes, the Residenz Palace and the Opera House. We had dinner in the Ratskeller just around the corner from the Marienplatz, where we ate dumplings that would sink the *Bismarck*!

Salzburg is of course famous for Mozart and *The Sound of Music*. I had been longing to visit ever since I first saw the film all those years ago at the Majestic cinema in Leeds – and it didn't disappoint. How delightful to see Mozart's birthplace and then to re-enact your favourite film on the steps of the Mirabell Palace Gardens! I had great pleasure choreographing the tourists to dance around the fountain and sing, 'Doe, a deer...'

Venice is a city that I would recommend to any couple as it is so, so romantic. We usually approach the city from the port area, where the many cruise ships are moored. The boat takes us along the Canale di Fusina to the mouth of the Grand Canal, and we moor along from the Bridge of Sighs. This means we get an amazing view of St Mark's Square, the Custom House and Santa Maria della Salute. If you're planning a visit to Venice, you cannot let your trip go by without experiencing a gondola ride or having a cocktail at Harry's Bar. Exquisite!

Rome is really two cities in one, with the Vatican the cream on top of the cake. The Colosseum, the Forum, the Trevi Fountain... All show the beauty of ancient Rome. And of course for a Catholic boy like myself, it is always moving to see the Vatican and the Sistine Chapel: the most precious jewels in the Catholic crown. During this first series we also took in my old stomping ground, Barcelona, where of course I had been guiding coaches at the tender age of eighteen. The city holds many dear memories for me so I felt enormously proud as we headed down the Ramblas with a camera crew filming my every step.

As for the contestants on this first series, well... The range and mix of the different ages and occupations was typical of the cross-section of people we would have on the show. As ever, there were many larger-than-life characters and many who made a big impression on both me and the viewers.

Pete and Barbara, for example, had never been out of the UK before and were interested in everything we did. However, Pete pushed another contestant, Pasquale, during the vote and consequently left the show. Pasquale and Bob were our first gay couple. They disliked a fellow traveller, John, the eighty-year-old Lancastrian who had taken part in the pilot, who had paired up with the hippie guitarist, Jaki, for the series. Unfortunately, his comments about not wanting to travel on the coach 'with two poofs' were overheard, despite him making them 'in the privacy of the toilet', or so he had thought. Unfortunately, these comments, along with some strong opinions about his personal hygiene, led to his downfall.

Bob and Pasquale also took against aspiring actress Sally and her sister Emma. They said that Sally's singing was horrendous and should only be heard in a loo and not in a theatre. They also rather unkindly called her a 'poisonous dwarf', thus destroying Sally's confidence.

Another memorable couple were Phil and Marion from Bolton. Phil was hopeless at eating foreign food, although funnily enough he was impressed with the German boiled ham and Germans in general. Unfortunately, he hated Italy, the Italians and Italian food, which rather offended one of the other contestants, Max, and led to Phil being voted off. Max and his friend Tom were both nice guys but they, in turn, had to go for partying into the wee hours and disturbing all the guests at the hotel.

In the end, the first series was won by Maggie and Paul, a mother-and-son team. Maggie was retired and Paul was a hairdresser. They were very sweet and kind, and certainly very popular – they were clear favourites on the coach and I was pleased for them that they won the prize. The finale was held in Paris on a fine autumnal evening, in the fresh green space of the Champ de Mars, with the illuminated Eiffel Tower providing a stunning backdrop to the grand conclusion of the show.

We completed series one in the French capital in early November 2004. I remember how beautiful the city looked in the autumn of that year. I felt quite exhilarated that we had finished the first programme, and proud that I had been able to do the job and act naturally in front of the cameras. On the train back through the Channel Tunnel, memories flooded back of my time living and working in Folkestone and working for Saga Holidays. I had watched this marvellous feat of engineering being created from its inception in 1988 and now was travelling through it at high speed from France to the UK with not a seasickness pill in sight. As I sat on the train back to Yorkshire from King's Cross, my mind was full of thoughts of the following spring. I knew that over the next few months all the filming would be edited by Matt and Andrew and made into a programme that would be aired in March 2005. I couldn't wait to see the reaction of my work colleagues at the Spa and, more importantly, that of my family and friends.

When I got back to Hawthorne Cottage, I took a week off before returning to work. After all the travelling I'd done, I didn't want to venture far, only to Scarborough, Whitby and Hunmanby to see my dear friends who welcomed me home. It was comforting to see my hens and ducks again and get back to some kind of normality.

Eventually, I returned to the Spa and took up the reins of preparing for our Christmas entertainment programme – the carol concerts and the pantomime – with everyone wanting to hear my news. How had it been? What was it like? Did I feel nervous? And, more importantly, when was it on TV?

* * *

In February 2005, just before the first series of *Coach Trip* was aired, 12 Yard invited me down to London for a few days. I was to appear on Channel 4's *Richard and Judy* programme to promote the new series, appearing alongside a young boy band called McFly. Well, goodness me. In my innocent way, I hadn't really considered the promotional work that might be needed for the show. I had enjoyed making the programme and afterwards, along with everyone else, I had just been waiting for it to be broadcast, keen to see how it had been put together. All along, I had just been myself – I hadn't even thought about how I might be coming across or whether I should have a public 'persona'. But now, I was to appear on one of the top TV shows in the country and be interviewed by such famous presenters that they were practically national treasures!

There was a PR team working to promote *Coach Trip* and they were all over me like a rash. They made me feel very important, and that in turn made me realize that I still had a job to do. It was a bit of a rude awakening – not to mention rather weird – but slowly it dawned on me that I would become something of the 'face' of the programme, as the contestants came and went but I always remained on the coach.

Luckily, I wouldn't be on my own for this first foray into the world of PR. Some of the tourists were going to be involved too. It was fun to meet up with the others from the filming, including Phil and Marion. We all travelled to the studios in a beautiful black Mercedes with Andrew Brereton. There I had my make-up done and was told to wait in the green room. This is a 'holding area' before you go onto the studio floor.

Before the interview, we met McFly, who were very nice guys and extremely young. They were surrounded by several older men in suits whom I presumed were their management team – they were watching their every move and being very attentive towards them. I tried to call Nikki Sweeney, my dancer colleague from the Spa, so she could talk to the boys – she was a big fan of theirs – but her phone was switched off and therefore she lost the opportunity of a lifetime.

The researcher went through our interview, giving us an outline of the kind of questions that would be asked, and we then went out onto the set and were introduced to Richard and Judy themselves. I was very nervous, both about meeting them and about the interview itself. Richard and Judy were at the top of their game – everyone watched their show – and so it was quite pressured. They were the first celebrities I'd ever met; it was a hell of a day. The interview itself seemed to go well, though I can hardly remember it as it all seemed to pass in a blur. The first question was directed at me and, now aware of my new responsibilities, I tried to take the lead in the interview, where it was appropriate, so as to give the show the best chance of success.

Afterwards, we went back to the green room, which had been transformed into a buffet and drinks area. I then got to talk to Richard and Judy off-camera, so to speak, and they were very nice and complimentary about the programme, saying it was a good format – whatever that meant – and should go really far. It was refreshing to see that they were just as lovely off-air as they are on it. We chatted to McFly again, and then our cars arrived to take us back to our respective hotels. We were handed goodie bags as we left, which was a nice surprise – in mine, there was a charming card thanking me for appearing on the show, alongside a bottle of champagne, a beautiful box of chocolates and some gentlemen's cologne. How the other half live! I then met up with some friends on Old Compton Street, but had an early night, as tomorrow was also going to be a big day.

The next morning, I put on my best suit as I was going to meet Adam MacDonald, the daytime commissioner of Channel 4, who had invited us to have lunch at The Ivy. This restaurant is of course famous for being the place where a lot of stars go to dine in comfort and peace without being photographed or disturbed. I had never been to such a fancy restaurant before, but Adam could see the writing on the wall, like a lot of others, and he had an instinct that *Coach Trip* was going to be a success. I still didn't really believe that the series would be anything more than a one-off, so I just treated it as an amazing lunch date.

Beforehand, I went to meet everyone at 12 Yard, in Livonia Street. Beth had moved on to the BBC by now and I missed seeing her, but all the other now-familiar faces were there: John Graham was beavering away at his desk, Mike Beale greeted me kindly, and Andrew Brereton and David Young spoke to me about how the programme was coming together nicely and how pleased everyone was with it. We got a car – yes, another private black Mercedes – to the Ivy and I sat in the back and felt like the Duke of Windsor as the sights of London passed me by. I was starting to get a bit too used to private cars.

Adam was a very gracious host. He commented on my future rising stardom, which made me blush, and we had a pleasant lunch while Mike, Andrew and Adam spoke about the broadcasting business and programming and all sorts of things that were way above my head. Although Adam was a powerful man in the TV industry, he was kind and polite to me throughout the meal, which I really appreciated. I was amazed at seeing people like Dickie Attenborough and Ross Kemp across the room, along with a host of other theatrical and TV stars. It was like a dream that a lad from Leeds could be sat here with all this carry-on. In fact, it was well beyond my wildest dreams.

I was dropped off after lunch to do some shopping in Oxford Street and later that night, at a performance of *Joseph and the Amazing Technicolor Dreamcoat*, which I attended with Andrew Wilton, I unexpectedly found myself filling up with tears of happiness and joy. I had not felt this happy in a long time: it was as if a page had been turned in the diary of my life – a fresh page, white and clean and ready to be filled with all the adventures to come. We stood up at the finale of *Joseph* and danced along with the cast to 'Any Dream Will Do'. My dreams were being fulfilled at that very moment and have continued to be so ever since.

The following month, the series was aired on television and I had a stream of well-wishers phoning me up to congratulate me and tell me how much they were enjoying the show. But after the transmission, life pretty much went back to normal at the Spa complex and I threw myself into my work. I felt that I was back in the 'real world' again and that my adventure into the realms of television had been just that – a one-off adventure. I had no expectation that anything more would come of it.

But then I got a call from Johnny Graham to say that Channel 4 were interested in another series. 'Oh my goodness,' I thought, 'here we go again...'

CHAPTER 17

Here We Go Again!

THE SECOND SERIES of *Coach Trip* was to start in Madrid, travelling through several southern European countries and ending up in Milan. Andrew Brereton was the executive producer again, but Matt was away travelling (though not on the *Coach Trip* bus) and couldn't take part; otherwise the team was largely the same as for the first series, except for one key difference. Paul Donald, a new driver who has remained with the show ever since, came on board for series two, and we hit it off straight away.

Paul is a steady, careful, professional driver. He is also my friend up front in the coach. He makes me tea whenever I get a break and we always discuss our routes and how to get there. If his satellite navigation system goes up the creek, I am the one who will try to guide him to our next destination. Paul is a very patient man too, sometimes having to wait around all day while we are off having fun filming, which is no mean feat. He brings his sun lounger so that when we have disappeared for the day he can read a book or paper and lie in the sun and top up his tan. We cockle along together and we have fun discussing all the places we shall visit on our days off. He has driven us all over Europe and into Africa and out again, and I get on with him tremendously well.

Sometimes Paul is replaced by Jamie or Malcolm, who fly in to cover for him when his hours have reached their limit and he needs a day or two off. There may be many pretenders to Paul's throne but Paul is the king: it takes a special kind of guy to drive us all around Europe year after year with our safety paramount in his mind at each turn of the wheel.

As it happened, I was once again on holiday in Torremolinos, visiting my friend Robert, when filming started, so I flew over to Madrid from Malaga airport to begin filming. And so the roller-coaster tour began all over again...

The highlights of the trip for me had to be when we went to visit Segovia and Salamanca, two of my favourite 'Real Spain' cities with fantastically beautiful palaces, aqueducts, cathedrals and plazas. I also loved Lisbon in Portugal, and Seville in Spain, with its magnificent cathedral housing the tomb of Christopher Columbus. Other memorable excursions included visiting Jerez in Spain, the home of sherry; the Alhambra Palace in Granada, one of the oldest Moorish palaces in Spain which dominates the city; Gibraltar and the HMS *York*; and Verona, Italy, the birthplace of Romeo and Juliet, with its magnificent arena.

On the morning of day twelve, we discovered that the coach batteries had failed due to a crew member leaving them on all night in Marbella, which was quite a problem as we were due to depart for the port of Algeciras in Spain immediately so that we could have a day in Morocco. I had taxis on standby, but luckily Paul managed to get the coach going so our trip to Africa could take place exactly as planned.

Our visit to Marseille in France was quite some day too, but sadly for all the wrong reasons. When I tell you we were filming there on 7 July 2005, the day of the London bombings, you might understand the reason why.

We had spent the morning horse-riding, which had been tremendous fun. As we returned to the coach to drive to our destination for lunch, the producer and director took me aside and told me that four bombs had gone off in London and that it was serious: people had died, many were badly hurt. I was horrified, immediately concerned for my friends who lived in the capital, and shocked to the core.

It was my responsibility to tell the contestants what had happened. I got everyone onto the coach, and had to break the awful news to them. I choked up as I tried to explain what had happened, and almost couldn't get the words out, but I had a responsibility for them all and I had to rise to the occasion, so I held back my own emotion to tell people calmly what had gone on.

I'll never forget those scenes on the coach. People were distraught. A lot of the crew were based in London and they were in absolute floods of tears, worried for husbands, wives, sisters, brothers, parents, friends. Everyone was trying to call their loved ones, but we were stuck deep in the south of France and we couldn't get through to anyone, which was enormously worrying. I tried to call Andrew Wilton, but got nothing. It was only later that I found out he was OK.

Our venue for lunch was a lovely old farmhouse that turned out to be full of French ladies. We slowly made our way inside, our grief clear on our faces. The response of the women really took my breath away; they were so kind. Each of them came up to us, pressed our hands, and solemnly communicated that they were '*très désolé, très désolé*' – very sorry, very sorry.

Over lunch, we told the contestants that if they felt they wanted to leave the show, to go back to England to be with their loved ones, then of course they should. Two young girls, Jess and Becky, who were frightened for their mums in London, and concerned about their workplaces too, decided that this was the best choice for them, and so we made arrangements for their journey home. Everyone else decided to stay. We had a rollerblading activity planned in the afternoon, but we cancelled this immediately, along with the evening's vote, and people had the time to themselves instead. I spent the afternoon alone in my hotel room, intermittently trying to contact Andrew and learning about the disaster on French TV, which was on continually, transmitting those awful scenes to those of us who were far, far away.

The next morning, we all resolved to carry on with the tour with determination and courage. It was an example of the true British spirit shining through: none of us were going to let this beat us; we were going to continue and not be knocked by the attack on our homeland.

We travelled that day to Sainte-Maxime on the French Riviera. It's just opposite Saint-Tropez, and just as lovely, but Saint-Tropez gets all the glory, partly because it was brought to international attention by the 1956 Brigitte Bardot film *Et Dieu…Créa la Femme* (*And God… Created Woman*) and has never looked back since. We spent the morning taking a boat trip around the beautiful bay, for which we were joined by a special guest – footballer David Ginola, who famously played for Tottenham Hotspur as well as the French national team. He lives in Sainte-Maxime with his wife and children, and the producers had arranged for him to join us for the day's activities. He too had been shocked by the bombings, and I think he just wanted us all to have a good time as he showed us round his home town.

As I have previously mentioned, I suffer from horrendous seasickness, and so the boat trip that morning was not exactly my favourite activity. David could not have been more kind. He gently put his arm around me and led me to the front of the craft, telling me to keep my eyes on the horizon. There I was, in one of the most glamorous locations in the world, with the arm of a rich, handsome footballer around my shoulders, both of us bathed in glorious sunshine, and all I could do was swallow weakly and hope I didn't throw up on his shoes.

David showed his sense of humour along with his kindness. We had our second gay couple on the coach at that time, Paul and Tim, who were lovely guys, very funny and camp. Paul had noticed David's concern for me and I think he seemed a little jealous of the attention I was getting from him. David spotted this too and thereafter completely hammed it up, which was very funny to see.

I got on really well with Tim and in fact we have stayed in touch after the show; the only contestant that I really keep in regular contact with. He is a very sensible young man and he was always interested in all the places we visited, so I really warmed to him during the series and our friendship has continued since then. However, Paul, who hailed from Scarborough, mysteriously went missing after his return from filming *Coach Trip*. Poor Tim, along with Paul's family and the police, tried in vain to trace him, but he has never been seen since and is still classed as missing as I write today in July 2011.

In the afternoon in Sainte-Maxime, David joined us for a game of beach football, which was fantastic fun, although slightly surreal too. Fancy that, Brendan Sheerin playing football with an international professional! My brother Patrick would never have believed it. I just about managed to resist the temptation to do an Irish jig in goal...

This series was to prove quite enlightening with regards to people's behaviour. Connie and Betty, two lovely funny ladies, were stabbed in the back on day five at Tomar. Clare and fellow passenger Joe had the most awful row in Seville, which left Clare in tears and the tourists arguing in the street.

In fact, it proved to be a fiery series in more ways than one. John and Irene from Doncaster had to leave us on day three after Irene was ill with the heat. At Mijas in southern Spain, I met up with Robert, Pat and Joan, my friends from Torremolinos, but the easy-going atmosphere turned out to be short-lived. At the vote,

Clare and Kat's departure sent Alan and Lorenzo on a drunken spree in which they ran up a bar bill of €460 and I had to red-card them for bad behaviour and running amok in a four-star hotel!

Father and son Joe and Marlon, along with Freddie the doll, drove me mad all day, every day. Freddie the doll went everywhere with Joe and I think became more of a friend than his own son, who was clearly embarrassed about his father's antics. Joe would talk to Freddie constantly, and insist that he had his own drink, his own meal – just like a child would do with their favourite toy. It was always Freddie this or Freddie that. It drove me – and the other contestants – up the wall. When we arrived in Benidorm, however, my prayers were answered when Freddie disappeared into the sea, never to be seen again. We had to have a minute's silence for him (of course) but oh, such joy that he had gone!

That happy incident aside, I was actually quite sad to visit that area of Spain again, and to see how it had changed. Benidorm is now an absolute nightmare as a holiday destination, not like in the late seventies when I used to work in Calpe, just up the road. It was a lovely resort back then.

The series came to a close in Milan. We spent our final afternoon at an exclusive fashion house in the city, where we all learned to be models and strutted our stuff on the catwalk in a *Coach Trip* fashion show, and then we held the final vote in the beautiful garden of our hotel. Paul and Joy, a middle-aged married couple, were our very deserving winners of the series. They were a lovely duo and really nice; I loved the fact that they'd joined in with everything and was very happy that they won. Their prize was to stay on in Milan for a few extra days' private holiday, and so we left them in that gorgeous city the following day while the rest of us headed back to the UK.

All in all, it was great fun and I visited some wonderful places. But after series two transmitted, in May 2006, everything went quiet and it looked like *Coach Trip* wasn't going to be recommissioned.

The series was shelved by Channel 4 and, once again, I thought that that was the end of my brush with TV fame. I was naturally quite disappointed, and yet I knew how lucky I was to have filmed those two series in the first place. I had no control over the matter, and there's no point trying to change things you cannot change. I simply accepted that that was it and I started to look to the future.

During the next three years, I made several life-changing decisions. After much soul-searching, I decided that it was time to leave Hawthorne Cottage. I was so sad to go, as the place was full of such wonderful memories, but it was a massive three-bedroom cottage with a big garden and in truth it was just too much for me to manage on my own. Les and I had looked after it as a team, and without his careful attention and our shared maintenance, the place overwhelmed me a bit, especially as I was working full-time.

Yet that wasn't the only reason. I was ready for a change. It was time to stand on my own two feet, to build a life of my own making, and to think only of myself for the first time in twenty-five years. A fantastic opportunity came up and I decided to help my friend Robert Chatterton expand his restaurant business, Bistro Europa in Torremolinos, and in so doing move back to Spain. I had always wanted to return there after I had had to leave the country prematurely due to Les's ill health. This fulfilled a dream I had long had to live back there again and to integrate myself into the Spanish way of life.

It was a golden opportunity that I couldn't pass up. Robert had offered me a 50 per cent share in the business, so I would be able to work and earn a living in the country that I had long felt so at home in.

Nevertheless, I had to think long and hard about my decision, as I would be leaving behind my life in Scarborough and the wonderful friends and work colleagues I had met through working at the Spa complex. But I knew it was the right thing to do. I had to move on, otherwise I would have been standing still in some kind of time warp.

My friends and family weren't surprised by my decision. I think they always knew I would go back to Spain eventually, and they fully supported my choice. My dear neighbour Sandra helped me to pack up Hawthorne Cottage. I gave a lot of things away. I would be moving to a small apartment in Spain, so there wasn't a lot of room for all the furniture and other bits I had acquired over the years. Many friends kindly looked after things for me that I couldn't take and yet couldn't bear to part with; they're still looking after them today, patiently and with good humour, and I do so appreciate it.

The hens all went to good homes, given to neighbours and friends as gifts. It got so that people were afraid to come to the house for fear of being given a bird as a leaving present! But I was happy to see them settled with people I knew would treat them well.

And then I was ready. I left the Spa complex, sold Hawthorne Cottage and said goodbye to Scarborough. My new home would be in Andalucia, right in the south of Spain, opposite Morocco. I was moving to Torremolinos, in the Malaga area. It was a fairly new part of the country for me, as my tourist work had all taken place in the north, although I had visited the town a long, long time ago when it had been a tiny resort. Now, it had changed and grown larger, drawing in a steady stream of tourists and ex-pats. It was easy to see why. The busy town, with its picturesque white-washed buildings, is perched high on the top of a hill, with the beautiful beach spread out below it, tempting in visitors with its azure sea. There are lots of shops and bars and restaurants, and the town benefits from a direct railway service to Malaga; it takes me only 15 minutes to get home from the airport.

It was good to be back in Spain. Robert and I worked very hard indeed over the next few years. We started by moving the restaurant, Bistro Europa, to new premises just down the street. We then turned the old restaurant into an Irish pub called Sheerin's Bar, to cater for the vast number of Irish visitors to the Bajondillo Apartments opposite, and we both worked in both venues, channelling all our energies into them.

Over time, we made the business a great success, in spite of the many problems and all the bureaucracy that a foreign country can throw at you. I learned a lot about myself in the process. I loved working front of house and taking orders and looking after people. It has been something I have done all my life and I really enjoyed building up a relationship with our customers. I firmly felt that my future lay in working in this bar.

However, as I should have realized by then, one never knows what the future has in store, and everything changed again when Channel 4 came knocking at my door once more in May 2008...

CHAPTER 18

A New Direction

JOHNNY GRAHAM FROM 12 Yard Productions phoned to tell me that a new commissioner for daytime television, Helen Warner, had seen the format of *Coach Trip* and thought it still had potential. So she had taken it off the Channel 4 shelves, dusted it down and decided to commission a third series.

I said I would have to discuss the opportunity with Robert first, then get back to him. After all, Robert was my business partner and I had to consider his position. I owned a 50 per cent share in the business and with that 50 per cent of the responsibility too. We discussed our options at length over lunch and Robert not only agreed I could do this series, he told me I *had* to. 'Coach Trip would not be the same without you, Brendan,' he said, generously. Robert would figure out a way of running Bistro Europa and Sheerin's Bar for the six weeks I would be away filming, and we agreed that on my return he would go off to Las Palmas in the Canary Islands to rest and recuperate.

I was filled with excitement at the news and that night began to get out my notes on the most popular European cities, in preparation for Matt Walton's visit to Torremolinos to brief me on the new series. And the nerves in my tummy began to churn yet again…

Series three was going to have a new series producer, Josh Elliott, who had worked on *Come Dine with Me*, assisted by Keeley Van

Dyke. The new production manager was to be Adrian Pegg. Andrew Brereton had left 12 Yard and moved to another production company; Matt Walton had rejoined the company as Executive Producer, but was also involved with other productions; and John Graham was handling all the projects as Head of Production from his office in London – so they would not be coming on the road with me this time.

Matt, Josh and Adrian flew out to meet me in Torremolinos and we all had a working lunch of paella at El Yate de Cordobes, one of my favourite fish restaurants. I learned that the route this time would take us across Europe again from Antwerp to Prague and we would be visiting countries such as Croatia, Czech Republic, Hungary, Lichtenstein and Luxembourg for the first time. Although 12 Yard map out the route we will take, we always discuss it as a team in detail beforehand, and I will raise any concerns I might have, or point out places we could take in along the way. Being an experienced producer, but new to the show, Josh was worried that not enough funny stuff would happen each day to fill the programme. I laughed and replied, 'Josh, it's *Coach Trip*, funny stuff always happens!'

It was good to meet up with the new team and to discuss what we wanted to do with the third series. It was important to get the planning right, because if this series proved to be successful, then it seemed likely that other series would follow.

I flew to London during the first few days of September 2008 to meet the other members of the team: Caterina Turroni, who was production co-ordinator; Karen Spence, contestant associate producer; Louise Allen, location researcher; and Ross Clutton and Sarah Phillips, the production runners. Jon Padley, Chris Stone and Jon Dibley were on cameras and Rob Garcia and Chris Youle-Grayling were on sound. Little did I know at that time how some of these team members would end up becoming good friends and working on all of the future *Coach Trip* series with me.

As the trip began, we left London and headed for Dover for our ferry to Calais. By nightfall, we had reached Antwerp in Belgium. Over the next thirty days, we were to visit many magnificent cities, with my personal highlights being Reims in France with its glorious cathedral (and of course its champagne!), the snow-covered Mount Titlis in the Swiss Alps (where one of the contestants, Ivy, memorably asked what a glacier was), the peaceful Lake Garda in Italy, and Vienna, an elegant city of palaces, waltzes, coffee shops and cakes. It was also interesting to visit some eastern European cities, such as Dubrovnik, the jewel on Croatia's coast; Budapest, split in two by the powerful blue Danube; Zagreb, the city of Croatian kings; and Prague, with its awe-inspiring beauty.

It had become usual to amass a collection of big personalities on the coach. The casting process is handled by 12 Yard, in particular the casting producer Natalie Grant, who does a fantastic job. In order to shortlist all the applications we receive, she holds interview sessions all around the country, where budding tourists practise various games, as well as the all-important vote. Natalie then chooses who will start each series, as well as lining up the couples who will replace evicted contestants. For my part, I know nothing about the tourists in advance. The first time I meet them is when they walk out of the hotel on that very first morning, or when they're parachuted into Europe to join us mid-tour. It's better that way as the camera can capture my honest reaction on meeting them and there's no hidden agenda. Natalie comes up trumps time and time again with an amazing variety of individuals who by turns charm, infuriate, inspire or irritate – a winning combination that makes for a brilliant TV show. Well, this third series was no different with certain personalities shining and others completely losing the plot as the trip went on.

Graham and Ivy were an interesting couple who started out well, but then got involved in too many cloak-and-dagger voting tactics.

When voted off, Ivy's comment about the group being as dry as 'toast with no butter' still makes me smile. I heard they got married naked on another TV show.

Jackie and Suzanne were the largest ladies I have ever had on the coach, both in terms of physical size and personality. Changing their hotel room in Luxembourg solved the problem of them banging into each other as they shared the small space.

William and Deanne were a real pair of shrewd players, interested in everything I said and showed them. William was a courier's delight and we often discussed the history and geography of the places we visited. Another enthusiastic and lovely couple were Colin and Diane from Wales, who particularly enjoyed visiting the Surrender Museum in Reims. I always like it when the travellers are genuinely interested in the sights they are seeing.

Delia and Jacqui are, in my opinion, the only people who have ever passed through the auditions who should never have made it onto the coach. They wanted to party instead of enjoying the sights of Vienna, and they walked off the tour after only sixteen hours on the coach, which is the shortest time anyone has ever stayed. Thank goodness or I would have red-carded them myself. As for Mark and Ann from Nottingham, they might have lasted longer if Ann had not grabbed Tom by his penis and hung on!

Holly, Taryn, Matt and Tom were my favourite young couples on series three. Love blossomed as far back as day six for Holly and Tom; I know as I saw them together in the hotel in Lucerne. They are now happily married and living in Brisbane, Australia, with Matt living close by, funnily enough. Romance does actually bloom on the coach for some people and Tom and Holly are proof of that.

Ann and Grace described their home in Gipton, Leeds, as a place where cats carry machetes and dogs have flick knives. I see Gipton has not changed since I used to go through it on the number six bus on my way to Corpus Christi. I must admit I have never laughed so much as I did with these two girls during an accordion performance we witnessed together in Conero, Italy. A local musician was playing the instrument quite competently, but the facial expressions he was making while doing so were so funny (like he was orgasming) that the whole group had a laughing fit and couldn't stop giggling.

By contrast, Daz and Betty were a genteel mummy and son combination, although Daz soon woke up to the fact that ruthlessness is a necessity on the coach if you want to stay on it – he turned into a complete firecracker at voting time. Luckily, Michael and John from Newcastle added some much-needed humour to the trip, so it wasn't all drama.

The series ended in the beautiful city of Prague, with Hannah and Katie, two lovely girls from Bushey in Hertfordshire, being the well-deserved winners.

Series three was transmitted in May 2009 and immediately became a success both with the viewing public and for Channel 4, attracting an astonishing 2 million viewers. I had started to record a video blog diary for this series after each day of touring about how I felt about the day's events, and this was also gaining popularity on the Channel 4 website. Many people would watch the programme and then log on to the blog to see my thoughts on the day, my reaction to the votes or my concerns over alliances and suchlike. It all helped to make the series more popular.

It was while series three was being broadcast that I started getting recognized in the street as being 'Brendan from *Coach Trip*'. It was odd to begin with, and I was a bit embarrassed, having never experienced that kind of adulation before. However, it was really gratifying to hear the viewers' comments. I would often get people coming up to me at airports or while I was visiting London or out and about in Torremolinos. I found out I was very popular amongst airline staff and anyone who dealt with the general public, such as hotel receptionists. I'd often get airline staff asking me if I had a few yellow or red cards handy to give out to that nasty bitch in row 9D, who only paid for an economy seat but thinks she's travelling in first class...

When I do meet people in the street, most people have a favourite place or activity they have seen on the show, which they want to discuss with me. Others refer to particular characters or to a nasty or vindictive vote. I often hear the same things: 'Wasn't she a cow?' 'Isn't that one evil!' 'I wouldn't last two minutes; they would vote me off straight away!' Another favourite comment is: 'Oh, I just don't know how you keep your patience with them.' That one always makes me laugh, as sometimes I don't know how I do it either.

Wherever we are, the conversation generally ends with a photo and a thank you and a nice comment about how much the person enjoys the show. I must admit it is lovely to be part of such a brilliant programme and I am deeply grateful for the opportunity to be able to continue having so much fun on *Coach Trip*.

In May 2009, I decided to sell my 50 per cent share in Bistro Europa, which was a very sad outcome for me as I had thoroughly enjoyed the challenge of operating our own restaurant and bar. As I write, Robert's Bistro Europa still sells the best sirloin steaks in Torremolinos. I had discussed my dilemma with Robert beforehand, as I knew I had to make a choice. I couldn't keep going away for weeks on end, leaving him shattered while I was off on one of my amazing adventures. I resigned from the business that spring because I knew that series four was being finalized for filming in the coming September, with a broadcast slot booked for the following February. I would continue to live in Spain in my home in Torremolinos when I wasn't on the road; it was a lovely lifestyle, after all, what with the clement weather and the beautiful setting, and I didn't see any need to return to the UK just yet. But *Coach Trip* now became my main job – an outcome I certainly hadn't foreseen when I had emailed Beth Davies all those years before.

Series four was to be quite an epic as Channel 4 had decided that they wanted fifty episodes, which meant fifty days of filming, from Portsmouth in the UK to the Sahara Desert in Tunisia, Africa. We would start filming on 7 September and finish on 27 October 2009. Wow, that was to be a long time away. It was a massive enterprise, involving a lot more work from everyone involved, and it was going to be intense. I have to confess I wondered if I could manage such a lengthy stretch on the road. Even I had never been to some of the places we were planning on visiting. We were going to cross practically the whole of Europe, then into Asia, and then make our way south to Sicily and then beyond, sailing to Africa to finish in Tunisia. What an adventure!

We had pretty much the same team as the previous series, but with a few changes: Chris Iliffe was production manager, Salvatore Assenza and Charlie Carpenter were helping with locations and cameras, and there was a new sound man along for the ride, Matt Johns.

Natalie Grant and Sarah Phillips were the formidable team responsible for looking after all the tourists and myself. I first met Natalie on series four, on arrival at the Aerodrome Hotel in Croydon, our departure location, and instantly warmed to this Yorkshire lass from Wakefield. We remain great friends and along with Sarah she is a key member of our *Coach Trip* crew family.

On the first day of filming, Portsmouth harbour slipped away as we headed out into the Channel for St Malo and France. We spent six days in France, which the group complained about, even though I took them to such beautiful cities as Paris, Dijon and Chablis.

In Milan, we treated them to a trip to the San Siro football stadium and then on to some culture in the cathedral, where I had to deal with an obnoxious lift operator who insisted on splitting up my group. This complicated the filming of our visit, although we quickly found a solution and simply recorded the tour once everyone had come up in the lift.

In the afternoon of day eleven, we were joined by a gay couple called Jon and Bruce from London, who will be remembered for the famous fight scene on the coach. Jon was a London cabbie and Bruce was an embalmer at a funeral director's. I made them welcome and had a lovely chat with them before we started the afternoon's activity. They were really nice guys and I could tell they liked me even though it was obvious they did not hit it off with everyone else in the group.

Jon and Bruce soon recognized that an alliance had formed between some of the younger members of the group: Gemma and Jodie, Tam and Jayson, and Paul and Matt. It was clear that this group was starting to get on Bruce's nerves, especially Jayson, who seemed to wind Bruce up for no reason at all. This animosity continued through dinner that night, so that by the time we were ready to depart for Vincenza the following morning, Bruce had already made his mind up to burst the group's bubble during the vote that coming evening.

At breakfast, the younger group decided to celebrate their twelve days on the coach together and produced some balloons and streamers while we were on our way to Vincenza. We departed Lake Garda on time and made our way to the motorway with the younger six celebrants in the front of the coach. Bruce and Jon were at the back and were getting annoyed at the noise of the little party – to which they hadn't been invited – which was disturbing the rest of the travellers. I heard some words exchanged between Bruce and Jayson that I didn't particularly like, but that passed off quickly. However, another comment came later, at which time I noticed we were still thirteen kilometres from the nearest Italian motorway services.

I advised Paul Donald to stop at the services whatever happened, as I could feel the tension mounting in the air. Words were going back and forth from the front of the coach to the back and getting stronger and more disturbing each time. The argument centred on Bruce and Jayson, with Bruce criticizing Jayson's party and claiming that his little alliance would be destroyed by that evening's vote. By this time, Bruce was getting really wound up. His partner Jon tried to calm him, but then Bruce started another tirade of abuse at Jayson, which included the words, 'I'll kick your fat ass all round this coach.' When he was challenged by Tam, who stood up for his friend, Bruce then completely lost his temper. He pulled off his microphone, undid his seat belt and leapt up to attack Tam and Jayson. I was up on my feet immediately and managed to separate them both, using my body and arm. Also within seconds Ross Clutton, a production researcher, threw himself into the fray, gathering Bruce around the waist and pulling him out of the coach just as Paul entered the motorway services.

By the time we had parked the coach, everyone was upset. Many of the ladies were crying and the men were very shaken up.

We had a long coffee break and a chat to calm everyone down, and we assured them that Bruce and Jon would not be joining us again. The consensus was an instant red card, which I delivered to Bruce in the car park of the motorway services. Of course this meant that Jon would have to go too. I really felt sorry for Jon as he was losing out because of Bruce's behaviour, but it was evident they had tarnished the journey for everyone so there was no choice. Only the day before, they had expressed a wish to go to Venice, which we were visiting the next day, so they really missed out due to their actions. But this sort of violent behaviour will never be tolerated on *Coach Trip*.

As for the remaining tourists, we all made a decision to put the incident behind us and to continue enjoying the rest of the day ahead of us in Vincenza. We all had a great time seeing the wonderful sights and taking part in the amazing activities, which were stone-carving and a visit to a grappa distillery, where we learned how to make the local liqueur – and how to taste it, too. We also all enjoyed our trip to Venice the following morning. It was a perfect day, with lovely blue skies, plenty of sightseeing, handsome gondoliers and the Lido beach in the afternoon. Well, almost perfect. I stepped into a massive lump of dog poo on the beach, which really turned me off the place, but Natalie helped me to remove it using something like six packets of wet wipes. Urgh!

At Nis in Serbia, the mood changed. I have never seen a group so silent and respectful as when we visited the Nis Concentration Camp and learned about the atrocities that took place there during the Second World War.

As we entered Turkey for the first time, there was a distinct difference in the scenery and the culture, with the beautiful spires of the Edirne mosques piercing the skyline of the city. We visited a four-star hotel in Tekirdağ and had massages, before wrestling each other Turkish-style in the grounds, covered in olive oil. This activity was interrupted when we were nearly landed on by a helicopter, as we were wrestling where the driver wanted to land! We then continued into Istanbul – such an amazing city, where west meets east. I have to say that to step into Asia, to sail on the Bosphorus, and to show people around the Blue Mosque is an extremely large feather in the cap of an international tour guide. I was very proud of myself that day.

At Xanthi, I promised the group mud baths and mud baths they got... Well, one massive concrete bath filled with mud, grass and leaping frogs. As we tried to cross the bath from one side to the other, heroically pulling ourselves through the dense, thick mud, it was one of those hilarious moments where you try to be serious but you just break down into uncontrollable laughter. It was an amazingly funny afternoon and is remembered fondly by us all.

Athens was a first for us on *Coach Trip*. Although I had been there before, it was lovely to revisit the Acropolis and to spend time in the Archaeological Museum. It was in Athens that the friendship that had developed between the tourists Paul, Matt, Carla and Angie was severed completely. They had all been such good pals, enjoying many comical moments together and dispensing with many of their adversaries, and yet the rift was beyond repair. Oh, how quickly the relationship deteriorated and how quickly the claws were ready to strike. That's *Coach Trip* for you. The girls voted for the boys to go home, and so Paul headed back to my old stomping ground, Scarborough, while Matt returned to Kent.

In Olympia, I upset the local guides by letting my tourists run bare-chested in the Olympic arena. I was told to get my clients dressed by several female Greek guides. My goodness – during the ancient Olympics, the Greeks used to run naked! I think it was the sight of pale, white, English chests, along with socks in their sandals, which had offended the Greek women. We made up in true Greek style with kisses and shrugs of shoulders – and no, the police did not turn up.

My Geology lessons at Corpus Christi, Leeds, came to life as we ascended Mount Etna in Sicily on day forty-five. That was a particularly special experience for me. The volcano is only dormant, with clear evidence of fissures weeping smoke and sulphurous gases. The lava flow is quite evident too and a stark reminder of the power of nature. I found it quite incredible.

Our last days were to be spent in Tunisia, which I had never visited before. However, I had worked in Morocco during my years with OSL and I found the locations to be very similar – think date palm trees and lots of camels. At the time of writing, Tunis is ablaze with revolution… How quickly things change. Kairouan was where I shouted at Nathan, 'Bring back that goat's head! We need it for the stew!'

Finally, as if we were in a dream, the Sahara Desert spread out before us. We had driven to it on our coach, then challenged the dunes in four-by-fours and now, riding camels, we traversed into the heart of the desert. It is one of the most remote and desolate places on Earth. There are no buildings, no landmarks – nothing in any direction for an hour's drive or more. All you can see are miles and miles of sand dunes and it is very, very hot. The only people there are the Bedouins, the only creatures the camels. We were about thirty kilometres from the Libyan border and I found the whole setting incredibly impressive. It was amazing to think that we had started our journey in Portsmouth, with fish and chips, and had ended up here, in this distant and different land. The contrast was incredible.

The contestants were perhaps less struck by the setting than I was, however. I could not contain my laughter as I heard Mukesh screaming like a queen at the top of his voice for Syreeta to turn his camel around and away from the steep dunes, which were frightening him silly.

I had imagined it would be the perfect end to a perfect trip. Our desert tents lay waiting for us, heavily decorated with thick carpets, Lawrence of Arabia-style, with servants to wash our hands and prepare the feast for us to eat. It was going to be the end of a long tour of fifty days and I was looking forward to a restful final night. But I had forgotten about human nature, and how Syreeta had developed a dislike of fellow traveller Ann.

After the sumptuous meal, as the sun began to set across the empty desert, I clearly heard Syreeta shriek at Ann: 'Vinegar tits!'

Human nature. It's a wonderful thing.

CHAPTER 19

Celebrity Status

AFTER SERIES FOUR was transmitted on 15 February 2010, it was apparent to all at 12 Yard and Channel 4 that the programme was a tremendous success for the network. The viewing figures were reaching 2.3 million and we were top of our slot, beating BBC1 and 2, ITV and Channel 5 practically every day. My blog, which I film daily, was even beating other famous programmes like *Shameless* online, getting 2,000 hits a day, which really made me proud. The show was sold to Australia and New Zealand and I watched myself a few times while visiting my Auntie Edith and my cousins in Perth, Western Australia. I could not believe it when someone came up to me in the middle of the main shopping precinct in Perth and asked for my autograph and went on to say how they absolutely loved *Coach Trip*!

With the show becoming such a success, and Channel 4 keen to commission more programmes, I decided it was time to get myself an agent. I'd cockled along until now on my own, but 12 Yard were starting to negotiate a new contract with me, and with things appearing to be more serious and long term now, I felt I needed someone to represent me.

I was introduced to my agent, Paula McKie, by a dear friend, Cindy Ritson, who works on Channel 4's *Countdown*. I was looking desperately for an agent and over dinner at our mutual friend Janey

Walker's house in Hutton Buscel, Scarborough, Cindy suggested that I get in touch with Paula. Janey Walker's dinners are renowned the length and breadth of North Yorkshire, by the way. She not only makes a beautiful main course and starter, but she also always offers three desserts, served on a trolley! *And* you can have second helpings!

I had previously emailed and telephoned lots of agents in London, starting with the As. One agent who had been recommended to me never called me back, even though I called them at least six times. 'Well,' I decided eventually, 'what is London's loss is Ilkley's gain,' and I picked up the telephone and called Paula. As soon as I spoke to her, I knew she was the one. We talked at length and she agreed to represent me in all my negotiations. She has had some sticky moments to deal with but we have always been fair and honest in all things and I know she has my best interests at heart.

She has her own agency, Agency Oakroyd, which is based near Ilkley in West Yorkshire, and she is a Yorkshire lass herself. We have a wonderful working relationship and I trust her completely. We love our free time together, spending many a happy hour in Betty's Tea Rooms in Ilkley, eating fat rascals (big scones, for those readers not from Yorkshire) and drinking Betty's tea. I adore chasing her two boys around the house and playing hide-and-seek with them – they make me feel so young. I have also met her lovely husband Andrew, who works at Leeds University and is very clever. Paula has played an integral part in furthering my new career and I'm very appreciative of all she does for me. With Paula on board, it felt fantastic to have someone fighting my corner in this brave new world of TV.

It turned out that 2010 was to be a great year for *Coach Trip*. Not only were we a ratings hit, but we started to receive critical acclaim too. We were nominated for Best Daytime Programme at the 2010 Broadcast Awards, and the whole team attended the glamorous awards ceremony at the Grosvenor House Hotel, Park Lane, London. These awards are where the great and the good from all walks of television life are seen in one place, dining, preening themselves, networking and hopefully bagging an award or two.

I had flown in from Malaga for the ceremony and John Graham and Matt Walton came to my hotel to pick me up. It was a special night – a tuxedo night – as we had been shortlisted for such a prestigious award, so there was an air of anticipation around us. I met Helen Warner, the commissioner for daytime television at Channel 4, in the cloakroom area as we proceeded to the drinks reception. It would be a difficult night for Helen, as she also had *Come Dine with Me* running against us, but she wished us luck and said, 'May the best man win.'

The large ballroom at the Grosvenor House Hotel is one of the most impressive rooms I have ever seen, decorated with dozens of chandeliers. It really has that wow factor. I was interviewed by online forum Digital Spy, who are real fans of *Coach Trip*, and they all wished us luck as we descended into the ballroom for dinner. The awards doubled as a social occasion for all from 12 Yard who worked so hard on the show: Josh Elliott, Keeley Van Dyke, Peter Dann (the production accountant), David Young, Sarah Phillips, and Trevor Hotz from HotCam – who provide a lot of equipment for the show – to name a few. I think we all enjoyed having a good dinner and some drinks together without worrying about the next activity or whether we were on schedule or not.

During dinner, you could not help noticing the celebrities on their tables or wandering around the ballroom, greeting friends or looking for the toilets. Newsreaders, *Top Gear* presenters, the cast of *EastEnders* at one end of the room and the cast of *Coronation Street* at the other, *The Inbetweeners*… The list went on and on.

After dinner, the awards commenced. We faced really stiff competition as we were up against *60-Minute Makeover, Come Dine with Me, Deal or No Deal, Homes Under the Hammer, Land Girls* and *Life Class: Today's Nude.* Factors to be taken into account included ratings, audience response and critical reaction.

Well, *Land Girls* won the award, and there was a deep sigh of disappointment on our table. Everyone on the programme works extremely hard to make it what it is, so I was sad for everyone. Sometimes you just have to accept the things you cannot change, however, so the night proceeded and we all cheered the winners and commiserated with the losers. At 12.30 a.m., a sleek black Mercedes car drew up outside the Grosvenor House Hotel on Park Lane (posh or what!), and took one sober gentleman from Beeston in Leeds back to his smart hotel for a nice cup of tea and bed. What a night... Fabulous!

It was in May 2010 that my own celebrity status really started to take off, with a request by ITV to take part in *The David Dickinson Show.* Sherrie Hewson was also appearing in that episode. I remember Sherrie not only from her work with the *Carry On* franchise, but also the many plays she has done. My role was to be a travel consultant to the programme and I was to comment on the new advertising posters for British resorts. As I had worked in tourism in both Scarborough and Folkestone, I was quite enthusiastic about the guest appearance.

I flew from Malaga to Heathrow, where a car sped me into London's Holborn area to my five-star hotel. I had a swim in the beautiful pool to freshen up, then took a taxi to Old Compton Street to Balans Café, where I met up with Tim Basset, my friend from series two, for an early dinner. Tim and I had a lovely meal and we enjoyed reminiscing about his time on the programme. Like many, he is amazed at the success of the series and we always end up laughing as we recall some of our misadventures on the trip. I returned to the hotel after dinner as I had to be up early the next morning for the car that was being sent to take me to the studios.

On the morning itself, I felt very nervous, as this was the first time I had been a guest on a TV programme in my own right, rather than simply promoting *Coach Trip*. As my car pulled up at the ITV studios on the South Bank, I was met by a member of the research staff, shown to the green room and given a hot cup of tea to calm my nerves. I then met some of the other staff, including the lady responsible for directing the programme. We went through some question cards together, which listed the various resorts that would come up and the types of questions David would ask me, so I was not left completely in the dark as to how the interview might flow.

After make-up, I was shown onto the set and noticed that the audience were already *in situ* as the programme was being filmed live. As I waited by the side of the set, along came Sherrie Hewson, who introduced herself to me and immediately said how much she loved *Coach Trip* and that she should get in touch with my agent to have me on *Loose Women*. 'You would be fantastic, Brendan!' she said. I was really taken aback but she kissed me on the cheek and said, 'Don't be nervous, it will be a lot of fun.'

As we made our way onto the set, David Dickinson came over and said hello. We went through the Q cards again, then before I realized what had happened he had spirited them away. I thought, 'Oh my gosh, he's only gone and put them on the table, now I won't know which order they're in.' But just at that moment the director shouted 'Action!' and that was it: I just had to wing it when it came to my turn to be interviewed. I remember talking about Scarborough and other resorts, we laughed a lot and before I knew it David was thanking us and we were escorted off the set and back to the green room. I find it astonishing, the speed at which these things are over and done with: it was all over before I knew what had happened. The production staff thanked me for coming and said everything had gone well and they were very happy indeed. And that was that!

A car took me back to the hotel, waited while I got my luggage and then deposited me at King's Cross station. Paula had timed my diary very well indeed, as I was immediately going to start filming the next series of *Coach Trip*, series five, from my home town of Leeds. I would just have time to see all my family beforehand, and have lunch with Paula at Betty's in Ilkley.

I got the train up to Leeds and while on the train, I texted my old school friend Matthew Kent from Corpus Christi – the boy I used to share cigarettes with – and asked him if he was driving my train from King's Cross (if you remember, he was the one who had loved watching trains so much as a child that he had gone on to drive them for a living). No, he said, he didn't drive 125s – but when I told him which train I was on, amazingly he said he was driving a local train behind me and I would pass him at Doncaster railway station! He went on to say he would be finishing his shift on arrival at Leeds and we could meet for a cuppa. So it was arranged that we would meet at the Queen's Hotel in City Square, where I had a suite booked, as soon as he had finished.

The memories came flooding back as soon as I walked into City Square towards the Queen's Hotel. It was the first time I would be checking in there as a guest. As I stood on the steps, I looked back at the square, which is now lined with bars and cafés. I remembered how I used to get the number six bus to Corpus Christi from outside the main Post Office, or the number one bus to take me home to Beeston after school. I recalled Auntie Dolly and me watching *Doctor Zhivago* at the Tatler cinema when it first came out. I remembered many hours waiting endlessly to meet John, who was always late. Oh, he would have made a fine dancer – he would probably have had his own dance school by now if he had lived. I remembered how Dominic and Isaac were so scared of our first sojourn to a gay bar, and how Isaac and I had stood watching all those posh people go into the Queen's Hotel for lavish dinners while we waited for John on that fateful first night out. I remembered how my beloved Les would pick me up in his car here when we were courting, to go shopping in Bradford or for lunch at the Flying Pizza in Roundhay Road, which was very smart indeed. And there, in the middle of the square, throughout it all and still standing, stood the majestic equestrian statue of the Black Prince, Edward, who would never be king.

I turned and went into the hotel and checked in with the beaming receptionist. She recognized who I was instantly, while behind me the porter carried my luggage. 'Oh my goodness, Brendan,' I thought to myself, 'just look how far you've come.'

Matthew joined me in the terrace bar at the top of the hotel, which has spectacular views over the whole of Leeds. We just picked up where we had left off the last time, as if we had never been away from each other. It's strange but we always seem to do this whenever we meet. He talked about Jan, his wife, and their two boys, and I signed some photographs for his family and friends (which he hated asking me for as I'm just Brendan, his oldest friend, and not some celebrity to him, but of course I was happy to oblige). We agreed to meet the next day too, as he was tired and had to get home before the rush hour started.

I sat there savouring the moment and looking out over my birth city, from one of the best hotels in town. I thought, 'Well, you haven't done badly for a lad from Hunslet, Brendan,' and I went back to my suite and got ready, as the Sheerins from Cross Green were descending on me. There would be my cousin John, my dear Uncle John (who always reminds me of my own dad as they look similar and their mannerisms are the same), my cousin Dymphna and her husband Paul, their son Stephen, and our Jonathan, who is my cousin Dawn's son. Dawn sadly passed away at the very young age of forty-eight as a result of cancer, which she fought bravely in St Gemma's Hospice in Leeds. I was able to visit her before I left to make series four of *Coach Trip*, but she died the night we were travelling from Patras to Ancona. Patrick, my brother, texted me the message that the family wanted me to carry on filming, so I did.

My next lot of visits took in my brother Patrick, sister Margaret and her husband (also a Patrick), my brother Martin and his girlfriend Julie, and my brother Terence, along with my dear school friend Nina Krupianka from Corpus Christi and her husband Owen. It was wonderful to have all the family together, to catch up on the gossip and to show them my suite which they all ooohed at – and also to tell them all about series five, which would be starting filming the very next day.

* * *

Series five left from the Oulton Hall Hotel in Leeds, but not before I had gone into the kitchen of the hotel and had my photograph taken with the cook, who had made me eggs and bacon for breakfast and was a fan of the show. I left that lovely Yorkshire lady with a great big smile on her face and her manager looking on in awe.

I was really excited about series five because we were going to some new countries, namely Sweden, Norway, Denmark, Estonia, Latvia and Lithuania. These were countries I'd never visited so I had done lots of research and was thrilled at the prospect of seeing them. It was going to be another thirty-day series, and we would be filming from May to June 2010. The powers that be had decided fifty days in a series was just too long, and to be honest I think the viewers agreed too. That fourth series felt like it went on for ever and ever and ever, amen. Thirty days seems to be the most popular length and so it was decided that we would return to this format for series five.

We set off first for Hull, my old shopping and stomping ground. We were going to do maypole dancing with some more lovely

Yorkshire ladies, then we were visiting The Deep aquarium, and after the vote we were to catch the overnight ferry to Holland.

My dear friend Gary, who still lives in Hull, met us at the aquarium and watched us film there. I shall never forget the look on his face; he was beaming with pride as he saw the cameras trained on me while I was being interviewed or conversing with the new tourists. It was as if Hollywood had arrived in Hull.

This tour would take us to Amsterdam where, after a pedalo tour of the canals, we would get risqué with some burlesque dancing. We had to ask the dancer to cover her breasts before filming as she had originally wanted to dance naked. Heaven forbid!

We drove through Bremen, losing contestants Mo and Marg from Kidderminster due to illness on day four. In Hamburg the next day, a surprise awaited us: the familiar faces of Ray and Glenys joined us at the submarine tour. This couple had started out with us on series four, but had been cruelly voted off by the group after only two days, so I hadn't really got to know them at all. On returning to the UK, they had immediately applied to come on the show again. Unfortunately, as Ray had verbal diarrhoea, they were voted off early once again, after just three days.

At Gothenburg, we ate the most horrendous smelly fish sandwich in creation. Apparently, the Swedes love it, but all I shall say is that they can definitely keep it. In Stockholm, we were busy admiring the lovely city sights when Paul took us into a tunnel and our roof camera suddenly descended on top of us through the skylight, which was quite a shock. The tunnel was only 3.6 metres high and we needed 3.8 metres to clear it with the camera. We always double-checked the heights of bridges and tunnels from that moment on!

At the Hartwall Areena in Helsinki, we tried – 'tried' being the operative word – to play ice hockey, one of Finland's favourite sports. Glenn from Northamptonshire actually crawled from one side of the arena to the other to start playing, and then found out he was at the wrong end and had to crawl all the way back again. He could not stand upright on the ice and in fact ended up under the goal rather than in it. The sauna island trip that afternoon was to make up for the aches and pains we endured at the hockey. Everyone relaxed, enjoying beating themselves with silver birch twigs rather *too* much, I would say. Unfortunately, there was a shock for Charlie and Sam, who received a yellow card and were none too pleased. I have never seen two posh boys so boiling mad.

Gun shooting in Tallinn, Estonia, left us all shocked at the power and might of firing live ammunition. It was not an activity I would like to repeat, but Sam loved it as he shoots grouse at home, when they are in season, of course. Nicki, meanwhile, loved the 'Butler in the Buff' activity – and the feeling seemed to be mutual, with the bronzed butler exchanging numbers and kisses with her. Naughty!

A double whammy was waiting for us all on day fourteen, when we lost husband-and-wife team Martin and Margaret for canvassing for votes, and mother and daughter Teresa and Katie through the red-card vote. On day fifteen, we lost Lauren and Chris due to the scheming of Amanda and Nicki, who were playing a blinder of a game. They avoided being red-carded no less than thirteen times on this series, which is quite a record.

I have coordinated some really difficult votes in my time, but one of the worst was in Vilnius, Lithuania on day seventeen. Somehow everything went very wrong for Charlie and Sam that day. They had made the mistake of breezily saying that they could leave tomorrow and it wouldn't bother them as they'd had such a good time on the show. Well, on *Coach Trip*, you can never forget that the other couples are always looking for an excuse to vote people off, and this kind of comment was a clanger. Some of the other tourists picked up on the remark and Charlie and Sam became an easily defensible choice for nomination that evening. The red card was coming their way and the whole group sensed this. Nicki and Amanda started to cry, followed by Glenn and Becca, followed by sisters Janet and Beryl. I had to walk into that semicircle in the midst of all this emotional turmoil, and as I stepped onto my mark, right next to Charlie, I heard him start to cry too. A large lump appeared in my throat and I could hardly get my words out. As I started to fill up myself, Jon Lloyd, the director, asked me to leave the semicircle and take a breather. But just a short while later I had to go in and deliver the red-card vote and leave the group to say their goodbyes. It remains one of the saddest votes in the history of the show.

Other departures included Nick and Mark, who walked because they were tired and could not stand any more pork (pronounced *pawk*). 'NOT MORE PAWK, AIM SICK OF PAWK, WE 'AD PAWK YESTERDAY!' Then there were Chris and 'I love you lots, like jelly tots' Carmel, who left due to work commitments in Liverpool. But for the rest of us, it was on with the tour...

On day twenty at Klaipeda (also in Lithuania), we cheered everyone up with a training session with the dolphins and a wet kiss from the biggest sea lion in the world. The following day, in Malmö in Sweden, the young nude Swedish men made grandma Maggie chuckle as she and her grandson Chris went for their massage. As for me, I had two dips in Copenhagen harbour on day twenty-two, as my kayak was unbelievably light and tipped over at the slightest touch. Thank goodness the harbour's water is the cleanest in the world!

We all returned to our childhood at Odense, the home of Hans Christian Andersen. Amanda was quick off the block to flirt with Jack from Cardiff as we re-enacted *The Princess and the Pea* in the open-air theatre, much to the amusement of the passers-by.

Norway was a wonderful new destination for us and, after visiting Munch's Museum in Oslo, we travelled by train to Bergen and the magnificent fjords. What a spectacular, scenic country Norway is, and to finish our final vote in Voss, in front of that towering waterfall, was stunning.

Grandma Maggie and her grandson Chris were deserved winners, but Becca and Glenn, and Amanda and Nicki, all made *Coach Trip* history, as they were the first couples to last the whole thirty days of the trip. I had become closer to them all due to their achievement, as I don't normally get to spend so much time with the tourists; the nature of the programme means that the contestants come and go regularly. I was pleased to see them do so well as they really played the game; they were very clever about it. The more popular you are, the longer you stay, and these couples had really sussed that out and made the most of their knowledge.

The countries we went to in series five were for me the most beautiful we have ever visited in terms of scenery. I had never been to the Scandinavian countries before and I was so impressed, both with the cities and the natural environment – but the scenery truly was divine. I shall never forget my room looking out at the top of the Hardangerfjord with its beautiful view of the fjord itself and the sea. The green fields of the fjords are absolutely breathtaking, and the whole setting was so calm and peaceful. I have been lucky enough to see many sights in my life, but this was one of the most memorable. Yet again, another fantastic series.

CHAPTER 20

No Rest for the Wicked

S ERIES FIVE WAS due to be broadcast quite soon after filming, with the transmission starting on Channel 4 on 30 August 2010. While the production team busied themselves editing the footage we'd captured in May to June, there was no rest for the wicked as we ploughed straight into filming series six, with only a few weeks off in between. Despite the quick turnaround, I still found time to do my research and to dig out the notes I needed for the tour, so I was all ready to go by the time the start date came around. It can take me weeks to do my preparation for the show, depending on my prior knowledge of the destinations involved. I always aim to get 75 to 100 per cent of the prep done before we set off. Once we're on the road, I only have my evenings free to do any extra work required, and after filming for 12 to 14 hours, I often won't have the energy required.

I try to make my research as wide-ranging and broadly informative as possible, so that I'm able to speak not just about the actual destination, but also the history surrounding it, perhaps biographies of any key players (whether monarchs or architects), facts about unusual items we might be making or using – basically any offshoot that might come up, or anything that I anticipate the tourists might want to know about. It's important to be prepared – if things go off course in terms of our schedule, my extra knowledge might just save the day or lift the episode, so I do as much prior work as I can.

Each time we start a new series, I do get excited about the itinerary and what my passengers are going to be like. Series six, filmed virtually back-to-back after the previous one, in July and August 2010, was no exception.

Milan was to be our starting point for this series – a beautiful cathedral city famous for its opera. We began our first day at the opera house itself, La Scala, and then tried to sing operatically in the main square for our supper. I made €4, which was enough for an ice cream. This is clearly not normal behaviour for an international tour guide, but when you're hot and want an Italian ice cream, well, you will do anything.

Lake Maggiore was next, and we went for a dip in it on one of the hottest days of the year. The boys from Southampton, Phil and Bob, shocked everyone by stripping off and getting their trunks on without so much as a by-your-leave or any consideration for the sensitive ladies – though mind you, some, like teachers Jane and Jayne from the West Midlands, just loved it! (And I noticed Wendy from the Wirral had a good look too.)

At Zermatt, my plans were foiled when I attempted to take the group skiing and discovered that the whole area had been closed off. I don't have much luck in Switzerland with cable cars not operating, as it had also happened in the previous series. I remembered that the last time I had been to Saas-Fee, in series four, the boys Paul, Matt, Tam, Jayson and Lloyd had all got incredibly drunk on schnapps, and I certainly did not intend to repeat that adventure. No, we would have to do something simple and educational, like a museum. This itinerary did not go down at all well, but sometimes you have to be firm about these things. Oh, and by the way, I was sick of telling some members of the group that the Matterhorn is *not* a musical instrument, it's a blooming Swiss mountain!

It was in Zermatt that our extreme sports activity became a bit too extreme. We were planning an afternoon on 'extreme scooters', wheeling ourselves around the mountain tracks. A race was set up for the tourists, where they started at the top of a hill, descended the slope, raced around a big rock at the bottom and then back up the hill to be named the winner. Phil and Bob were up first and they both had plenty of competitive spirit. The race began and they went for it – but as they scooted around the rock, disaster struck. Phil smashed into it, coming off his scooter and badly injuring his knee. He ended up being carried down the mountain to have stitches put in his leg. We immediately cancelled the rest of the activity for safety reasons. Phil's leg got worse and sadly he and Bob both had to leave us – but not before they had descended into the packed dining room of the hotel and paraded around in their mankinis. They were good fun and it was a shame they had to go.

I am sometimes apprehensive about the activities we do on *Coach Trip*. I am briefed on the itinerary and schedule before we set off so I know in advance what's coming. I've never refused to do anything, but sometimes I don't take part in the high-risk excursions, such as bungee jumping, for safety reasons. Imagine if I injured myself on day one of a tour – the rest of the planned trip would be a write-off.

That said, I've still participated in plenty of heart-racing stunts – abseiling springs to mind, and riding a zip wire in Norway. Now that was memorable: you read 'zip wire trip' on the schedule and you think, 'How pleasant,' recalling calm descents in homely forests in the UK, with plenty of pine needles beneath you to break your fall. So I find myself on this zip wire, merrily traversing a beautiful green meadow full of pretty wild flowers, and then suddenly the meadow and the trees surrounding it fall away and I'm crossing a wide gorge, a river gushing 140 metres below me, clinging on for dear life.

My favourite activities are the white-water rafting and the Segway tours we take to sightsee around cities. The latter are just so much fun to ride on, as well as providing a very quick way of jetting between sights to ensure we can pack in as much as possible. I had done white-water rafting before *Coach Trip* – my first time was on a trip to the South Island of New Zealand, on the Shotover River, during a holiday Les and I took after his transplant – and enjoyed it very much, so every time that's on the itinerary I'm thrilled. I love the excitement of racing over the rocks, not knowing if the next wave to hit will capsize you or if you'll be safe and dry for another few metres at least.

That's not to say that I always enjoy a soaking, however. On Lake Geneva during series six, Barbara and Elaina from London nearly pulled my leg off as they got into the water to wakeboard. Cries of 'Dear sweet Jesus!' and 'Lord save us!' rang through the air as they insisted on taking me in with them. I literally had to force their hands off my thighs.

After Bordeaux – and some oysters – we carried on into Spain, where I always feel very much at home. At Pamplona, I led a tour of the famous *Corrida* or bull run, which is held annually in July during the festival of San Fermin, the patron saint of Pamplona. The tour threads its way through the city, ending at the famous bull ring.

Unfortunately, Bollywood had arrived in town to make a film, which rather scuppered my plans. However, we found out that they were going to film a bull actually running through the streets and I thought it would be amazing if we could get nearer and watch, as the tourists would see at first hand what Hemingway had described so well in *The Sun Also Rises*. We tried to get permission, but due to health and safety issues, they would not let us near even to see the bulls, so we left disappointed. It was frustrating, as we had not intended to run with the bulls like the participants of the fiesta do, we just wanted to watch.

Instead, after the truncated tour, we ended up playing cricket in the central plaza and educating the locals as to how loudly Mary could rally her team and generally scream at the top of her voice. I thought at one stage she was going to have some sort of hysterical attack, but it seemed she was just extremely excited at being made team captain – a decision I was to regret with every second that passed in that beautiful plaza in Pamplona. I don't think I had better go back there until the dust settles on yet another embarrassing visit to one of Spain's premier tourist hotspots.

On day eighteen in north-west Spain, it emerged that would-be MI6 agents Andrew and Leah from Liverpool had taped a conversation with Cumbrian husband-and-wife team Hilary and Terry, which revealed some underhand tactics and alliances. Well, they certainly chose their moment to reveal this fact, playing the tape just outside the Cathedral of St James in Santiago de Compostela. We were at one of the most important sights in ancient Christendom, and all our group was concerned about was the vote and the taped conversation. The convents, the cathedral, the beautiful monasteries, the statues, the churches and all the important ancient sights flew by as everyone discussed at length the blessed vote. No one saw anything except for Margaret from Newcastle, as she and I stole off to view the ancient Portico de la Gloria and the Botafumeiro, one of the largest thuribles in the world. Unbelievably, the revelation about the tape didn't even lead to a yellow card that evening; Hilary and Terry hung on by the skin of their teeth and were in the clear for another day.

Lisbon always intrigues me, especially the fact that Vasco de Gama found a route from here to India as early as 1498. Unfortunately, as we traversed this city in electric golf-cart buggies on day twenty-two, I simply couldn't find our route out of the castle district – but we had a lot of fun trying, in spite of the locals' protestations at our mode of transport on the tiny streets.

Seville is one of my favourite cities in the world, where flamenco reigns supreme and the Madonnas of Macarena and Triana vie for devotion. Christopher Columbus is buried in the cathedral – apparently he travelled more after he died than when he was alive, as everyone wanted to claim him. The Santa Cruz district is filled with patios and passageways just wide enough to take a table for two and the tapas are wonderful; I would urge you to take advantage of these things if you ever visit.

We returned to quite a few places that we'd visited before on series six, but I always love going back to destinations; they never get old and there's always more to see. We only spend a very short space of time in each location, so the chance to revisit old favourites is always welcomed by me. And for the tourists, of course, it's a whole new experience.

After Seville we journeyed to Cadiz, home to the Spanish fleet and the golden-domed cathedral of St John of God. The castles, fortresses and the beautiful old town with its beaches within walking distance make Cadiz an unexplored treasure for most of us. We made my favourite Spanish dish, paella, on the beach and it tasted delicious, with what you would call in Spanish a '*buena pinta*' or 'good look' about it.

Tarifa's beaches and sun helped us to relax before our final journey over to Morocco in Africa. This was a new and different world of belly dancers and souks, couscous and lamb tagines. It was a fitting end to what had been an amazing tour and the couples – well, some of them at least – played a brilliant game. As ever, there was an extraordinary collection of characters, many of whom met a sticky end.

Despite being on their honeymoon, Ruth and Steve did not endear themselves to the group from the outset and were off by day three with some harsh words said on departure. Jayne and Jane walked because they missed their children and were not enamoured with the less than five-star accommodation. As for Wendy from the Wirral and her son, although they were very funny, they too were off by day five.

Nav made us cringe when he told us about the seven body piercings he has below his belt. I wonder if he sets off the alarms when going through the security checks at airports? Unfortunately, he and his girlfriend Anna were voted off after only two days.

Father and daughter David and Amanda – Barnsley's own and full of true Yorkshire grit – were intelligent and interested in everything we did, but it was not enough, as David's descriptive narratives were too much for the group to cope with. They were red-carded after three days on day nine.

Niece Jasmine and Aunt Rara were given chances, but it was obvious from the start that these party girls would party too hard in the end. With great pleasure – and after a lot of apologizing to the hotel staff – I instantly red-carded them for disgraceful drunken behaviour in Bordeaux.

Barbara and Elaina were a lot of fun and laughed a great deal on this trip. But Elaina's screaming could be heard in Oslo. When she was warned to keep quiet at the horse-riding activity, she took no notice and screamed so hard that the poor horse bolted. She did a delightful impression of Calamity Jane – thankfully no bones were broken.

I really must apologize to Val and Margaret, as I have never seen anyone so ill on a boat before, myself included. The boats really did start rocking as we hit the swell off Gijón in northern Spain but the Geordie gals did well and had a great time otherwise. Tressa and Sharon, two funny girls from Morecombe, also enjoyed every minute of their trip and laughed through most of it.

Husband and wife Darren and Mary would have lasted longer if Mary had not reached a new record of loudness, several decibels above the norm, while captaining her cricket team in Pamplona. Wayne and Emma were also a lot of fun, constantly bickering between themselves, much to the amusement of the rest of the group. They lasted twenty-one days, which is probably longer than they had ever lasted together before. It was a great shame they missed out on the last day due to Wayne's illness.

Mike and Shane disappointed everyone as they had hyped up their macho active lifestyle, but it never really surfaced on the tour. They also got bored very quickly and distanced themselves from the group. I was starting to get worried about Shane's constant staring at me, as he appeared somewhat starstruck. They were voted off after only three days. The demon red card was also the downfall of Ben and Karen, who were stabbed in the back by the group after only one day.

Shaun and Tom and Lucy and Sarah all enjoyed their time on the tour but could not dislodge the remaining two couples – Rob and Timmy and Hilary and Terry – who were the powerhouse of the votes. So by the time they joined, it was easier for them to sit back, relax and enjoy the ride to the finish. David and Daniel also only joined us at the very end, but at least they got to see the sights and sounds of Morocco and the Costa del Sol.

Rob and Timmy, best friends from Essex, played a blinder of a game with a few moments of anxiety thrown in for good measure. They even confronted their own relationship head on at times, but in the end they won the game and were one of two couples that had lasted all the way from Milan to Morocco. Thirty days: what an achievement.

The other couple who remained from start to finish and who admitted to having 'more faces than the town hall clock' were Cumbria's Hilary and Terry. There were moments when I thought they would be red-carded and asked to leave but somehow, to everyone's surprise, they had more lives than a black cat. Was there an alliance? We shall never know – but one thing's for sure: whatever you thought of them, they played the game to their best advantage and got to enjoy thirty days of activities, thirty days of hotel accommodation and food, and thirty days of seeing the sights of Europe from Milan to Morocco with Switzerland, France and Spain thrown in for good measure. A fantastic journey, an amazing adventure – but then again that is what always makes *Coach Trip* so special.

CHAPTER 21

A Starry Series

AFTER I GOT back from filming series six in August 2010, I thought life would start to calm down again, but it was not to be. My agent Paula and I usually touch base with each other every Thursday to discuss my diary and any new business opportunities that have come in. During one of these calls shortly after my return, she told me that I had been invited to appear on *Big Brother's Big Mouth* with Davina McCall on day eight of the *Ultimate Big Brother*.

Well, of course I accepted. I flew to London and met up with my old friend Andrew Wilton and we had a very early dinner in the centre of town. I was quite amazed at the number of people who said hello to me while we walked around Soho; even Andrew commented on it. Although it was slightly surreal for him, I think he was thoroughly pleased for me. He knows how hard I work on the show and, for him, this was my recognition for all the passion I pour into it.

That evening, I went to see *Priscilla, Queen of the Desert* at the Palace Theatre, starring Jason Donovan. I really enjoyed the show and the music was fantastic. I had travelled the length and breadth of Australia with Les in 1981 and we had visited the outback, just like in the musical, so it was a very special place for me and the show brought back many memories.

Australia is an amazing country. On my last visit, I hired a camper van – a posh one, I might add – and travelled down the west coast from Perth through Bunbury, Margaret River, Albany and across the bush to Esperance. I stayed on beautiful beaches and in national parks and met many lovely people. I remember a couple in Esperance who loved the programme and were so surprised to see that I had made it all that way on my own. I think they half expected to see the coach with its Union Jack-emblazoned wing mirrors trailing along behind my camper!

The day after seeing *Priscilla*, I prepared to go to Elstree Studios for my appearance on *Big Brother's Big Mouth*. I had watched *Big Brother* before I moved to Spain, but since the move I hadn't been able to keep up with it. However, with the knowledge of my impending appearance on *BBBM*, I had made sure I was fully up to date with the latest series. A car came to pick me up, and as I got into the black Mercedes and sped north, I found myself musing excitedly that Elstree was where so many fantastic films had been made, from *Murder on the Orient Express* and *Star Wars* to *Indiana Jones* and *The King's Speech*. My goodness, it was like going to England's answer to Hollywood! Of course, Elstree is also famous for being the home of *Big Brother*, and here I was, about to appear on its spin-off show with the comedian Bob Mortimer and racing pundit John McCririck. As the car arrived at Elstree, depositing me within a few steps of the *BB* set, I felt very nervous and was amazed at the size of the place. I was met by *BBBM* staff, who took me to a dressing room that I shared with Andrew Stone from *Pineapple Dance Studios*.

After make-up, I had some supper and was then shown onto the set with Bob Mortimer, who was really kind and reassuring. Davina McCall came over and welcomed me, saying it was so nice to have me there. She is a very warm person and loves *Coach Trip*.

We were all there to discuss the blossoming relationship between *BB11* winner Josie Gibson and John James Parton, as well as *Ultimate*

Big Brother itself. Josie had been in the *UBB* contest, but she had walked on day three, so as to be reunited with John, who wasn't in the house. They were both in the studio with us that night and their new relationship was a hot topic.

Many thought that John, who was from Melbourne in Australia, was simply an opportunist. He was very blond, very surf-boyish and very handsome. When we questioned Josie, it was clear she was obviously smitten with him and was quite coy with her answers. John McCririck was his usual blunt but honest self. I just hoped they would be happy with each other, but you never know when people are thrown together on television as it's not real life. I really enjoyed the show and we all ended up dancing till the credits had rolled. All in all, it was an amazing evening. I felt so natural just talking and in the car going back to my hotel, I thought, 'Well, it just cannot get any better than this, surely?'

I did not realize how popular *Coach Trip* was among other celebrities, actors and TV presenters until Paula was contacted the following month by the BBC London breakfast show. They asked me to do an interview on 3 September with Paul Ross and Gaby Roslin. I agreed and we actually did the interview by phone with me at my home in Torremolinos, which was easier for me than travelling all the way to London. Paul Ross was a big fan of the programme, so he led on all the questions and seemed very excited to be talking to me. Of course, I was very excited to be talking to him too!

Our next *Coach Trip* adventure was to be the starriest series yet. A long while back, some time during the making of series three, Matt Walton and John Graham had mentioned to me that there was a possibility of making a celebrity version of *Coach Trip*. I have to confess that the thought of me wandering around Europe showing celebrities the sights filled me with complete fear and foreboding. These were people who were famous, who had been on television hundreds of times. They probably holidayed in Martinique or the

Maldives, or had private houses in Thailand, the Bahamas or Australia. Maybe they even had private jets! So why would they want to come on a coach with me for ten days to make a daytime programme that aired in the afternoon on Channel 4? Didn't they have more important things to do in their glitzy celebrity lives?

However, once that seed had been planted in my head, I couldn't help but wonder what it would be like guiding a group of celebrities, wickedly fantasizing about what would happen if I ordered them about or had to chastise them if they were late down with their luggage. After all, a coach tour is a fairly humble way to travel. What would I do if they complained and how would they react to being red-carded by their fellow celebrities? All these questions and more kept running through my mind but my main thought on the subject was clear: I should treat them just like any other passengers I have ever looked after – that is, with patience and understanding.

Yet I also knew I would not tolerate any celebrity antics: it was my coach and they would have to conform to my rules and play the game just like anyone else, and I would have no nonsense or dramatics on board. They could keep that for their other lives. No, I would make no exceptions – the celebrities were just normal folk to me, and that is how I greeted them on the morning of 14 September 2010 in Prague, as we started to make our first ever *Celebrity Coach Trip* with a prize of £1,000 for the charity that the winning pair of celebrities chose.

I had flown from Malaga to Prague a few days before filming started to prepare for the new series, and also to have some time in the city to visit the castle complex and Gothic cathedral. Most of the celebrities were arriving on Monday 13th, and although they were staying in the same hotel as me, we would not meet until the first morning, as I was sightseeing in the city centre and my room was in a different part of the hotel. The production company, 12 Yard, preferred me not to know who the celebrities were until I actually met them when they walked out of the hotel.

I waited outside the Clarion Congress Hotel in Prague with our driver Paul and Jon Lloyd, who was the series producer, while Keeley Van Dyke was filming inside the hotel with the celebrities. Then the first couple, Alex Ferns and Ricky Groves, came out of the hotel and I recognized them immediately from *EastEnders*, though I do not watch the soap avidly. I introduced myself and told them to leave their luggage at the side of the coach, just like I would a normal couple. They said hello, shook my hand and got on.

Glamour models Bianca Gascoigne and Imogen Thomas were next and to tell you the truth, I knew they were models of sorts simply by the way they looked, but as to who they were or what they were famous for, I did not have a clue. They were very nervous indeed, particularly Imogen, but I ended up giving them both a hug of reassurance to help them get on the coach.

Actress Carol Harrison and TV presenter Ingrid Tarrant were next. I had no idea who they were either, but I welcomed them and got them onto the coach and they all started to introduce themselves to each other.

Paul and Barry Elliott were my final couple and of course they were well known to me as the Chuckle Brothers. They had often filled the Futurist Theatre in Scarborough, especially during the school holidays, and I thought they were very entertaining indeed. I had never met them before, but they were a Yorkshire institution, and legends in their own right with their catchphrase, 'To me, to you.' Within seconds, everyone was saying it on the coach.

We set off to our first activity in the centre of Prague with the Czech National Ballet and I pointed out the main sights en route. After the introductions on the coach, even I managed to find out what everyone did and what they were famous for. The ballerina Veronika Iblova must have wondered who on earth I had brought to her, but I must admit all the celebrities joined in enthusiastically with the activity. We all got changed into our tutus, did our warm-up with the prima ballerinas and had a lot of fun. The Chuckle Brothers did a few routines that made us all laugh and it was nice to see everyone enjoying themselves and getting to know one another.

After lunch, we had a surprise waiting for us with the late arrival of *Big Brother* contestant Ben Duncan and *Apprentice* star Raef Bjayou. Once again, I did not have a clue who they were until they were introduced to me. They were late in arriving because they had both had social functions to attend in London the previous evening and Ben's had gone on extremely late. And of course, when the champagne is flowing, it's hard to pull oneself away, darling!

Ben made a faux pas during his introduction when it became clear he thought Ingrid was someone else of the same Christian name who was a writer for *Majesty* magazine, rather than a broadcaster in her own right and the ex-wife of Chris Tarrant. He did not score any brownie points after dropping that clanger, I can tell you.

In fact, Ben was extremely extrovert and outrageous in everything he said and did. He told me quite forthrightly that he never sees the early side of noon and only ever gets up at 12.30 p.m. for the lunchtime news. I replied equally forthrightly that this would have to change immediately, as on *Coach Trip* we have people to meet and activities to complete, so the average wake-up call would be 7 to 7.30 a.m. He looked at me completely horrified while I chuckled at his distress.

Raef's dress sense really impressed me; I have never seen such clothes. He always looked extremely smart indeed and in the past he would have been described as a proper dandy. I would hate to see his monthly wardrobe bill. After studying the competition, old man Raef confidently told Ben that he thought it was clear that he and Ben were the most famous couple on the coach and that they would have no problem getting rid of these nobodies as soon as the voting started. What a charmer. But I had to take my hat off to his drive and energy: he apparently runs five companies and had always checked in on all of them and the stock market by 8 a.m. every morning, which I found commendable.

That first afternoon, I took the group tank driving, which was a barrel of laughs, especially as Ben and Raef were not dressed properly for the activity in their smart London suits and shoes. We donned some uniforms (which sadly for Raef and his suede shoes didn't include a change of footwear) and waded through the mud in the ex-Russian tanks. Everyone had plenty of fun.

The first yellow card was awarded that night to Ben and Raef – despite or perhaps because of Raef's earlier cockiness. Although they networked with everyone after arriving late, they had not really impressed anyone with their posh accents, especially the down-to-earth *EastEnders* boys who were 'not 'avin it, mate'.

Our second day saw us in Pilsen in the Czech Republic, where we went to a puppet theatre. The group was split into two and asked to write and perform their own puppet show. It was obvious from the script of Alex and Ricky's show that Ben was in the firing line with a few pointed jokes about his bouffant hairstyle. Poor Imogen and Bianca were also not very happy as they couldn't get a word in edgeways – their performances had been completely hijacked by Alex and particularly Ricky, who stole the show from them. The other team, consisting of the Chuckle Brothers, Ben, Raef, Carol and Ingrid, all did very well at the puppetry, but in truth were outshone by Alex and Ricky's performance.

After lunch, I took them for the now-famous Pilzen beer bath. I shared a bath with Ingrid and Barry Chuckle, for my sins, and we had a lot of fun. Paul and Ben opted for massages, Raef had his own bath and Imogen and Bianca shared their own. Ricky and Alex did not do themselves any favours after they decided to get out of their bath and streak around the bath house, showing everyone their private parts, front and behind. Imogen and Bianca were shocked and clearly felt very embarrassed.

Ingrid, whom I was warming to, simply laughed it off. I found her to be a very intelligent, kind and caring person. Like me, Ingrid has travelled extensively and we became friends that day in the bath. I wondered what ever could have made Chris Tarrant jeopardize his relationship with such a lovely, beautiful lady.

There was a lot of tension at the vote that night, especially between Imogen and Bianca and Ricky and Alex regarding the boys' streaking. As it happened, the girls picked up a yellow card that evening. By this point, I also noticed that Imogen and Bianca were becoming very friendly with Ben and Raef, forming an alliance with them. I always find it fascinating watching the relationships ebb and flow on the show.

Sausage-making in Ravensburg, Germany, was the order of the morning on the third day, though it was not to everyone's taste – after only fifteen minutes' filming, Alex made his way to the loo and threw up, as he could not take the smell of the sausage factory. Everyone had a go at making the sausages and afterwards Ricky displayed his chef's skills in the oldest sausage cookhouse in the world by the banks of the River Schussen. The afternoon was spent cruising down the river on a lovely boat with a beer keg on board to loosen everyone's tongues. Even though the beer flowed freely, it was evident that the girls could not shake off the previous day's flashing escapade, and tensions were still high at the vote. Alex and Ricky unsurprisingly got the yellow card.

In the German town of Passau the following day, we made a visit to the cathedral, where they have the biggest organ in Europe. I was quite surprised when everyone became fairly spiritual there. Ben wanted to confess his sins immediately, until I told him that we didn't have six hours to wait for his confession and he should see to it on his return to London. Our accordion lesson followed, and as the day wore on into the evening vote, it became obvious the travellers had hatched a plan to share the yellow cards around to avoid people being voted off. Well, we couldn't have that – so I decided that we would implement an instant red-card vote from now on, as everyone was getting far too comfortable spreading the yellow cards amongst all the contestants quite safely.

The next day, the red terror hit Linz. Everyone was worried about the outcome that evening. This was an instant red-card vote, intended to shake the celebrities up – and shake them up it did. From now on until the end of the show, there would be a red card every day. The result was a tie between Raef and Ben and Alex and Ricky, so after some deliberations the group had to decide between the two couples. In the end, it was Raef and Ben who were sent packing that evening.

The next morning, two new celebrity couples joined the party. Interior designers Justin Ryan and Colin McAllister joined us for our trip to Salzburg and we also added eighties pop star David Van Day and DJ Tony Blackburn to our group when we arrived in the city.

We all ventured off on to our Segway PTs – two-wheeled balancing electric vehicles – as I led a tour of the city of Salzburg. I must admit David Van Day was a nightmare, crashing into everyone before we had even started. Poor Paul Chuckle fell off because he went into the back of Justin, who had just stopped for no reason at all. Justin kept falling off repeatedly too and was camping it up like Mary Queen of Scots and showing everyone his grazed knee. Finally, as we neared the Mirabell Gardens, Carol came off her Segway as well. It was a bit chaotic to say the least, but we made it all in one piece and no one had to be hospitalized.

Being the massive fan of *The Sound of Music* that I am, I got the group to sing on the steps of the Mirabell Palace and re-enact Maria von Trapp's choreography, with the celebrities dancing around the fountain and running through the maze. It was one of my favourite days on the trip and it was so nice to get to know Tony Blackburn, whom I had listened to on the radio and watched on *Top of the Pops* while I was growing up. He was so charming and kind, a real gentleman. It was such a pity he had been partnered up with David Van Day, who was becoming quite a nuisance, singing his head off at every opportunity.

During the vote that evening, the group red-carded Imogen Thomas and Bianca Gascoigne. The die had been cast in Linz the day before with a misunderstanding between the girls and Carol and Ingrid, so the older ladies were gunning for the girls at vote time. I had warmed to Imogen and Bianca; they were lovely girls and I was sorry to see them go. I remember when I asked them about boyfriends Imogen just shut up and said her relationship was complicated. Well, of course it turns out that 'complicated' was a bit of an understatement, my dear – but never mind, Brendan won't say a word...

At Innsbruck, the group got a bit of a shock with the arrival of football legend Rodney Marsh and ex-Bucks Fizz singer Cheryl Baker. They arrived at our second activity disguised on a bobsleigh and immediately during the introductions it was evident that there was huge friction, in fact downright animosity, between Cheryl and David Van Day. This – combined with David's constant joke-telling and song-singing – was the undoing of both David and Tony, and they were red-carded unanimously by the group. Poor Tony Blackburn had to leave as they had come as a partnership, but he did it with good grace and he understood that everyone's feelings were not directed at him. He was definitely the innocent party.

The coach broke down and while we were all sat inside it, waiting for taxis to come and take us to the hotel in Innsbruck, the group asked Cheryl to explain why she had reacted so strongly to seeing

David Van Day. It turned out that David had joined Bucks Fizz for a while after original member Mike Nolan had left (following a serious coach crash), then after this incarnation of the group had broken up, he had continued to use the Bucks Fizz name on his own, despite not being a member of the original line-up. A legal battle ensued between David and founder member Bobby G, who had acquired the legal right to the band name. Eventually, the case was settled out of court, but clearly the dispute had been bitter and feelings still ran high.

I sat in my guide seat transfixed at all this. I found it fascinating to hear all this juicy showbiz gossip from the horse's mouth, so to speak. I was so disappointed when the taxis arrived to take us all into Innsbruck!

Unfortunately, Cheryl Baker's problems on the show didn't end there. The partnership with Rodney Marsh was to do for her in the end, as it seemed that Rodney's dry sense of humour did not endear him to the group. No matter what he said, he managed to offend people with his comments, and therefore the following day both he and Cheryl were voted off with a red card, despite our being so entertained by Cheryl's gossip.

The beautiful Italian city of Verona was next on our itinerary. Juliet's balcony scene dominated the morning, with Alex and Carol acting out Shakespeare's sonnets to the enjoyment of the crowds. Carol took her role very seriously and you could see why she is such a good actress. She told me she was writing a musical, so she is clearly a clever lady too. It's impossible not to feel romance in the air at Juliet's house, which attracts lovers and couples from all over the world. I have a lump in my throat every time I visit this most romantic setting, but as Tennyson reminds me: ''Tis better to have loved and lost / Than never to have loved at all.'

Two Transylvanian pop stars joined us as we sang in the beautiful amphitheatre at Verona – yes, the Cheeky Girls were coming on board! I must say I wasn't impressed with the Cheeky Girls' singing – they were all short frocks, high heels and long legs. They had brought their minder, Ray, who went everywhere with them. Apparently, their mother normally accompanies them, but Ray had got the job for *Celebrity Coach Trip* so he never took his eyes off the girls and carried all their bags too. They are quite a gimmick, but it clearly works for them, so why not? In Verona we lost Justin and Colin, who departed with a red card, which was a real shame as this was our penultimate day and I had forgotten to ask them about colour schemes for my apartment in Malaga.

The glorious city of Venice featured on our last day and I made sure the celebrities got to see everything. While showing off the beautiful mosaics in St Mark's Square in the middle of Venice, I got accosted by some British tourists and asked for photos. This was quite amusing as, apart from the Cheeky Girls, not one of the actual celebrities was similarly approached, which was quite an eye-opener for me. I am still surprised by the attention I get and I think it's lovely that people enjoy the programme so much.

The final vote took place on the rooftops of Venice, with everyone nominating their favourite couple travelling on the coach that day. The group chose Paul and Barry, so I was delighted to declare the Chuckle Brothers the winners. Paul and Barry are really lovely gentlemen and thoroughly deserved to win. They had entertained us throughout the tour and been kind and pleasant to everyone on board, and it had paid off with a cheque for £1,000 for a charity of their choice.

We all dined that night in a beautiful Italian restaurant and reminisced about all the places we had seen, the activities we had completed and the people who had been voted off, and after our desserts we said our goodbyes to each other. I felt a great sense of relief that I had managed to complete this first *Celebrity Coach Trip*, and also the satisfaction of a job well done.

My experiences of travelling with the celebrities, getting to know them, talking and laughing with them were fascinating. Ultimately, I just treated them like ordinary people, because that is what they are at heart: ordinary people, just with extraordinary jobs to do. So if you ever come across a celebrity who's snotty or rude then please pity them, for they have forgotten where they came from, simple as that.

The next day, my Air France Airbus 320 took off from Marco Polo airport on its way to Charles de Gaulle airport in Paris, and banked right. From my window, I could see the whole of Venice before me – one of the most beautiful cities in the world glistening in the morning sunlight. I settled down ready for my French breakfast and reflected on my experiences of the last couple of weeks, thinking to myself, 'I really am the luckiest international tour guide in the whole world.' Then I quickly had to pull myself together before I started to fill up!

CHAPTER 22

The Show Must Go On

I HAD ONLY recently returned from filming *Celebrity Coach Trip* when I found myself on the road again, taking the train to Malaga airport to catch a flight to London Heathrow. On 7 October 2010, I was once again nestled comfortably in the back of a private car, the roads outside passing by soundlessly through the blacked-out windows, heading for Wood Lane and the home of the BBC. It was one of those 'oh my goodness' heart-stopping moments. I was going to the headquarters of the BBC, Television Centre, where *Strictly Come Dancing*, *Top of the Pops* and *Blue Peter* are made, as well as many other classic programmes that I had watched when I was a child, such as *Bill and Ben*, *Andy Pandy* and *Jackanory*.

I was to appear on *Harry Hill's TV Burp*, which despite being shown on ITV is actually filmed at the BBC. Harry Hill is a great fan of *Coach Trip* and he practically always features it on *TV Burp*. As the car arrived, I was met by one of the staff, signed into the building, given a guest pass and then shown to my dressing room.

I was to make a surprise appearance with Harry, and then close his show dressed as him while he came on dressed as me. This was all filmed in front of a live audience, which by now didn't really bother me as I was starting to get used to it. All I wanted was to do my scene with Harry Hill correctly, which luckily we managed first time.

Glenn from series five of *Coach Trip* was also appearing on the show, as Hans Christian Andersen. The episode of us visiting the Hans Christian Andersen Museum in Odense, Denmark had recently been broadcast so it was, as always with *TV Burp*, a very topical take on the show. It was nice to meet up with Glenn, his mum and his sister, and we had photos taken afterwards in the gardens of the BBC. Unfortunately, I couldn't attend the after-show party as I had an early flight to catch back to Malaga the next morning, so I was soon whisked away in my private car, back to the centre of London and the comfort of my hotel.

Just a month later, I found myself returning to the English capital for another promotional interview – perhaps my highest profile one yet. The *Celebrity Coach Trip* we had just filmed had been edited in super-quick time and was already due to hit screens. On Tuesday 9 November 2010, I appeared on *This Morning* to promote the new series, along with Paul and Barry of the Chuckle Brothers and Raef Bjayou and Ben Duncan, as the series had started transmitting on Channel 4 the previous evening.

Phillip Schofield and Holly Willoughby actually came out of their London studios to do the interview on our coach. This completely put me at my ease because the coach is my domain, so it was a very comfortable interview. With the celebs around me, too, it made it seem totally normal, just like we were back on tour. Holly and Phillip were very professional and very sweet, and the interview went brilliantly. I had a lot of fun with the celebrity tourists; we were all teasing each other and it turned into a free-for-all conversation once the key questions and promotional points had been covered. I have done quite a bit of TV work now so I didn't feel too nervous; it's amazing what quickly becomes second nature to you in this life. We also got to meet Lesley Joseph and Coleen Nolan, and had a fascinating tour of the *This Morning* set while the programme was on air.

After the show, I met with Matt Walton and John Graham from 12 Yard, who had come down to the *This Morning* studios to watch the interview. We had lunch in the OXO Tower, which has wonderful views over the Thames to St Paul's Cathedral, which is such a quintessentially English icon. As I flew back to Malaga again, I thought about returning home to live in the UK – but then, when I saw the palm trees on the seafront of Torremolinos, I thought, 'Well, not just yet.'

As November turned into December, however, I was back in England again, this time for a longer stay to accommodate the latest twist in my new celebrity career. Yes, now I was Brendan Sheerin, pantomime star! I had been asked to appear in *Aladdin* at the Southport Theatre and Convention Centre on the front, playing the Sultan. Vivian and Jim Wells from Pele Productions, who are based in Liverpool, had contacted my agent Paula to ask if I would be interested in taking the role, and I'd jumped at the chance. I knew what good fun pantos were from my time at the Spa complex, although I found it unbelievable that I would now be the one on stage. If you'd told me all those years ago, as I organized the tickets and scheduling for the pantomimes at the Spa, that one day I'd be taking part in a panto myself, I never would have believed you in a month of Sundays. It was going to be very strange to move from front of house to backstage and performance. I only hoped that I would have the high energy required for our month-long run.

The show also starred Michelle Heaton from Liberty X as my daughter Princess Yasmin. I wasn't familiar with the pop group, although I knew that they'd been very successful, and I found Michelle to be a delight to work with, as indeed was the whole company. Widow Twankey was played by Jamie Greer, Joe Mills was Mustafa, Hannah Wing was the Slave of the Ring and Aladdin himself was played by David Flynn. Mark Stuart Wood was the villain Abanazar and Britain's tallest man, Neil Fingleton, was the genie, and what a genie he was – all 7 foot 7 inches of him!

I had first met the team back in September, when we'd gathered for a photo shoot to enable the producers to get some early promotional shots of us, so that they could make up the poster and other PR material. I was excited and yet very nervous, which wasn't helped by the fact that I'd had a *twelve*-hour trip from Malaga thanks to ridiculous flight delays. But the company was lovely and I was made to feel really welcome by one and all, and so I left looking forward to the adventure ahead.

Simon Rawlings directed us and although I had to act quite out of character as the stern, cruel Sultan, I was still Brendan from *Coach Trip* – so I yellow-carded Yasmin and referred to people being voted off if they didn't behave. I thoroughly enjoyed the rehearsal period, as I practised my lines until I knew them by heart, and piece by piece the production slowly came together.

The first night, on 9 December 2010, was very exciting for everyone, from the dancers to the crew to the cast. This was also the press night, so we had to impress the critics and the VIPs who had been invited to the theatre, which was practically full to its 1,700 capacity. We were all nervous trying to remember our lines and quell the churning in our stomachs, but one thing that really impressed me was the tremendous camaraderie of the company. It was like a family and everyone looked after everyone else. Even though some of us had only met for the first time in rehearsals, everyone forgot their own importance and looked out for each other – Jamie Greer in particular helped me with my lines over and over again during rehearsals.

When I walked out onto the stage for the first night, I was a true pantomime virgin. I would go on to perform my best every evening, but that first time it was frightening to say the least. I remember putting on my costume and applying my make-up beforehand, using the mirror in front of me with the lights all around it, just like you see in the films, which made me feel like Noël Coward or Dame Maggie Smith. Jamie had kindly coached me on how to do my face, and so I ponderously applied foundation and accentuated my eyes; the make-up was necessary because of the powerful stage lights, of course. It had been a long time since I'd worn stage make-up – I think the last time was probably during the Corpus Christi production of *West Side Story*, a lifetime ago. If Mr Bloodworth could see me now...

I shared a dressing room with Jamie, but as he had already gone on stage in his role as Widow Twankey, I was left completely alone as the seconds ticked down to my debut. I just stared at myself with my make-up on and thought, 'Oh heck, here we go again! What are you letting yourself in for this time, Brendan?'

Then Sarah, the stage manager, called out my full name: 'Calling Mr Brendan Sheerin to the side of the stage... Mr Brendan Sheerin, your final call!' and I had to get ready for my entrance as the Sultan from Agrabah. I stood at the side of the stage, blessed myself and walked on with the first lines in my head ready to say to Yasmin.

The welcome I received from the audience in Southport that night I shall never forget in all my life. All I could hear was people applauding and children calling out: 'Brendan, we love *Coach Trip*!'

I also remember the fans of *Coach Trip* who stood at the stage door and wanted autographs every night, even in the freezing cold snow. I felt very special and sometimes quite overwhelmed. To open the stage door and see the car park full of waiting people – well, that's what pop stars or famous actors might expect, but I certainly didn't. There was always a mixture of fans, too – from grannies to teens, young kids to twenty-something students – and I happily signed away for everyone, because that's what people wanted.

Even now, I sometimes get a bit shy when I am recognized in the street, but I am always civil and kind to people. I once asked the

Chuckle Brothers how they coped with their celebrity status and they said it is part of the job, so I have always remembered that when I sign autographs and have my photo taken. Quite recently, I was flying from London Gatwick to Malaga on Monarch when I was spotted by some English students who were going on an exchange holiday to practise their Spanish. Not only did I have a photo with practically every student, I ended up being photographed with all the airline crew as well. It's funny how such occurrences end up slotting into your everyday life.

I was very touched that a group of *Coach Trip* contestants came to see the show. Daz, from series three, organized a reunion for some of them and they came along to support me in Southport one evening. It was lovely to see them and we all had drinks afterwards and chatted about old times.

While I was appearing in *Aladdin*, Russell Grant phoned me at the Southport Theatre to ask me to do an interview for his Christmas show. I had looked after Russell when he had appeared as a guest with the Scarborough Spa Orchestra at the Spa complex, when I was duty manager all those years ago. He remembered me well and we had a lovely conversation reminiscing about the Spa and the orchestra. He had tickets to come and see the panto, but unfortunately the snow came down and covered Southport completely for several days, and sadly he had to miss it. I did manage to appear on his show, however, doing a pre-recorded interview for his radio programme, which went out on Christmas Day. It was a brilliant end to an extraordinary year.

* * *

After Christmas, I had a few months off to recharge my batteries, before I was swept up into the celebrity whirlwind again. *Coach Trip*'s production company, 12 Yard, have offices at Granada Television

Studios, Manchester, and on the morning of 28 March 2011 I found myself walking – yes, walking for once, no black Mercedes this time – through the streets of Manchester on my way to a meeting with Tim O'Connor, the production manager. We were going to discuss the preparation for the second and third celebrity series, as well as series seven and eight of regular *Coach Trip*, all of which had already been confirmed as going ahead, such was the popularity of the show now. I'd had a medical with the doctor ahead of this long stretch of filming, as I would be on the road for roughly five months in the coming year, filming the programmes pretty much back to back, with just short breaks in between. The doctor had told me to lay off the chocolate, but other than that I was fit to work on the forthcoming productions, and so it was with a spring in my step that I went to meet Tim.

While I was at Granada, I also met my old friend Sarah Phillips, with whom I had worked previously, and Ross Clutton, who is an ace at finding activities for me. By chance, I also spotted Barbara Knox, who plays Rita Sullivan in *Coronation Street*, having a coffee in the café area of the studios, but she was talking to someone so I did not want to interrupt her.

After the meeting, Sarah and Tim had a surprise for me: I was given my own personal tour of the *Coronation Street* set. I had photos taken behind the bar and in the back room of the Rovers Return, walking down Coronation Street, sat at the sewing machines of the factory and outside Kevin's garage. There were clear signs of the rebuilding that had taken place since the tram had come off the rails and caused that amazing disaster. This tour was a real treat for me as I had grown up with the likes of Elsie Tanner and Ena Sharples, the Ogdens, Bet Lynch, Kevin Webster and, of course, the queen of *Coronation Street*, Annie Walker. I thought their surprise was so thoughtful, but that's the kind of people I work with on *Coach Trip*, and why it's always such a pleasure to make.

The second *Celebrity Coach Trip* series – which was filmed over two weeks – set off in April, and was its usual roller-coaster ride, with highs and lows aplenty. It is being edited as I write, so we shall wait to see which events make the final cut – I shall be watching with just as much anticipation as you when it hits our screens in autumn 2011.

More excitement was afoot later in the year when comedy panel show *Celebrity Juice* invited me on as a guest on 5 May 2011. The day before I was to appear on the programme, my agent Paula came down from Yorkshire to be with me. I took her on a tour of London and showed her some of the sights. It was a chance for us both to talk about the future and have some quality time together.

Celebrity Juice is made by Talkback Thames at the Riverside Studios. When the car pulled up at the studios in Hammersmith, we were welcomed by one of the runners on the show. Everyone was very attentive indeed; even the comedian Paddy McGuinness came over in reception to say hello and shake my hand as we signed in.

After make-up, producer Dan Baldwin introduced himself and asked if everything was OK. We had dinner by the river before I went on, and then we were shown to the side of the set. Keith Lemon (Leigh Francis) is the presenter, and I was to open several boxes and introduce myself. Davina McCall was also there and said hello, hiding with me in a box as Keith tried to find her later in the show. She remembered me from *Big Brother's Big Mouth* and was just as friendly as she had been on that programme. I told her she ought to come on *Celebrity Coach Trip* as she adores the show, but she has three young children and she said she couldn't possibly leave them.

The other guests were French DJ and producer David Guetta, comedian Rufus Hound, TV presenter Fearne Cotton, and Max George and Tom Parker from boy band The Wanted. The programme was really fun to film and I had an absolute ball.

After the show, Paula and I had a drink in the bar, said goodbye to everyone and then I signed some autographs for the audience (who are allowed to stay behind after the show), before hopping into one of those big black cars and heading back to my hotel. It had been a wonderful, surreal evening, and yet such events were becoming less and less of a rarity. As I settled down to sleep in my comfortable hotel bed, tucked up in its luxurious sheets, I marvelled at how my life had changed so dramatically over the past few years. What had started as a fun experience had become the most extraordinary day job. From one little email my life had turned completely upside down, so that this topsy-turvy world of celebrity appearances and TV shows had become as familiar as fish and chips. Ah well, you know what they say: it's funny how life turns out.

CHAPTER 23

Torremolinos

M ost mornings, I sit out on my terrace and have breakfast. I still live down in the Bajondillo district of Torremolinos, in the Malaga area of Spain, a short five-minute walk from the beach.

I love to look out at the Mediterranean, to notice if it's smooth or rough, and to watch out for passing cruise liners from Malaga port. I also take note if there is any wind, and which direction it is blowing through the palm trees that line the seafront promenade.

My apartment overlooks the pool and Emilia, the Argentinian *portera* or caretaker, comes down most mornings and cleans the pool. I usually have a word with her in Spanish, the usual topics being the weather – of course – her work for the day, and when I am off filming again. She always says how nice it is to see me resting. We also discuss my pending visit to Argentina, as it's one of the countries I haven't been to yet. Don't worry: it's on my 'to-do' list.

I love swimming in the pool, but prefer the sea. Lying on a beach reading a good book or a newspaper is a proper indulgence for me. I also love doing the bilingual crossword in the local paper *Sur* – the clues are in English but the answers are in Spanish and it is one of my favourite pastimes. I also walk the promenade in Torremolinos and can clock up over two kilometres doing that, which enables me to justify eating a bar of chocolate while watching the latest film on Spanish television if I stay in for the night.

After a good Spanish lunch – a Malaga frito or paella or just calamares, all with salad – I usually siesta. It's a Spanish habit I love and it gets you out of the heat of the day, which can be forty degrees Celsius at times. It also recharges my batteries and makes me ready for the evening. Most nights, I walk up to Nogalera Square where I sit and drink tea in a local café, watching what seems like the whole of Torremolinos pass by and checking out the many different nationalities of tourists. I adore people-watching and I always seem to be accosted by some Spanish ladies, who talk about their health problems, the heat, the Spanish economy or the youth of the day. In summer on balmy warm nights, I stay out till midnight, sometimes meeting friends for a drink. When I return to the apartment, it is filled with the musky scent of night jasmine, which comes in from the garden and perfumes all the rooms.

I have become used to living on my own. I am very self-sufficient and I have grown to like the feeling of not being beholden to anybody. I love the peace and quiet and freedom, and I am quite content to enjoy my own company. With so much of my life now spent on the road with a large group of tourists plus crew in tow, time to myself has become precious, and I value my own time and space.

That said, I'm hardly a recluse. At least twice a week, I visit my dear friends down in Fuengirola – by train, as it is too busy in the summer months to use the car. Parking is a nightmare in the summer anywhere on the Costa del Sol. On Sunday evenings, I visit friends in Malaga, where we talk and drink tea and coffee and put the world to rights. I also lunch with Frank and Graham, my friends from Los Alamos, and we often attend the little English theatre in Fuengirola, where we may see a play or a musical revue. Graham is sometimes a participant in those plays and it's lovely to see him shine.

My family and friends – both at home and abroad – are very important to me and I always like to keep in touch by phone at least once a week. I have kept my friendships since my early years as a courier and my days working for Saga Holidays. My friends are astounded at my success: sometimes they think it's a dream, but one thing they are sure about is that they shall always have their Brendan as a friend. They know I shall never become someone who I am not, far from it – I like being me and not some diva.

During the summer of 2011, I have been filming series seven of regular *Coach Trip* and the third series of *Celebrity Coach Trip*, as well as writing this book, so I have been extremely busy. The show is so popular now that we have taken to filming the series back to back, so that Channel 4 can keep it on our screens as often as possible throughout the year. As long as I have enough time to prepare my research notes before each series starts, I'm thrilled about this packed schedule. The programme has only just taken off and I am more than happy to ride the crest of the wave, to go with the flow and see where it takes me. For the moment, I'm thoroughly enjoying every tour we go on, and I'm willing to continue for as long as it may last. As I write this, I am about to have a few weeks off before we begin to film series eight, which I know will start from the UK and head to Europe, but the exact route is not yet fully finalized.

At the time of writing, none of the new series I have already filmed have yet been transmitted by Channel 4, so I cannot divulge the contents of those shows. What happens on the coach stays on the coach – until it's ready to be revealed, that is. Suffice to say, you are in for a treat. The characters on the regular show are just as unique as always, with some outstanding couples. There is a lot of fun with the activities, plus some extraordinary voting tactics, and the same bickering and disagreements between the couples as ever, which is what makes the programme such compelling viewing. You will not be disappointed when the episodes hit your screens.

The second and third celebrity series also have some interesting personalities lined up to entertain you. You may have already heard through the press grapevine that Michael Barrymore and Wagner from *The X Factor* are appearing on series two of *Celebrity Coach Trip*. How long will they last? Do they get voted off? How do they network among the other stars on the coach? Will they have any alliances with other celebs? All these questions and more will be answered very shortly indeed. We start our tour in the south of France on the Côte D'Azur in the wonderful resort of Nice... But beyond that titbit, my lips are sealed.

Come the autumn, I will be preparing for pantomime season again. This time, I will be appearing in *Snow White and the Seven Dwarfs* at the Southport Theatre, which is where I did *Aladdin* in 2010. I really enjoyed my debut last year and when Vivian and Jim Wells called Paula in February 2011 to say that Southport wanted me back and they could offer me a part as Herman the Henchman in *Snow White*, I just jumped at the chance. One thing about pantomime is that it is a lot of fun and therefore you enjoy yourself just as much as the audience does. The reaction of the children in particular is amazing. They are so spontaneous with their comments and all seem to adore *Coach Trip*.

I will also enjoy being back in England for Christmas. Although the panto schedule is hectic, and we only get Christmas Day off, it is magical to be in my homeland for the festive season. To hear the kids singing carols, and to go to the local church in Southport for Midnight Mass – these are special things that mean a lot to me. With Les having died on 28 December, Christmas will always be tinged with sadness, but as my friends and family rally round me and we join together to toast the season, it's a bittersweet sadness that slowly tastes less bitter with every passing year.

With the commissioning of more series of *Coach Trip* and the development of *Celebrity Coach Trip*, my life path has taken a dramatic and exciting turn. When Helen Warner courageously decided to commission another series after the programme's hiatus, it catapulted me into a life beyond my wildest dreams. A life where private cars pick me up from the airport. Where I am recognized and smiled at (especially by the lady immigration officer at London Gatwick airport, who beams only at me and no one else). Where children and grandmas share their favourite bits of the show with me when they see me. Where students, especially, all seem to have worked out a 'foolproof' strategy for winning the game if only *they* were on the coach. Where, in spite of all the fame and celebrity the programme has given me, I am still ignored in Torremolinos by the majority of people and am only spotted by a few discerning viewers. Fortunately, my anonymity is protected there and that is why I so enjoy living there and the peace and the quiet it affords me.

I love returning to the UK and especially to Flixton. I have wonderful memories of this lovely Yorkshire village where Les and I were so happy and contented, and many wonderful friends still living there, such as Sandra, Jenny and Georgina. They, in their turn, miss me terribly and try with all the persuasive talent that Yorkshire-women possess to get me to buy So-and-So's house in North Street or that detached in Main Street. I shrug and laugh it off. Maybe one day I shall return to my beloved Yorkshire, who knows? But for the moment I like where I live.

Usually when I visit, I stay in Scarborough and get fattened up by the biggest Yorkshire puddings you could fit on a plate, made by my dearest friend Brenda and served up by her lovely daughters. I am also treated to fantastic dumplings with mincemeat – all winter fodder because I usually hit Scarborough in the snow and ice of winter. Although it's cold outside, the welcome is extremely warm at Meadow Drive.

At the Kam Sang Chinese Restaurant on North Marine Road, I meet up with my old colleague Nikki Sweeney (now Nikki Sweeney Chisholm following her marriage) and family, who update me on all the entertainment news in Scarborough and the rest of the north of England. I recently visited the newly completed multi-million-pound renovations at the Spa complex, where I used to work. It is a beautiful building and still the jewel in Scarborough's crown.

I also return to the place where I had to say my goodbyes to Les and start, very slowly, to pick up the pieces and begin my life anew. Even now, eleven years later, the piercing heartache can return with such speed and suddenness that my tears will begin to flow quite freely. Yes, I know, I am not the first or the last person to suffer the intolerable grief of losing the one you love. And although I remember that period of my life as the most painful, I am forever grateful to my immediate family and friends who helped me through the various stages of loss, from anger, resentment and bitterness to acceptance and faith – and not forgetting gratitude for having had the opportunity to be loved by the same person for twenty-five years, which by any standards is a remarkable feat.

My only wish is that anyone who wants to be a ballet dancer like John, or a Geology teacher like me, may do so without fear, hindrance or prejudice. It is so important to be free in this life, to soar like an eagle, to be yourself and to shine in your own way, like the golden sun, and more importantly to love freely and to be loved. I have had an amazing life already and I am so grateful for all that has happened so far.

When I was asked to write this book, I felt inadequate and fearful, but as time has gone on, I feel that if it will do someone some good then it is worth it; if it entertains and makes people laugh, then what a joy that would be; and if it merely satisfies someone's curiosity about my life and myself as a person, then so be it. If asked, would I change my life, I would say no, because the different experiences I have had have made me what I am today. I love my life; I love the joy of family and friends; I love peace and quiet; I love shopping; I love a calm sea to swim in and a hot beach to lie on; and finally, I love a good bar of milky chocolate (fat-free, of course!).

I have always described *Coach Trip* as an amazing adventure, where you travel and get to see the many beautiful sights and sounds throughout Europe. Where activities test your abilities, your strengths and your weaknesses. Where you will like some of your fellow passengers, and not others. Where you can make alliances to further your cause or make mistakes and live in regret. Where you are liked one minute and stabbed in the back the next. It's not a million miles away from life itself in all those respects. Whatever your reason for watching, it is always an incredible journey – and long may it continue to entertain the millions of viewers who watch it over all the networks.

All that's left to say is: sit back, relax… and enjoy the ride.

Index

The initials BS in subentries refer to Brendan Sheerin.